The Challenge of Neutrality

The Challenge of Neutrality

Diplomacy and the Defense of Switzerland

By
Georges-André Chevallaz
Former Federal Councilor and
President of the Swiss Confederation

Translated By
Harvey Fergusson II

Foreword By
Joseph E. Persico

LEXINGTON BOOKS
Lanham • Boulder • New York • Oxford

LEXINGTON BOOKS

Published in the United States of America
by Lexington Books
4720 Boston Way, Lanham, Maryland 20706

12 Hid's Copse Road
Cumnor Hill, Oxford OX2 9JJ, England

British Library Cataloguing in Publication Information Available

Library of Congress Cataloging-in-Publication Data

Chevallaz, Georges-André.
  [Défi de la neutralité. English]
  The challenge of neutrality : diplomacy and the defense of Switzerland / by
Georges-André Chevallaz ; translated by Harvey Fergusson II.
    p. cm.
  Includes bibliographical references and index.
  ISBN 0-7391-0274-5 (cloth : alk. paper)
    1. World War, 1939-1945—Diplomatic history. 2. Switzerland—Defenses. 3.
Neutrality—Switzerland. I. Title.

  D754.S9 C4613 2001
  940.53'25494—dc21

                                                    2001029628

Printed in the United States of America

∞™ The paper used in this publication meets the minimum requirements of American
National Standard for Information Sciences—Permanence of Paper for Printed Library
Materials, ANSI/NISO Z.39.48-1992.

Contents

Preface

In the preface to the French edition of his imposing *Histoire de la Neutralité suisse*, Edgar Bonjour discusses the difficulties the historian faces in achieving the complete objectivity that is normally had in what may be termed the "exact" sciences. He points out that "in the final analysis, every assertion carries the brand of its author, a man of his times. The historian does not cease to make value judgments, even if he is unaware of doing so. To make a selection from especially abundant material is already to take a position."

With his basic honesty, Bonjour applies this judgment on history's relativity, on the difficulty of reaching the truth and absolute impartiality, equally to himself in his quiet survey. It is difficult to reach perfect objectivity in narrating and interpreting events, given the complexity of the facts, and more so of the people who influenced them, "these creatures which fate puts in circulation on earth for its personal use," as Jean Giraudoux says in his *The Trojan War Will Not Take Place*. History cannot provide absolute truth. It will always be research, subject to revision. This does not in the least deprive it of its interest, even its necessity, at first through natural curiosity and then because the past, if it does not determine the present and the future through a necessary continuity, brings with it an inventory of recurring themes, experiences, traditions, and convictions that it would be careless to reject. History can suddenly take revenge on illusions of an utopia.

But it is true that, in this work that is at once problematic and passionate, it is easy to give in to the temptation of a Manichean vision of history, separating the good from the bad grain, the reprobates consigned to Hell and the elect destined to an eternity where a good memory of them lives on. This a human tendency that even computer-aided operational research with its allegedly quantifiable parameters cannot rectify.

vii

Bonjour justifies his "refraining from pushing concern for nuances too far," because, he adds, "it is incumbent before anything else to bring the necessary moral and political judgments to bear on the matter at hand, without manipulation, even at the risk of putting in doubt the purity of one's intentions."

The historian, however well aware he may be of his fallibility, assigns himself first the establishment of the facts and an understanding of people's intentions and the relations between them before he brings "moral and political judgments to bear . . . without manipulation." According to Bonjour, the search for objectivity, in itself already quite relative, will be submitted to moral criteria or political prejudice. He is much closer to Bossuet than to Thucydides.

Our reflections will seek to bring some nuances to the understanding of this still controversial period, to the controversy between Manichean interpretations, and especially to the opinion of neutrality in the context of that period, without claiming in itself to achieve absolute impartiality and definitive objectivity.

We also need to understand the role of those who exercised the most important responsibilities, neither heroes nor traitors, acclaimed or unjustly disparaged, but both of these people saw their mission, their vocation, and temperament to keep Switzerland out of the conflict in peace, liberty, and solidarity and free of fanaticisms, ideologies, and unleashed interests.

I have attempted a reassessment that is as finely shaded as possible, on a human scale, neither extolling nor condemning. Except for verifying polls, I did not go deeply into the mass of archives which others have consulted or published with patient diligence. I have tried to sum up and compare the works that have used them, such as those of Bonjour, Bourgeois, Bucher, Gautschi, Lasserre, Marguerat, Roulet, Senn, and Urner, and the precious collection of *Documents diplomatiques suisses* published under the direction of Jacques Freymond and Oscar Gauye.

The sequence of chapters is more by subject than by chronology or biography. As a practicing politician, I was more interested in the decision-making process than the picturesque nature of events. As a result, some sectoral clarifications suffered repetitions which are useful for continuity. Given the abundance of books and documents consulted, the bibliographic notes are generally elliptic and incomplete, for which I apologize, since I have limited myself to an academic punctiliousness.

Without attributing to them any responsibility for this work, its imperfections, omissions, or errors, I would like to express my gratitude to those who have helped me with their opinions, encouragements, and corrections, especially Professors Louis Edouard Roulet, Jacques Freymond, François Schaller, Ambassador Maurice Jeanrenaud, and Pierre André Bovard. I salute the publisher of the original French-language text, Michel Moret, for his clear thought and courage. It is to those near me, especially my wife, for her patient rereadings and constant solicitude that I owe the most thanks. The discussion of Switzerland's actions during World War II have been very intense and unfair in the United States and Great Britain, for which reason some of my American and British friends have persuaded me to publish the present translation. I thank them, as well as all those who have helped, especially the American Swiss Foundation and its president, Ambassador Faith Whittlesey, as well as Georg Gysssler, Chairman of the U.S. Advisory Council. I am indebted to Harvey Fergusson II for his careful translation and to John Gardner and Don Hilty for their editing efforts. They all have contributed to strengthen the historical ties of esteem and friendship that unite our countries.

This book was originally published in French by Éditions de L'Aire in 1995, under the title *Le Défi de la Neutralité* and permission to publish in English has been granted by them. Gratefully acknowledged is partial funding by Presence Switzerland (PRS), The Sophie and Karl Binding Foundation of Basel, Switzerland, and The Ulrico Hoepli Foundation of Zurich, Switzerland.

Foreword

A number of years ago, I wrote *Piercing the Reich,* which included the story of Allen Dulles and the OSS in Switzerland during World War II. During my research, I had occasion to examine Switzerland's precarious role during the war and to come to a fair understanding of the principle of armed (as opposed to moral) neutrality. This policy, based on credible strength, has been practiced by Switzerland for more than 700 years and contributed greatly to the country's ability to maintain its independence and democratic traditions during World War II.

Former Swiss Federal Councilor and President Georges-André Chevallaz has written a masterful book describing Swiss diplomacy during the war as conducted primarily by Federal Councilor Marcel Pilet-Golaz. In Chevallaz's account, we see Pilet-Golaz as a shrewd and skillful diplomat, resisting German pressure while adhering to the formal requirements of Swiss neutrality, as he was obliged to do under international law. We see a tiny country holding its ground (literally and metaphorically) while completely encircled and militarily overmatched. Chevallaz offers insight into the private sentiments of the great majority of Swiss who were sympathetic to the Allied cause. We also learn about the internal political disputes and power struggles that eventually led to Pilet-Golaz's resignation.

At this critical juncture in history, Switzerland enjoyed the services of both an exceptional foreign minister and a deeply patriotic and courageous military commander, General Henri Guisan, a relationship illuminated by the author.

Switzerland avoided invasion during World War II because it embraced the belief that democracy is best preserved through preparedness—peace through strength. And Switzerland, indeed, made herself strong. However, as in most great conflicts, military strength alone did not suffice. Firmness of purpose had to be wedded to diplomatic skill.

For many Americans, Switzerland's unique circumstances and actions during World War II are sidebar stories. This account of Swiss endurance and survival is important, not least of all because Switzerland and the United States share many common values, including an abiding commitment to democracy, federalism, and the rule of law. Granted, the conduct of some Swiss during and after the war has provoked sharp criticism. The history of every wartime neutral reveals similarly behaving individuals. This readable translation of Councilor Chevallaz's book is valuable not only because it captures those shared ideals but, just as important, it gives the reader a more balanced and nuanced understanding of Switzerland during the war than has been presented to us of late.

Joseph E. Persico

Chapter One

The Choice of Neutrality

Why was it that Switzerland announced its neutrality when faced with the threat posed by Germany and its national socialist, authoritarian, totalitarian, and racist ideology? Why did it not immediately join the democracies, then limited to France and Great Britain, which had finally resolved, after much equivocation, to stand up to Germany?

The problem is more complex than simply a Manichean contrast between Good and Evil. First, Switzerland was not the only country to declare its neutrality in August 1939, even omitting the countries of central Europe that had already fallen into the Rome-Berlin axis or soon would: the Scandinavian countries, the Netherlands, Luxembourg, Belgium, Greece, and Portugal, as well as General Franco's Spain, which was indebted to Germany and Italy for the support they gave him in his conquest of power. Hostile by tradition to dictatorships, but disapproving of the way the European powers controlled the peace in 1919 and the following years, the United States did not enter the war until the Japanese attack on Pearl Harbor in 1941. If Franklin Roosevelt, who had been elected president in 1932 and remained faithful to the spirit of Woodrow Wilson, believed in the principle of collective security and was disturbed at the totalitarian and warlike development of Hitler's Germany, the isolationist majority in the American Congress remained hostile to any external commitments and thus passed the neutrality laws, which prevented aid to the democracies. In 1938, when German pressure on Czechoslovakia intensified, Roosevelt launched an appeal for peace to the European governments, but he publicly excluded American participation in case of a conflict. It was not until 1939 that Washington undertook a substantial effort and only in the autumn of 1940 that it gradually bent its neutrality policy and in March 1941 that the Lend-Lease Act allowed the United States to supply England with the

1

necessary weapons and provisions that allowed it to win the war. In the East, the Soviet Union, people were thinking, would not fail to discourage the expansion of the Third Reich because of the fundamental opposition of their ideologies.

This nearly general neutrality was to create surprise. Certainly six years of National Socialism had made it possible to take the measure of the regime's temperature long before the Holocaust: six years of totalitarian dictatorship, the parallel powers of the SA and the SS, the repression of all opposition, and the marginalization and persecution of minorities and Jews. But these very excesses made people doubt that Hitler's regime would last. Although he had been brought to power democratically through the support of the German nationalists and certain industrialists, there was thought to be no doubt that these allies would be able to moderate him and keep him from an adventure that could not fail to be disastrous for Germany. A number of foreign economists showed, with figures in hand, that the German economy was not in a position to sustain a long war, as it lacked financial resources and raw materials. This was also the view of certain German generals, too attached to the army, whose morale and discipline had been maintained in spite of the Treaty of Versailles, to commit it imprudently before they had completed their rearmament program. Finally, in this country with its firm spiritual tradition, one could rely on the churches, both Catholic and Protestant, to make peace prevail. The Franco-British alliance, that of "the best army in the world" with the most powerful fleet, would suffice to make Hitler see reason sooner or later.

Beyond this relatively reassuring view of the situation, Switzerland intended to base its neutrality on its consistent practice and its international commitments.[1] Neutrality, as Machiavelli teaches us, is in the nature of federations, frequently divided as they are on their foreign policy goals and thereby limited in their ambitions. Since the origins of the Confederation, neutrality had been a frequent practice both among the cantons and in its relations with foreign countries. Since the sixteenth century, after the defeat at Marignano in 1515 had forced Switzerland to take account of its limited forces, and the Reformation had accentuated domestic differences, the Confederation became devoted to neutrality in European conflicts, in virtue of customary right respected by the powers during the Thirty Years War and the conflicts of the seventeenth and eighteenth centuries. The invasion of 1798 by the armies of the French Directory opened a brief parenthesis of foreign and civil wars. By the Act of Mediation of 1803, Bonaparte reestablished the Confederation's federalist structures. He recognized that neutrality was Switzerland's natural vocation, as he accommodated the country to his interests.[2]

After violating Swiss neutrality in 1813, the Allies, who had conquered France, recognized it in 1815 as being in Europe's interest, declaring Swiss neutrality perpetual and giving it their guarantee. Swiss neutrality became both a right and an international obligation. The Constitution of 1848 made the Confederation a federative state, endowed with a permanent central power, a federal foreign ministry and army, and thus allowed it to declare this neutrality itself. It assured Switzerland's political independence in a Europe by then intent on conflicts that mercilessly affronted national sensitivities.[3] Thus, Switzerland was to remain neutral in the conflicts for Italian unity in 1859–61, for German unity in 1866, in the Franco-Prussian war of 1870–71, and finally during World War I in 1914–18.

In 1919, at the end of the latter conflict, Switzerland saw its guarantees of neutrality renewed by Article 435 of the Treaty of Versailles. On February 13, 1920, the Council of the League of Nations, which had just been established, declared that "the perpetual neutrality of Switzerland and the inviolability of its territory, as they are acquired in public international law, notably by the treaties and by the Act of 1815, are justified by the interests of general peace and are therefore compatible with the Charter of the League of Nations."[4]

However, Switzerland would have to assume the duties of solidarity incumbent on its membership in the League of Nations, including the obligation to participate in trade and financial sanctions that organization might decree against a state violating its Charter. It would be prepared for any sacrifice to defend its own territory itself in all circumstances, but it could not be required to participate in a military action, to allow the passage of foreign troops, or the preparation of military expeditions on its territory. This specific reservation of military neutrality made it possible for its people and its cantons to adhere, with some hesitation, to the League of Nations on May 16, 1920, by 414,830 yes votes against 322,937 no votes, and a majority of only one canton.

The League of Nations disappointed the hopes placed in it. It was not as universal as had been proposed. The United States, whose intervention in World War I had been decisive and whose President Wilson had played an essential role in settling the peace, did not ratify the Treaty of Versailles and distanced itself from the League of Nations and from European affairs. Germany was not admitted to the League until 1926, and withdrew in 1933, while the USSR entered the organization in 1934, in spite of Switzerland's questionable opposition.[5] On that occasion, Federal Councilor Motta pronounced a diatribe against the Soviet Union based more on law and ethics than on political opportunism and which was to weigh heavily when relations were resumed between Bern and Moscow. Pilet-Golaz, who was even questioning what purpose the League of Nations served, now resolutely opposed, in the Federal Council, the admission of the USSR to the League.

Under the dominant influence of France and Great Britain, then often in disagreement with each other, the League oscillated constantly between a move toward reconciliation with Germany, of which the Locarno Agreement in 1925 was especially conspicuous, and a policy of strictly applying the Treaty of Versailles, of which the League was the guarantor, to a Reich bereft of its colonies, forced to pay war reparations and strictly limited in its armaments.

From the moment beginning in 1929 that the economic crisis revived the nationalist demons, in the economic decline and unemployment, the League proved to be incapable of keeping the peace. It did not prevent the denunciations and successive violations of the Treaty of Versailles to which Hitler resorted—rearmament; the remilitarization of the Rhineland; the annexation, albeit consenting, of Austria to Germany; the Franco-British capitulation at Munich and the successive dismemberment of Czechoslovakia. Meanwhile, Mussolini had gone off to conquer Abyssinia. The economic sanctions with which he was punished, which were ineffective, threw Mussolini into the arms of the führer and sealed the "Pact of Steel" between the two dictators, before the Ribbentrop-Molotov Agreement of August 1939 opened the doors of World War II, sacrificing Poland as a propitiary victim of the unlikely collusion between Nazism and Communism which overthrew the order of strategic forces in Europe.

Given the powerlessness and decline of the League, Switzerland had extricated itself well from a badly run game, prudently, inconspicuously but without shame. The growing antagonism among the European powers and the fragility of the alliances dissuaded Switzerland from tying its fate to a League which no longer represented the community of nations. In 1938 it had its return to total neutrality recognized by the Council of the League.[6] Switzerland had only partially applied the embargo declared against Italy. It had shown debatable haste in recognizing Italian sovereignty on the Empire of the Negus. It observed strict neutrality during the Spanish civil war, a trial run for the war to come, in which Germans and Italians furnished General Franco with weapons and "volunteers," while the democracies extended only hesitant support to the Spanish Republicans.

The Swiss commitment to neutrality, traditional and confirmed by international law, recognized and guaranteed by the powers, could not be questioned. To remain credible, it implied constancy and duration and could not oscillate according to circumstances, opportunism, or the unpredictable dance of the alliances. On the other hand, in spite of its background in the political concepts of democracy and liberty, the Confederation could not declare solidarity with the disconcerting policy of France and England which was sometimes rigorous and sometimes lax, with their lack of firmness in the face of German rearmament, the insufficiency of their military preparations, and the lack of conviction in their public opinion, even if there was not a strong feeling of seriousness at the time.

Certainly the great majority of the Swiss people was not prepared to rally around the totalitarian order of the Axis countries. Nationalism, violent repression, and Germany's anti-Semitic outbursts caused a general revulsion, especially in the German-speaking part of Switzerland for the very reason of Germany's proximity and the linguistic tie. The same applied to fascism in Ticino, where some irredentist fires had long been burning. If Mussolini, with his dramatization and his Caesarean profile ("the trains run on time"), had been able to benefit from sympathetic understanding at the Political Department and the University of Lausanne, which had made him a doctor honoris causa for the courses he had taken earlier as a socialist refugee, the attack on Ethiopia and the Pact of Steel alienated most of the sympathy he had generated.

In Switzerland at the end of the 1930s, the movements at the extreme right, the "fronts," based on the Nazi and fascist models wearing colored shirts, made more noise than they gathered votes. "They are only marginal," said Jacques Freymond, the historian of this epoch.[7] At the height of their popularity, in the federal elections of 1935, they obtained less than 14,000 votes, 1.5% of the total, and two seats in the National Council, one for Zurich and the other for Geneva, where the fascistic National Union of Georges Oltramare was developing a lively effervescence. But in 1939 they were to disappear from both the Federal Parliament and the cantonal parliaments. Only some small groups of activist hotheads pursued their noisy propaganda in favor of the "New Order," with the obvious support of the German government and the Nazi Party. This does not exclude a generally discrete understanding if not sympathy for the German cause in the right wings of some bourgeois parties, in certain business circles, and among certain officers who were close to the German army by education and tradition.

On the left, the Socialist Party at that time had the greatest number of voters with 25%, but it was not represented in the Federal Council where four Radicals, two Conservative Catholics, and one representative of the Peasant Party sat. But the economic crisis and even more the rise of the national socialist dangers led to a fundamental revision of the socialist program. The party detached itself from the class struggle in order to adhere to the policy of collective contracts and labor peace. It rallied to national defense and the policy of armed neutrality. Its left wing, essentially French-speaking, came close to communism, and, placing its hopes in the USSR, pursued a policy of total opposition to federal policy. The ban which struck it from 1940 on, at the same time as the extreme right organizations were hit, did not prevent it from pursuing its activities with all the romantic and literary attraction of clandestinity.

Armed neutrality, to which the great majority of the Swiss and their leaders were devoted, was justified by the commitment in international law, the practical situation in Europe and the firm will to safeguard the country's independence and liberties by keeping it out of a conflict where its views would have little weight in the decisions of the powers and the variations in their alliances.

The status of neutrality is always problematical since it depends in good measure on the respect which belligerent powers accord it. Belgium in 1914 and 1940 and other states often underwent painful experiences in this regard. Neutrality in principle is less difficult under equilibrium conditions when two belligerents with equal forces face each other on the frontiers of the neutral country, as was the case with Switzerland in 1914–18. But the total encirclement in which the defeat of France was to place the Confederation in June 1940 made neutrality a true challenge.

However that may be, with tensions in Europe heating up, with the threat against Poland taking shape after the signature of the Ribbentrop-Molotov Agreement on August 23, the country was mobilizing everywhere. The Federal Council, with only Motta believing that peace was still possible, made ready its border troops on August 28. Motta convened the Federal Assembly on August 30 and gave an address to the effect that Switzerland's policy for centuries had dictated fidelity to the principle of neutrality, which it had freely adopted, which was recognized by most of the states and guaranteed by international treaties. Without becoming involved in conflicts among nations, Switzerland would fulfill its historic mission of serving the cause of peace and mitigating the sufferings of war victims. It would take the military and economic measures necessary to safeguard its independence. For this purpose the government was requesting a grant of extraordinary powers.[8]

On August 30, the Federal Assembly confirmed this desire of neutrality under all circumstances and with respect to all countries. It promoted Corps Commander Henri Guisan to full general and appointed him commander in chief of the army, which the Federal Council mobilized fully on September 2. Full powers were granted to the government on condition that the parliamentary committees controlled their use.

On August 31, the Federal Council addressed its declaration of neutrality to forty states. This took up the text used in 1914: the Confederation "would maintain and defend by every means at its disposal the inviolability of its territory and the neutrality which the treaties of 1815 and the agreements supplementing it have recognized to be in the true interests of Europe as a whole." If the joint neutrality with northern Savoy, agreed on in 1860 and abandoned in 1919 was not mentioned, Switzerland's commitment in favor of "the impartial activity of humanitarian work that can mitigate the sufferings a conflict would cause" was specified.

Germany confirmed its respect for neutrality in acknowledging receipt of the Federal Note. Italy did the same, while making its ports and railroads available to the Confederation. France greeted the declaration favorably, but its ambassador in Bern insisted that Switzerland authorize delivery of the antiaircraft guns already ordered, which was done. Great Britain confirmed its respect for neutrality, adding "insofar as this neutrality will be respected by the other powers." This reserve implied that England could decide to intervene on its own accord if it judged that neutrality had been violated. The Federal Council could not admit this conception: the intervention of a third power could not occur except on Switzerland's specific request. Germany had already admitted this interpretation; England adhered, withdrawing its reservation.[10]

A neutral state benefits from two essential rights: the right of respect for its territory and the right to maintain its relations with the other states. On the other hand, it commits itself not to participate in hostilities provided that its neutrality is not violated and to treat belligerents impartially. The universality of relations implies that there is freedom in principle to effect exchanges with the two opposing sides as with the other powers.[11]

As to war materiel, the Hague Convention of 1907 tolerated private trade in that commodity. On this point, the Federal Council's policy varied. The ruling on maintaining neutrality of August 4, 1914 prohibited all exports of weapons, munitions, and war materiel to belligerent states. But during the conflict the necessity of resupply and the fear of unemployment led to their authorization. The weapons trade with the various belligerents was relatively heavy.

The ruling of the Federal Council of April 14, 1939 on maintaining neutrality again prohibited export of war materiel to countries at war. It entered into force on September 2, 1939. But on September 9 the Federal Council already revised its decision in the face of France's pressing demand on behalf of materiel already ordered.[12] Certainly the "moral position of the country would be bolstered by keeping up this prohibition." But the strict observance of that prohibition could not be had except "at the price of very serious economic and financial difficulties, which would serve as a social destabilizer," in the words of the report of the Political Department. As a result, and on the condition that the belligerents be placed on an equal basis, that they supply the raw materials indispensable to their manufacture and that they provide payment guarantees, the government decided in principle that war materiel could be delivered to Germany, France, and England. The latter two were the main customers of private arms factories from then until June 1940.

To what extent did the state's neutrality policy imply neutrality in public opinion and the press?[13] Two irreconcilable attitudes faced each other: that of the totalitarian system where state and people were swallowed up in an allegedly unitary will, in a democracy pushed to the absurd, where the government, consisting of *Führer und Reichkanzler* Adolf Hitler, endowed with full powers, elected by the people and strengthened by subsequent plebiscites, supported by a single party, incarnated the one and indivisible national will.

Sharply opposed to this was the attitude of Swiss liberal democracy, in which authority flowing from the people, elected and collective, took power, but respected freedom of opinion in its critical diversity and its expression in an open and pluralist press. It is true that this liberty could not be absolute in that period of high tension, under permanent threat of attack and a blockade in reprisal. Reasons of national security led the Federal Council to ban the extreme right-wing and left-wing organizations as well as their press, since it was duly established that both, momentarily in agreement at the time of the Ribbentrop-Molotov Agreement, were financed and controlled at a distance by foreign powers for propaganda purposes that threatened Switzerland's independence and existence.[14]

Without any detriment to their freedom of expression, the newspapers were requested to be prudent and objective. Military security appeared of high priority. The responsibility for an a posteriori censorship was given to the army. However, it was not prepared for this essentially political mission and occasionally showed rather pedantic zeal. It even desired the establishment of prior censorship, which was denied. Beginning in 1942, the oversight of the press was to revert to the civil authorities, in this case the Department of Justice and Police.

But the German and Italian governments were already blaming the Swiss government for what was being written in its press that they did not like. *Oeri* of the Basler Nachrichten, *Schürch* of the Bund, and *Bretscher* of the Neue Zürcher Zeitung were especially noted both for their talent and their independence, and the government was requested to take their pens away from them. Pilet-Golaz, in his capacity as head of the political department, where he had succeeded Motta, had to fend off these repetitive requests, supported in addition by the Swiss Legation in Berlin and by a few nervous Swiss. He preached in vain his sermon explaining that a state's neutrality did not gag the press. He could also have replied that the German or Italian press was not exactly tactful about Switzerland[15] and that they were close to the Swiss government.

How did Swiss neutrality distinguish itself from that of other countries trying to survive in a Europe dominated by the Axis? Could one speak of neutrality as it applied to Portugal?[16] Antonio Salazar, the dictator whose regime was drawing near the Axis powers, stated in May 1939 that an open Atlantic and colonial activity were connected to the alliance with England, while proximity and peninsular solidarity—not to mention the support given to General Franco—increased fraternal amity with Spain. "The universality of our interests leads us to entertain the best of relations with all states." However, because of the geopolitical situation and strategic developments, its neutrality with respect to the Anglo-American allies was soon to pass from benevolence to connivance.

Concerning Spain, one may speak of the neutrality of variable geometry.[17] General Franco's regime and the support he had received from the Axis powers in its civil war, placed Spain nearer the dictatorships than the democracies. Initially neutral, it passed under the influence of Minister Serrano Suñer and the Falange, which grouped the regime's activists, with a "nonbelligerence" which approached an entente with Germany and Italy in the hope of reinforcing its positions in North Africa at the expense of France. This allowed Hitler to plan an operation on Gibraltar through Spain. But Spain's economic situation and England's commercial and political pressure, the influence of the church and the opposition of a cabal of generals to Serrano Suñer and the Falange brought an end to the project for an alliance. Hitler, in addition, refused to fulfill Spain's needs. Spain did no more than join a Blue Legion to the Axis troops in the Soviet Union, which Allied pressure led it to withdraw. In May 1944, a secret agreement was reached with the Anglo-Americans for commercial exchanges. However, Spain did not disengage itself from German political ascendency before the end of the war. It did not even refrain from openly engaging in an operative alliance with Germany, with a prudence in keeping with the country's interests.

Swedish neutrality does not have the perpetual status of Swiss neutrality guaranteed by the powers.[18] It was a current, not constant option, which did not exclude occasional or permanent alliances, in particular with its Scandinavian neighbors. In 1914, it had proclaimed its neutrality in concert with Denmark and Norway, but later, in the face of economic difficulties, its government reached an agreement with the Allies that intensified commercial exchanges. In 1939, the German fleet's mastery of the Baltic and its control of the straits and the power and range of the Third Reich's air force led to fears of encirclement where it would be difficult to maintain a neutrality which had not even been proclaimed. The strength of Sweden's armed forces rose from 89,000 men in 1939 to 256,000 in 1943, while the air force tripled the number of its aircraft during the war. At the end of 1939, Sweden reached trade agreements with the belligerents.

When the Soviets attacked Finland, Sweden abstained from declaring its neutrality. It facilitated the recruitment of volunteers in a gesture of solidarity with Finland and provided war materiel. But it refused passage over its territory to Franco-British troops, which would have established control over the iron mines of northern Sweden while bringing support to the Finnish army. Alone, Finland paid for its heroic resistance by the partial cession of Karelia and a port on the Barents Sea.

The unresisted invasion of an unarmed Denmark and the conquest of Norway by the Third Reich achieved the complete military and economic encirclement of Sweden, setting it at risk of an invasion. Germany gave up the idea, preferring to keep intact the iron mines that would eventually provide a quarter of its mineral supplies and which military action could have made useless. However, it imposed conditions on Sweden that were scarcely compatible with the rules of neutrality. Stockholm had to allow the transit through Sweden of thousands of "soldiers on leave" in uniform, actually relief for the German troops in Norway.

On June 22, 1941, when Finland, hoping for revenge, associated itself with the German attack on the USSR, Hitler formulated his requirements to the Swedish government: permission for his military aircraft to overfly Swedish territory, the use of Sweden's telephone network, the transport by Swedish railroads of materiel and provisions necessary for the German-Finnish operation, and the transfer of a German division with its weapons and ammunition from Norway to Finland by the same means. There was some political resistance, but, on the advice of the king and the commander in chief, government and parliament were obliged to give in. As Justice Minister Westman said later: "Neutrality is not an abstract idea, but a practical policy for the purpose of keeping us out of the war."

This pragmatism permitted Swedish policy to evolve when American power and Soviet resistance appeared. Sweden was forced to limit its supply of iron to ball bearings and cellulose, which comprised most of what Sweden supplied Germany. Based on troop movements in 1942, there was fear of a German attack, but after 1943, the Germans were disturbed about a possible Allied operation against Norway and the support it could find in Sweden. Swedish Foreign Minister Christian Günther reaffirmed the neutrality policy: "Sweden is determined on armed resistance to any attempt by either belligerent to force it into the war on its side. To keep Sweden out of the war is the objective of our neutrality. All problems are to be dealt with in terms of that objective. It is in this context that Sweden's neutrality during the war is to be understood."[19]

In this conflict, there were as many principles and practices of neutrality as there were neutral countries. This diversity is explained by historic, geopolitical and economic differences, by the course of events, the caprices of fate, and the capacity of the peoples and their leaders to overcome or undergo them. It is therefore not a question of classification by merit, which would be unjust because conditions were different in each country. But a comparison with other countries' policies of neutrality allows us to understand better how serious Switzerland's challenge was and how it was met by those who bore the responsibility for its foreign policy and its defense.

NOTES

1. Edgar Bonjour, *Neutralité (Synthèse)*, 1–120; Jean Monnier, *La Neutralité du Point de Vue du Droit International Public*, in *Neutres Européens*, 17–27; Jacques Freymond, *Neutralité Morale, La Neutralité*, 93–105; and Rudolf L. Bindschedler, *Die Schweizerische Neutralität, Eine Historische Übersicht*, in *Schwedische und Schweizerische Neutralität*, 149–54.

2. Auguste Verdeil, *Histoire du Canton de Vaud*, Lausanne, 1854, vol. III, 449 and 452. Addresses of the first consul to the Swiss delegates.

3. Edgar Bonjour, *Neutralität*, vol. I, 279–304.

4. *Documents Diplomatiques*, vol. VII, bk. 2, 321–22, 461–554.

5. *Documents Diplomatiques*, vol. II, 204–8.

6. Edgar Bonjour, *Neutralität*, vol. III, 203–81, notably 263.

7. Jacques Freymond, *Neutralité Morale*, 97.

8. Edgar Bonjour, *Neutralité*, vol. IV, 13–34.

9. *Documents Diplomatiques*, vol. 13, 324.

10. Edgar Bonjour, *Neutralité*, vol. IV, 17–21.

11. Jean Monnier, *Neutres Européens*, 14–21.

12. *Documents Diplomatiques*, vol. 13, 324.

13. Edgar Bonjour, *Neutralité*, vol. IV, 155–230.

14. Edgar Bonjour, *Neutralité*, 388–97.

15. Daniel Bourgeois, *L'Image Allemande de Pilet-Golaz*, in *Etudes et Sources*, 4, 92–94; and Edgar Bonjour, *Neutralité*, vol. IV, 191–234.

16. Carlos Bessa, *La Neutralité Portugaise dans la Seconde Guerre Mondiale*, in *Neutres Européens*, 135 ff.

17. Barrio Marquina, *La Relative Neutralité Espagnole*, in *Neutres Européens*, 109–33.

18. Sten Carlsson, *Die Schwedische Neutralität, eine Historiche Übersicht*, dans *Schwedische und Schweizerische Neutralität*, 17–29.

19. Wilhelm C. Carlgren, *Sweden's Neutrality Policy during the Second World War*, in *Neutres Européens*, 155–64.

Chapter Two

Marcel Pilet-Golaz, Federal Councilor

The career of General Henri Guisan, who headed the Swiss armed forces, is well known, thanks to a large number of biographies. In particular, Willi Gautschi's biography is remarkable for the quantity and precision of its documentation and interpretation, which are both critical and positive. In contrast, the career of Marcel Pilet-Golaz, apart from Erwin Bucher's *Zwischen Bundesrat und General* (1991), which is devoted mainly to Pilet-Golaz, has scarcely been the object of special study. Since the intention of this book is to interpret the political decisions of the period 1940–1944 when Pilet was responsible for the Political Department, that is, the Ministry of Foreign Affairs, biographic data is kept to a minimum here.[1]

Marcel Pilet was born on December 31, 1889 at Cossonay into a family of notaries, pastors, deputies, and magistrates. It was from this circle that he chose his wife, Mathilda Golaz, daughter of Donat Golaz, a state councilor and deputy at the Council of States. After secondary studies at Lausanne, Pilet entered the university there. He studied law and was president of the Belles-Lettres Student Society. He completed his studies at Leipzig and Paris, concluding with a thesis on civil law, which earned him a doctorate at Lausanne. Thereafter, he obtained his license to practice law and embarked on a career at the bar. At the same time he pursued a military career in the reserves, where he rose to battalion commander. With some hesitation he became a candidate in 1921 for the Great Council of Vaud Canton, where his competence and eloquence earned him authority in legal, fiscal, and financial matters. Beginning in December 1925, he was a member of the National Council, Parliament's lower house, where he was elected on the Radical ticket. What sort of a man was he and what did his contemporaries think of him?

In 1933, Edgar Bonjour, the future official historian of Swiss neutrality, had just been appointed to a supervisory position at the Federal Archives. He was received by Federal Councilor Pilet, vice president of the Federal Council, who abruptly asked his stupefied visitor, "What good are the archives anyway?" The young historian told me that he acquired a lasting mistrust of this minister who treated history so casually.

But the tone and substance of the question were very much in the sarcastic manner of Pilet, and reflected his taste for the disconcerting paradox which often motivated him. His wit was cultivated to the point of affectation, moving from quip to quip as at the student Belles-Lettres Society, where people would distinguish themselves by disrespectful sarcasm at the most serious of things — as they still do.

Yet he was not a success at Belles-Lettres, according to Pierre Béguin, editor of the *Gazette de Lausanne*, who had worn the green beret of the Belles-Lettres Society after Pilet. Béguin later sharpened his pen with an acute personal dislike, denying that Pilet had any wit at all. "He was always mocking things and trying to be funny; but he was just mean, acidic, and disagreeable, making people ill at ease with his negative sarcasm." It is true that Béguin afterward tempered his views, as conveyed to Jean Philippe Rau, but they gave an impression of settling accounts of reciprocally wounded personal vanities. However, they were mitigated by the calmer judgment Béguin pronounced in *Le Balcon sur l'Europe* concerning Pilet's speech of June 25, 1940, shortly after France surrendered.[2] "That day Mr. Pilet-Golaz failed to achieve that warmth he so needed to fulfill his difficult task of rallying the Swiss people. Such was the interior conflict of this man of superior intelligence, brilliant, undeniably devoted to his country, a great magistrate in whom an extreme reserve and perhaps an excessive shyness have always prevented him from expressing his emotions and for whom, because of this fact, establishing a rapport with crowds, as with individuals, has been denied him. He has often been reproached for his sarcasm, which has had innumerable victims, who most likely never suspected that he used it, above all, against himself."

Pierre Grellet, long a brilliant journalist covering the Federal Palace, evoked Pilet in his *Souvenirs d'Ecritoire*. "Perhaps Pilet-Golaz's career would have been longer if he had begun by restraining his brilliant and quick intelligence, which was dangerously tinted with sarcasm. His eloquence was lucid and rapid, but carefully prepared, to give the appearance of improvisation. There was a certain dilettantism in his ways, an air of treating the most serious matters lightly and taking inconsequential things seriously. In short, he did everything he could to disturb the people who found his superiority so difficult to accept, especially when it was accompanied by a certain casualness. But whether we liked it or not, we had to bow before a mind that moved with such perfect ease among the complexities of political life."[3] "What [Pilet] said was acute," said Bernard Barbey, chief of General Guisan's personal staff. "It contained some truths that hit the mark and struck or in some way hurt, even when the generalization seemed hasty, even when it bordered on the arbitrary or the unjust."[4]

Pilet truly enjoyed disconcerting people with his words, behavior, and clothes. He would wear gaiters and an elitist cape with golf trousers and a Basque beret to a military parade, standing beside prominent persons in derby hats, rolled-rim fedoras, and tight frock coats or colonels in stiff collars. And his effort to seek at all costs the formula, the unexpected word, or the discourse in rhythmic prose often troubled his audience, which was hard put to follow the glittering richness, at times forced, of a vocabulary that the Swiss found difficult to grasp. This undoubtedly led to frequent misunderstandings and gave the impression of a casual attitude that bordered on impertinence. It did not correspond to the innermost depths of his thoughts, but even among those close to him, it led to lasting resentment.

Georges Perrin, a journalist who long covered the Federal Palace and was quite close to Pilet and appreciated him, mentioned his difficulties in dealing with people. "He lacked that psychological sense that would have allowed him to make his points accessible to many minds less flexible than his. An aristocrat of the intellect, he was especially repulsed by certain forms of slow-wittedness. In short, he had very little esteem for Parliament. . . . He was quite arrogant with its members. A deputy had to take account of the interests of a certain number of voters, and his own interests did not necessarily fall into step with those of high policy or the national interest. Pilet had great difficulty admitting that, and it cost him the friendship of many of his colleagues."

"He failed to make direct human contact with other people," observed one of his political friends. "This weakness exposed him to more criticism, which affected him in spite of his rather cool exterior. If anyone took it upon himself to defend him, Pilet was neither satisfied nor grateful, since he was so sure of himself that he could not admit that anyone would criticize him or suspect even the least of his actions." The liberal Frédéric Fauquex concluded, "As a patriot, he believed that what he did was good, so that he never needed to defend or explain himself. In his mind, he placed himself above his adversaries' attacks."

In spite of his brilliant intelligence, decisiveness, and courage, Pilet set off alone on the perilous road of Swiss foreign policy in the midst of a raging Europe. He had a severe handicap—his difficulty of establishing a rapport with his colleagues and their ingratitude in return.

However, the election of Marcel Pilet-Golaz to the Federal Council on December 13, 1928, was hardly difficult. State Councilor Ferdinand Porchet, a strong man from Vaud, had declined to succeed Ernest Chuard, who had retired after nine years of firm and thoughtful management. Pilet, a deputy since 1921 in the Grand Council of Vaud, was thirty-nine years old. He had been a member of the National Council for only three years. His candidacy did not lead to dissidence in the Radical Party, in spite of some complaints in the German-language press in favor of the law professor Paul Logoz, deputy of the Geneva Union of Economic Defense. Pilet's candidacy received the support of the liberal newspaper *Gazette de Lausanne* as well as the backing of Heinrich Walther, the "kingmaker," the most influential president of the Christian Democratic faction then known as Catholic-Conservative, and of the *Vaterland* in Lucerne, its principal organ.[5] Pilet was elected on the first round by 151 radical, liberal, conservative, and agrarian votes. Professor Logoz received sixty-six votes, notably and paradoxically from Socialists, although his constituency in Geneva was rather to the right.

The left's opposition to Pilet-Golaz certainly dates back to 1926, when the law regulating government officials and their right to strike was debated. Pierre Grellet recalls Pilet's intervention on that occasion in the *Journal de Genève*. "The entire Chamber had gathered around Mr. Pilet-Golaz—there were no microphones then—and followed his commentary on the strike with interest. He was an incisive and sober speaker. The most subtle orators of the extreme left would be hard put to refute the precise reasoning by which he defined the role of the state and its officials in contrasting them with employers and employees in private firms. He showed that a strike by government personnel was the equivalent of a revolt against the people and the negation of democratic principles. It is rare that a new deputy earns his reputation with his maiden speech. Marcel Pilet made a great impression."[6] He placed himself on the political chessboard from then on, permanently on the right of the Radical Party and a target of the unions.

The Interior Department was entrusted to Pilet-Golaz during his first year on the Federal Council. At the time, this department was as lacking in interest as it was now saturated with work. Thereafter, Pilet-Golaz took over the Department of Posts and Railroads, whose technicalities were apparently unsuited to his political talents. He was soon again in conflict with government officials. The country was in an economic crisis. In 1928 there were 8,300 unemployed; in January 1936 there were 124,000. An effort was therefore needed to straighten out the federal finances, which had been seriously affected by the crisis. In response, Jean-Marie Musy, chairman of the Finance Department, proposed financial austerity measures.

Pilet-Golaz had under him the two large government corporations operating the postal system and the railways, with about 60,000 employees in all. He was firm in his desire to contribute to moderation in salaries, and he encouraged a simple lifestyle. He tried to show Parliament that it was possible to dine on 1.80 francs, or on *cervelas* (common sausage) salad for 60 centimes. The austerity of this simple salad earned him continuous notoriety and the lasting mistrust of the Socialist left, up to the gravest hours of the war. Certainly Pilet was fully aware of the fidelity and competence of these officials as well as their rights. He had personal, positive, and confidential relations with union representatives such as Robert Bratschi. But this infelicitous *cervelas* salad, if brought up, was to weigh on the stomach of the Confederation's employees for a long time to come, more heavily than the incompetence, injustice, or mistakes of the minister. Employee representatives still recalled that salad in 1975 when I was obliged as minister of finance to oppose an increase in real salaries. That is the risk involved with an expression that scores a point but is not forgiven.

Erwin Bucher, who took on the task of clarifying Pilet's personality and deeds so widely and stubbornly decried by public opinion in his *Entre le Conseiller fédéral et le Général*, cites a description of the federal councilor by Jacques Pilet, his son, which concludes:

"in sum he was simultaneously
—a pure intellectual, a bit of an elitist, gifted with a lively intelligence that allowed him to absorb and analyze problems of every kind;
—a man of letters with an acute sensitivity, a sparkling mind, and a great facility of expression;
—a decisive man of action who exercised his functions with authority."

Steeped in French culture, he had a very Latin mentality. In my view he was more like a graduate of the French *Ecole Nationale d'Administration* than a political figure from French-speaking Switzerland. That made him hard to understand for our compatriots from beyond the Sarine Pass.

We would add that for those close to him, he was often hard to live with because of the harshness of his demands and his sarcasm, according to confidences given us. Yet with his lively intelligence, his spirit of decision and authority, this was the man who was to direct our foreign affairs during the bleak circumstances of the war.

NOTES

1. Urs Altermatt, *Conseil Fédéral*, 366–71; Jean-Philippe Rau, *Pilet-Golaz*, Passim; and Gonzague De Reynold, *Mes Mémoires* (Geneva, 1963), t. III, 667–76.

2. Pierre Béguin, *Le Balcon sur l'Europe, Petite Histoire de la Suisse Pendant la Guerre 1939–45* (Neuchâtel, 1950), 159–60.

3. Pierre Grellet, *Souvenirs d'Écritoire* (Lausanne, 1952), 155–60.

4. Bernard Barbey, *PC du Général* (Neuchâtel, 1948), 45. Other testimony has been gathered by Jean-Philippe Rau in *Marcel Pilet-Golaz*, or has been given me directly.

5. Peter Menz, *Der "Königsmacher," Heinrich Walther*, (Fribourg, 1979), 100 ff.

6. *Journal de Genève*, June 18, 1926.

7. Erwin Bucher, *Zwischen Bundesrat und General*, 509–15.

Chapter Three

Threat on the Border

FROM THE "PHONY WAR" TO THE BLITZKRIEG

What was Switzerland's position on the chessboard of European strategy on March 10, 1940, when Pilet took over the Political Department (Ministry for Foreign Affairs)?[1]

In September 1939, Hitler invaded Poland with the connivance of the USSR, which took the eastern part of the country. On November 30, Soviet troops invaded Finland where they met vigorous resistance but were able to occupy the Baltic states without a fight by virtue of the Ribbentrop-Molotov Agreement. In order to cut off the Swedish "iron route" by sea, the French and British in April 1940 attempted a raid on the port of Narvik, in northern Norway. But the Germans got there first, in spite of the clear inferiority of their fleet. Taking out Denmark, which gave up any armed defense, on the way, they conquered Norway without much resistance and installed a government that they dominated.

On the French front, the French army and ten British divisions mounted an armed guard behind the Maginot line, in a demoralizing "phony war." Now that Hitler had cut to pieces what he called the Versailles *Diktat*, would the conflict stop there? Many people thought so. This was especially the view of some Swiss general officers, who asked in April 1940 that no more than two divisions be kept under arms. General Guisan, the commander in chief, did not share this cheerful optimism and maintained an alert position.

Hitler upset all predictions. Beginning on May 10, 1940, he brushed aside the neutral states of Belgium, the Netherlands, and Luxembourg; crossed the Ardennes, which were supposed to be impenetrable to tanks; conquered Paris; and pushed the French army to the area around Lyon. The new government, headed by Marshal Pétain, was forced to declare an armistice. Italy entered the war just in time to participate in the victory without having contributed to it.

On September 2, 1939, the Swiss Federal Council (the country's executive) decreed general mobilization, which brought 430,000 men under arms. During the winter there was a partial demobilization, in rotation, in spite of some alerts. The long periods of waiting, with reduced forces and scant ammunition, did nothing to improve the training of the troops or develop their combat effectiveness. The soldiers' morale, training, and motivation depended a good deal on the degree to which they were informed, on the spirit of initiative, and on the mood of the troop commanders, all of which were unequally distributed. However, vigilance remained, revived by the alerts. At the frontiers the border troops perfected their defensive networks. On the northern front, the divisions in the front line from Limmat to the Aare constructed an important network of countryside fortifications. Lectures given by the organization *Armée et Foyer* (Army and Hearth) contributed to troop motivation from November 1939 on. Beginning in February 1940, the establishment of an auxiliary women's service made a modest beginning to women's contributions to the army. Finally, on May 7, 1940, the Federal Council authorized the commander in chief to mobilize local voluntary guards, whose 128,000 men testified more to Switzerland's will to resist than to any reinforcement of operational dissuasion.

"A thunderclap in a calm sky," the German offensive in Flanders of May 10, brought the war's realities brutally to the fore. The Federal Council decreed general mobilization. In spite of the disquiet caused by some diversionary military maneuvering north of the Rhine, Switzerland did not appear to have been threatened by German plans in this strategic phase. But it was now totally surrounded by Axis forces, with the sole exception of the narrow corridor in the French department of Haute-Savoie, the last opening onto a very relatively free France. This was when the most disturbing part of the war began.[2]

Army Group C under General Ritter von Leeb, the left wing of the German forces, regrouped in accordance with the armistice agreements to a line separating the unoccupied French zone from the German-occupied one. It concentrated its thirty-seven divisions, four of which were armored, in Burgundy. But this was not a deployment for well-earned rest and recuperation after the campaign in France. On his arrival, von Leeb received the order to be prepared for a mission "for which orders will follow." But the reconnaissance he made on the following days along the Jura left scarcely any doubt on the nature of his mission. Furthermore, on June 25, the Army General Staff developed a plan for invading Switzerland. At the same time, the armored corps of

General Guderian, a specialist in armored combat who had regrouped to the north after a long triumphal campaign, received the order to move toward the Montbéliard region, since General Schörner's mountain division, which Himmler would visit at the border, had reached Pontarlier. Did this obvious haste to reach the Swiss border indicate the intention to launch an operation? Hitler gave Guderian his marching orders personally and directly. Hans Senn, however, interprets these moves as pressure in support of a threatening note of June 19 demanding the return of German aircraft interned during the campaign in France.

CONFRONTATION WITH THE MESSERSCHMIDTS

At the beginning of June 1940, with the theater of war moving to the area near the Jura, the Swiss air force was given an opportunity to test its strength in combat, confronting the German aircraft, both bombers and fighters, which had been easily violating Swiss airspace.[3] The alert patrols of six squadrons of Messerschmidt 109Es and four squadrons of Morane 3800s were in continuous action protecting Swiss neutrality in the air. As General Guisan noted in his *Report* at the end of active service, "Guarding our neutrality in the air was an excellent training ground which allowed us to develop our pilots . . . by giving them an opportunity to measure themselves against the German pilots. . . . Their aggressive spirit was a precious symbol of our will to resist." There was some significant air combat on June 4, when the Swiss patrol attacked a squadron of thirty German bombers, and on June 8, when a dozen Swiss fighters took on thirty or so German Messerschmidts.

The German command's reaction to these exploits was undoubtedly of a different kind. The all-powerful Marshal Goering, head of the German air force, regarded the dozen victories by the Swiss pilots, equipped with Messerschmidts recently sold by Germany, over the Messerschmidts of the Luftwaffe as a personal affront. The noisy festivities that celebrated these victories at the Payerne airport, whose echoes reached to the German Legation in Bern, were also offensive.

A planned sabotage operation against Swiss airfields was discovered through the vigilance of a Swiss railway employee and perhaps also the accommodating attitude of agents of the *Abwehr*, the German counterespionage organization, which was able from time to time to be of service to Switzerland.

However, the note that Köcher, the German minister in Bern, handed to the Political Department on June 19 was heavy with threats. It claimed that the Swiss fighters had intervened beyond the frontier and demanded apologies and reparations for the human and material damages. It had none of the conciliatory language characterizing previous démarches and ended with a threat having the tone of an ultimatum. If there were any further such incidents, the Reich would dispense with written communications and "resort to other methods" to defend its interests.

The reply to be given was discussed in the Federal Council in the presence of Commander in Chief Guisan. Had the Swiss pilots been operating beyond the frontier? Germany said they had. Inquiries by the Swiss command formally denied it. Guisan did not want the pilots' actions to be disavowed by the presentation of apologies, but he did not oppose any decision the Federal Council might make. He also thought that a negative response to the German note would imply "general mobilization." "And inevitable war," continued Pilet. He recognized the general's views, but brought out the probable reprisals in case of a refusal. This was primarily a matter of prestige, the prestige of the Luftwaffe that had had its pride wounded, the prestige of the Swiss Air Force that could have felt slighted by an apology. It would not be reasonable to go to war over a matter of prestige.

The reply note, which the Federal Council approved unanimously, stuck to the conclusions of the Swiss inquiries but admitted that the pilots could have gone beyond the frontier counter to orders and unbeknownst to their superiors. The Federal Council expressed regrets and apologized for the incident. It freed the interned German aviators and returned to Germany the aircraft that could be repaired, which violated the rules of neutrality. This was undoubtedly a regrettable violation, but it is easier to deplore it in the historical abstract than to oppose it amidst the doubts of the politicians, forced to choose between certain reprisals and the possibility of avoiding them at the price of lesser concessions.

The air incidents continued at a slower pace, and the Swiss air force continued to defend its neutrality. Germany supplied it with an additional group of Messerschmidts without too much rancor.

REALITY OF THE THREAT

The episode of these air incidents could easily have unleashed an invasion, given the impulsiveness of the Nazi leaders and the facts that the prestige of Marshal Goering was at stake and that Hitler was involved. But less anecdotal reasons could also have set in motion the powerful armada concentrated to the west of the Jura and enabled General Ritter von Leeb to carry out the preliminary order he received during the regrouping that had followed the armistice.

It would have been in Germany's interest to take advantage of the circumstances—the momentum conferred by the campaign in France, the obvious prestige of its victory, and the disarray of public opinion in Switzerland—to invade that country, add it to the Axis resources, and incorporate it into the new Europe that Hitler intended to last for a thousand years. The strategic argument of Switzerland as the alpine crossroads that assured control of swift communications between the Reich and its Italian ally and offered possibilities of maneuver and communication was added to an economic justification: a hand laid on a small, intensely industrialized country with a skilled labor force and a significant reserve of capital and available foreign exchange.

A political motivation was also present. The Swiss people appeared—in the majority, and more in the German than the French-speaking part—not to be very receptive to Hitler's "New Order" and were obviously hostile to the intense Nazi propaganda and the gesticulations of some "frontists" on the right in gray shirts. The democratic mill continued to grind on according to its centuries-old rules, and while observing prudent restraint, public opinion, the press, and the radio expressed themselves freely. Nazi ideologues and activists were burning to put an end to the provocations from this nest of democratic wasps and to annex Switzerland to realize *Grossdeutschland* (Greater Germany). Frustrated by their setbacks in the French Alps, the Italian fascists intended to annex Ticino, the Italian-speaking canton, and fly their flag over the Swiss alpine passes. Strategically, the moment would have been well chosen for a surprise attack; the German troops were still intoxicated by their victories in France.

Because of its obvious sympathies for the democracies, the Swiss population was unhappy and demoralized at the unexpected defeat of France. Some people were resigned; others dreamed of saving their furniture and their businesses. The available defense forces in the Swiss army were poorly adapted and ill-armed in spite of the strength of the forces—450,000 men had been mobilized—and coverage of the frontier was tenuous. In fear of a German attack, the bulk of our defenses had been placed on the northern border near Zurich, the Limmat, and the Aare. An attack from the west, passing easily over the Jura barrier, was hardly expected. The army's barely covered front line on the plateau of Vaud was weak in armaments, without tanks, and without adequate antitank defenses. The rustic valleys of Mentue and the woods of the Jorat did not permit easy defense of the terrain. Guderian's armored vehicles could find ample room here. "It would have been a disaster," according to the military historian Walter Schaufelberger.

If one is to believe a report coming from the private information bureau directed by Captain Hausamann, Hitler reportedly called a meeting of his closest collaborators for June 24, 1940 at the Reich Chancery in Berlin. They ranged from Air Marshal Goering, chief of the Luftwaffe and a leading member of the Nazi Party, to General Wilhelm Keitel, head of the Armed Forces Supreme Command, and included Foreign Minister Joachim von Ribbentrop; Rudolf Hess, the führer's deputy; and Joseph Goebbels, minister of propaganda.[4]

Two competing options were reportedly discussed. Ribbentrop proposed the immediate invasion and occupation of Switzerland by Germany from the north, from a line passing from Léman to the Lower Engadine, through the Alps around Bern, and the Gotthard and Splügen passes, with Italy taking over south of that line. Ribbentrop did not believe that Switzerland would offer any armed resistance. If it did, a quick aerial action would be enough to induce surrender.

The army representatives were reported to have recommended against the invasion. Keitel was not at all certain that an ultimatum would lead the Swiss to capitulate. If the army did resist, Germany would have to anticipate heavy losses given the nature of the terrain in the Jura and in crossing the Rhine. Losses would be heavier if the Swiss were to deploy on the alpine massif. This campaign would cost the German army hundreds of thousands of men, who would have been useful for the landing in England and later in an engagement in the USSR or other countries. Continued resistance by the Swiss in their mountains could encourage the rest of the world in its struggle against Germany. Of course the military leaders believed that the invasion as sketched by Ribbentrop would be desirable in the long run. The well-mannered young Swiss, like the Austrians, would make excellent German soldiers. The Swiss would offer significant military reserves, enabling better resistance against the British bloc.

However, it would not be desirable to sacrifice thousands of men in an immediate attack. It would be preferable to act through propaganda, encouragement of subversive activities, and demobilization of the army, which the economic situation could not fail to bring about. When the groundwork was laid in this way, German pressure and the threat of an immediate invasion would be assured of success. Hitler is said to have rallied to Keitel's opinion.

Did this summit meeting take place? Edgar Bonjour, who doubts the reality of an invasion threat, mentions Hausamann's report and publishes it without comment. Klaus Urner has demonstrated that the persons cited were all in other places on June 24. The meeting could therefore not have taken place in Berlin nor in the führer's general headquarters. Further, Hitler was scarcely used to convoking such gatherings and supporting the opinions of others so democratically. When asked later about what he was going to do with Switzerland, Hitler replied jokingly: "On launching the campaign in the west,

Switzerland would only be a diversion. I would leave it to Sepp Dietrich (the SS *Gruppenführer*) and my personal bodyguard!" Erwin Bucher points out how unlikely the meeting was and uses that to stress Hausamann's unreliability which Captain Waibel, one of the most qualified officers in the Swiss intelligence service, had already pointed out to its head, Colonel Masson.

However, whether the summit meeting was held or not, or whether it was in that form and in that place, the points made are perfectly plausible and served to convey the options submitted to Hitler and his followers. Hausamann did make up stories on his own, but these stories are often close to the probable.

Walter Schaufelberger published in the *Neue Zürcher Zeitung* of November 14, 1989, a note from the operations section of the German high command on a report presented on June 28, 1940, at the headquarters of Army Group C, giving the führer's decision: "Hitler is said to have declared that an invasion of Switzerland would be considered under certain conditions. For the moment, the problem was not urgent. We will not have troop concentrations and preparations—however, they were already under way—but we need to prepare ourselves for it intellectually."[5]

"As researchers have shown, Switzerland was at no time directly threatened by a military invasion from 1939 to 1945," Willy Gautschi feels able to write in his otherwise remarkable work on General Guisan.[6] Recent analyses of German documents and the findings of those such as Klaus Urner, Walter Schaufelberger, and Hans Senn contest that. Pilet faced "critical situations, some of which were most serious, but which never took form in the diplomatic notes." We should note here that Hitler usually attacked without warning.

Hans Senn, in *Anfänge einer Dissuasionsstrategie*, confirms from an exhaustive study of German projects that this threat was real at a time when, paradoxically enough, the Federal Council and General Guisan were proceeding to the demobilization of a large number of troops.[7] Senn mentions the order to prepare given to von Leeb and the inspection by the latter of the Jura frontier and Hitler's hesitation. The speech at the Federal Council on June 25 that announced a partial demobilization, together with the return of the interned aircraft and pilots, could have passed as an expression of desire for detente. The main German thrust would be against England; Army Groups A and B would move north, both to get ready for the invasion and to encourage the British to compromise, leaving Hitler a free hand for his attack on the USSR, which he was already contemplating in spite of the doubts of his generals.

But "Case Switzerland" was still on the schedule. Large troop concentrations were at the Swiss border. In mid-August 1940, the German Twelfth Army and its three corps were in Franche-Comté and one corps was north of the Rhine. The operational plans code-named *Tannenbaum* were continuously being refined. The deployment of most of the Swiss army in the redoubt (see Chapter 8) led to the reinforcement of troops set aside for the invasion. It was not until November 11 that the high command announced that the operation was no longer being currently planned.[8] Was this the result of the Swiss will to resist? Or did it derive from the need to straighten out the Balkans where Italy was doing badly, or more remotely, from the idea of the Russian campaign that Hitler was pursuing?

ITALY'S DESIRES

Arriving late and ingloriously to the armistice meetings of June 1940, Italy alternatively followed German intentions for Switzerland, undoubtedly disturbed at seeing its ally deployed at the Alps, but desiring at least to participate in the division of the Confederation, thought to be an obsolete survival of shepherds' democracy.[9]

If Pilet had no doubt of Hitler's aggressive intentions, he was less categorical with respect to Mussolini's attitude. The Duce did not want to see Germany installed at the Alps. He had a certain sympathy for Switzerland, which was expressed in his good will, especially in the economic field. Pilet observed, however, that "Mussolini would not hesitate to sacrifice his sympathies to his politics of grandeur; and, moreover, he did not have enough influence to make Hitler change his plans. Everyone knows that no one could do that when Hitler made up his mind, not even his generals."

Pilet also notes that the army intelligence service had contemplated sending an emissary at a crucial moment to the Duce to plead Switzerland's cause. Pilet disapproved of the plan. "It would be like putting our finger into the machinery of the Axis, which would grind us to a powder and swallow us whole."

On June 7, 1940, under the signature of General Roatta, the Italian army's General Staff gave General Vercellino instructions in case of a violation of Swiss neutrality. On June 10, Vercellino transmitted his operational plan to the high command. On June 17, German Minister Köcher in Bern confronted his Italian colleague Tamaro. To the Italian's astonishment, Köcher asked him about plans for dividing up the Confederation if "Switzerland has not lost its reason for being included in the Europe that will arise from the war." For a year the Italian General Staff would work on plans for the invasion and partition of Switzerland, parallel to the operations of the German General Staff.

Let no one harbor any illusions about the good intentions that Mussolini officially announced with respect to Switzerland. "I have my eyes focused on Ticino, since Switzerland has lost its cohesion and will disappear one day like so many small states," he said in March 1939 before the Grand Council of Fascism.[10] On October 19, 1940, Mussolini gave Hitler his interpretation of the situation. "It doubtless will not surprise you if I number Switzerland among the last continental positions of Great Britain. Switzerland is posing the problem of its existence by its attitude of incomprehensible hostility."

NOTES

1. On the period from September 1939 to May 1940, see Hans Senn, *Dissausionsstrategie, Etat-Major VII,* 172–224 and Willi Gautschi, *Le Général Guisan,* 83–102.

2. On the situation in May–June 1940, see Daniel Bourgeois, *Le IIIe Reich . . . ,* 107–29; Klaus Urner, *Die Schweiz muss noch. . . ,* 13–73; Erwin Bucher, *Die Schweiz im Sommer 1940* in *Revue Suisse d'Histoire,* 1979 vol. 2, 356–89; Hans Senn, *Dissausionsstrategie, Etat-Major VII,* 229–40; Willi Gautschi, *Le Général Guisan,* 175–226; and Edgar Bonjour, *Neutralité,* vol. IV, 79–106.

3. *Documents Diplomatiques,* vol. 13, 785–87.

4. Klaus Urner, *Die Schweiz muss noch . . . ,* 62–63; Erwin Bucher, *Zwischen Bundesrat und General,* 233–34; Edgar Bonjour, *Neutralität . . . ,* vol. VIII, 42–44, vol. IV, 77.

5. Walter Schaufelberger, *Neue Zürcher Zeitung,* November 14, 1989; and Schaufelberger, *Militärische Bedrohung der Schweiz 1939–1940* (Zurich: ETH, 1989), 42.

6. Willi Gautschi, *Le Général Guisan,* 738; and Marcel Pilet-Golaz, 9, 13, 14.

7. Hans Senn, *Dissuasionsstrategie,* 273–78.

8. Hans Senn, *Dissuasionsstrategie,* 240–42; 246–58.

9. Alberto Rovighi, *Un Secolo di Relazioni Militari tra Italia e Svizzera 1861–1961,* Documents of the Italian General Staff (Rome, 1987), 488–563; Giorgio Rochat, *Les Troupes Italiennes de Montagne Pendant la Guerre Mondiale 1940–1943,* Actes du XVII Colloque de la Commission Internationale d'Histoire Militaire Publiés par Louis E. Roulet (Bern, 1993), vol. 2, 322–23; and Hans Senn, *Dissuasionsstrategie,* 260–72.

10. Georges-André Chevallaz, *Les Plans Italiens Face à la Suisse 1933–1943* (Pully, 1988); and Edgar Bonjour, *Neutralité,* 200–01.

Chapter Four

Confusion of June 1940

This was the situation that the Federal Council and Marcel Pilet-Golaz, president of the Swiss Confederation for the year and since March 1940 chairman of the Political Department (minister of foreign affairs), confronted at the end of June 1940. His predecessor in office, Giuseppe Motta from Ticino, who had been seriously ill for several months, had died on January 23. Surprisingly for this period of acute tension, Pilet-Golaz officially took over the Political Department only in March. He did not do so happily. "I would be afraid to hazard myself in an area as closed as that of international politics," he had written in 1927. "I must obey knowing that I have been sacrificed," he said to Gonzague de Reynold[1] in 1940. But he hardly had a choice. "No one more qualified was available," noted Bonjour. Baumann was at the bottom of the list. Obrecht, who had prepared the war economy remarkably well and stated "that he would not go abroad on a pilgrimage," referring to other European heads of state making the trip to Berchtesgaden or Berlin to hand their countries over to Hitler, was seriously ill. Wetter was a financier, not at all interested in foreign affairs. Enrico Celio was little known in Parliament, to which he had just been elected on February 22. Etter, a cultured lawyer, was a serious candidate because of his large sound mind, cooperative attitude, and patriotic convictions, but the corporatist tendencies of his youth and the influence of Gonzague de Reynold placed him too far to the right for certain radicals of the left wing. Pilet could not escape. As he said, "Since I couldn't be a lion, I forced myself to be a fox."

As the dangers mounted under the latent threat, the Federal Council clearly indicated its desire to have Swiss neutrality respected. On April 18, a directive from the Federal Council and General Henri Guisan, the commander in chief, warned against a surprise attack. "News broadcast by radio, in pamphlets, or other means that casts doubt on the will of the Federal Council and the army commander to resist must be considered as lies of enemy propaganda. Our nation will oppose the aggressor to the end and by every means, whoever it is." The text was signed by Pilet-Golaz, Leimgruber, the chancellor, and General Guisan.[2]

On May 10, at the moment Hitler unleashed his offensive in the West, the Federal Council was meeting in the presence of the general. President Pilet-Golaz spoke on the radio: "Three friendly countries have been dragged into the infernal torment. We may be faced with dreadful circumstances. We must be ready. That is why the Federal Council, convinced of the people's will, is resolved strictly to fulfill the duties of our centuries-old neutrality which has been proclaimed, scrupulously observed, and solemnly recognized. We must make it respected by everyone, and against everyone. This morning, the Federal Council made the decisions dictated by circumstances. The entry of foreigners into Switzerland will be subjected to redoubled vigilance. The army will be entirely remobilized. The nation's burden will be heavy. The soldiers will do their duty calmly and unemotionally. Firmness and solidarity. Let us redouble our vigilance and courage. This is no time for discussions or hesitation. Let us stick together. Desire to act. . . . Let us have confidence in the authorities. They are watching. They will give you confidence."[3]

But near the battlefield, in the furnace of open war and under the threat of bombardment, it was hard to keep one's nerve. Panic was noted in certain regions.[4] From 20,000 to 30,000 people from Basel fled south between May 14 and 16 to take refuge in the Pre-Alps, where their welcome was far from cordial. But had not the Federal Council encouraged this exodus in October 1939 by anticipating a general authorization to take up residence in other regions and in giving the cantons the power to prepare an evacuation? A wave of mistrust grew against a "fifth column" that was sometimes real but often expanded by fantasy and anxiety. Then, after the defeat of France, there was collapse and confusion, where the population vacillated from hatred of Germany to the fear that it inspired and, in spite of everything, to the prestige conferred by victory. Would it not be better to adapt our political apparatus, to harden this permissive democracy to which the defeat of France was severely imputed? From right to left there were astonishing reversals. The Socialist *Berner Tagwacht* found that there was a check on "capitalist democracy mined by its contradictions and weaknesses with its feet of lead, not gold." Was resistance still possible, not only against the military forces of the Reich but against the popular movement, the social renovation that had taken hold of this people whose minds had been taken over by the swastika regime?

A shattered France surrendered. An isolated Great Britain regrouped its squadrons and mobilized its home guard. Why didn't we demobilize?

"Morale has fled the scene," noted Bernard Barbey in *PC du Général*.[5] A report from the army's press and radio division stated that "there is a total lack of directives." Amidst the general wavering and contradictory rumors, we feared that foreign propaganda would get the upper hand over our completely unsettled public opinion.

Between June 21 and 25 *La Gazette de Lausanne* oscillated between the will to resist of some and the acceptance of adaptation of others. On June 21 it wrote, "We must hold." On the 24th, "Switzerland must adapt or resign itself." On June 25, the paper leaned to adaptation. "We must adapt to the hard necessities of the present and learn the lessons from the terrible events unfolding in Europe. In particular, we must make a greater effort than we have up to now to become familiar with and understand the new political and social concepts now impregnating public life in the two great states bordering ours, which are dividing control of Europe." And in the editorial section of that newspaper: "We must either accept the totalitarian point of view and recreate a work ethic, a love of discipline, and a spirit of sacrifice for the community or let our stronger neighbors impose their economic and other conditions on us, since we will continue to place private interests—with the differences they entail—above those of the nation. We need a spiritual renovation of our country." The press and the elites did not resist any better than in other times against the prestige of victorious force, contagious passion, and the emotions of our European neighbors.[6]

This moral panic even won over some distinguished humanists. Marcel Raymond, in *Le Sel et la Cendre* (pp. 147–48), quotes a letter to his wife: "All hope is lost; all illusions have been snuffed out; a voice tells me that the only course to follow is to try to accept. A few years ago, or perhaps only one year, my revolt would have been significant. But this revolt is in vain. Of course to accept does not mean to approve, to join anything in spirit, but only to conform one's thoughts to what really exists." And in that period, another elitist, the classicist André Bonnard told me: "Hitler had announced that he would remake Europe for 1000 years—I'm afraid he's right!" Resignation was gaining over the will to resist.

Even Gonzague de Reynold, one of the pillars of Swiss conservative identity, seemed resigned to the inevitable. He believed that the Axis would win, writing on June 17 to Etter that Switzerland had virtually lost its independence, its neutrality being good only as a museum piece. A few days later he encouraged Etter to eliminate liberal democracy and restore federalism as it had been before 1848, in order to reach an agreement with the Axis powers.[7]

Certainly this resignation was far from unanimous. It had less of a hold on public opinion than on the emotions of certain intellectuals or the interests of some businessmen. Certain journalists—Oeri in Basel, Schürch in Bern, and

Bretscher in Zurich—were the subject of complaints by the German government to the Federal Council because of their firm attitude. Willy Bretscher, in the *Neue Zürcher Zeitung* of June 6, echoed the order of the day of June 3 issued by the commander in chief to encourage calm, confidence, and a firm will to resist in the army and in public opinion. "The order of the day is an appeal to affirm unconditionally our community's will to resist. It should be echoed on the fallow fields of our domestic politics and rouse sluggish hearts."[8]

How did Pilet live through this period of acute tension? "Considerable overwork. Part of the personnel mobilized. Meetings that eat up our time. Very few hours for official business properly speaking. Even less for reflection, however important. There is a limit to my strength. Obrecht's is irretrievably lost," he noted on July 3.

Gonzague de Reynold, who visited him the evening of May 15 with Philippe Etter, described him walking with long strides through the corridors of the Federal Palace. Pilet told him, "We expect to be attacked tonight," and entrusted to him an exploratory mission to Mussolini, from which he would return empty-handed.[9] On May 25, Pilet received German Minister Köcher. The Swiss president stated that he had no sympathy for the French, who were responsible for the situation they had gotten themselves into. He ironically advised Köcher, in case he was obliged to do so, not to burn the legation files in the garden facing the street, "as others have done." When the minister stated that he was very disturbed at the agreements between Switzerland and the Allies, Pilet answered that he would not be able to admit the promise of assistance from a third country unless Switzerland had expressly requested it at the moment it was attacked.

Was Köcher alluding to contacts between the Swiss and French general staffs, then compatible with neutrality, which were made public in the documents discovered later at Charité-sur-Loire? Did Pilet act in bad faith in his reply? There were no negotiations involving political responsibility. Bonjour establishes the difference between this and technical preparatory bargaining between military men. The latter had previously occurred during World War I between the chief of the Swiss General Staff, Sprecher von Bernegg, and General Weygand, of the staff of General Foch, chief of the French General Staff in 1917. A support agreement in good and due form, under the seal of the governments, would have constituted a breach of neutrality. Pilet, from then on, had responded in good faith, which the German minister confirmed to his government.[10]

But in his increasingly frequent and insistent visits, Köcher noted to Pilet that Swiss public opinion was basically hostile to the Reich. Retaliation was to be feared and, with the momentum from their conquests the German army could cross the Jura mountains. Justifiably concerned in this moment of crisis, Pilet had recommended urging calm and objectivity in the press. He did not mean to gag it or forbid it from expressing its sympathies on condition that it was moderate in its views. There were two views on the press's responsibility. One was defended by General Guisan, who recommended both the introduction of preventive censorship in the civil authorities and not the army that had been responsible up to then. The transfer—though without preventive censorship—was made only in 1942. This view that insisted on the responsibility of the press was clearly inspired by the strong reactions in German newspapers and by the official intervention of the Reich's government, as transmitted by its diplomatic representatives. Gonzague de Reynold echoed this. "It would be regrettable if we were dragged into the war because of the imprudence of some irresponsible journalists." It should be observed at the outset that this was, "also the concern of the entire Federal Council and if I may say so, of the general."

The alternative view of a free press, which included a sense of responsibility, was especially defended by Willy Bretscher. As editor of the *Neue Zürcher Zeitung* he recalled to his committee "that the Swiss press had had the merit of warning public opinion against the technique of annexation without fighting which had grown up in previous years." This freedom of expression had to be maintained, because, "in recent times, neither naive courtesy nor friendliness have saved any country from aggression and occupation." In 1943, in a conversation with National Councilor Feldmann, himself a journalist, Pilet put the press's influence on events into its context: "There was plenty of influence in the sense that, in my view, the press cannot tip the balance in the case of a deliberate decision to attack Switzerland; but a decision can also be made under pressure of emotion provoked by certain press statements. We need to avoid this danger. Hitler is a complete lunatic."[11]

On June 18, 1940, the day after Marshal Pétain, who had just taken over the French government, requested an armistice, the president of the Confederation met with General Guisan; Federal Councilors Etter, Minger, and Baumann; Minister Bonna, head of the Foreign Affairs Division; Colonel Logoz, legal advisor to the General Staff; and Bernard Barbey of Guisan's private staff. Guisan summed up the situation: there were important German concentrations in the Black Forest. We did not know whether they were assigned to break through the Maginot line or to attack Switzerland. A mechanized group coming from Champagne was heading to Besançon and Pontarlier. This could have induced the French troops to take refuge in Switzerland and therefore cross the Jura mountains. The Swiss army, most of which was facing north, hastily set up a line of defense on the Mentue and the forest massif of the Jorat. Some internment would arise. Would we have to evacuate Zurich?[12]

NOTES

1. Gonzague de Reynold, *Mes Mémoires,* t. III, 643, 668–69.

2. Edgar Bonjour, *Neutralité,* vol. IV, 69; and *Gazette de Lausanne*, April 19, 1995.

3. Edgar Bonjour, *Neutralité*, 72–74; and Jean-Philippe Rau, *Pilet-Golaz,* 24–25.

4. André Lasserre, *La Suisse des Années Sombres* (Lausanne, 1989). Recalls fluctuations in public opinion during this period, especially 69–87. Daniel Bourgeois, *Le IIIe Reich . . . ,* 186–91; and Marcel Pilet-Golaz, 12–13.

5. Bernard Barbey, *PC du Général*, 24.

6. *La Gazette de Lausanne* for the indicated dates; and Jean-Philippe Rau, *Pilet-Golaz,* 31–33.

7. Erwin Bucher, *Zwischen Bundesrat und General,* 522.

8. Willy Bretscher, *"Der Tagesbefehl des General," in Neue Zürcher Zeitung,* June 6, 1940.

9. Gonzague de Reynold, *Mes Mémoires*, 640–50.

10. Edgar Bonjour, *Neutralité*, vol. V, 9–41; and Bernard Barbey, *Aller et Retour* (Neuchâtel, 1967). This officer, who was very active within the General's private staff, drew up the journal of the negotiations he conducted with the French officers.

11. *Documents Diplomatiques*, vol. 13, 668; Edgar Bonjour, *Neutralité,* vol. V, 173–97; Gonzague de Reynold, *Mes Mémoires*, 650; and Willy Gautschi, *Le Général Guisan*, 544–62.

12. Bernard Barbey, *PC du Général*, 20–21.

Chapter Five

The Speech of June 25, 1940

With an obvious threat at the frontiers and in an atmosphere of disquiet and confusion dominating the population, Pilet, in his capacity as president of the Swiss Confederation, delivered an address over French-speaking Swiss radio. This undoubtedly led to more commentary afterward than it attracted attention at the time, in spite of the gravity of the circumstances. He had been thinking it over for three days, according to his notes, with the army and the press waiting from one moment to the next for an official comment at the time when France's surrender was overturning European assumptions. He sketched out its principal characteristics in an untidy manuscript of June 23. He discussed the text on the evening of the 24th with Etter, who delivered the text in German; Minger; and National Councilor Théo Gut, liaison officer for the press between the army command and the government. Enrico Celio would read the text in Italian. The other members of the Federal Council were not consulted in advance, but they gave their approval that day by requesting that it be delivered that very evening.[1]

SPEECH OF JUNE 25, 1940
BY THE PRESIDENT OF THE CONFEDERATION

My fellow Swiss, you have probably asked why I have kept silent for weeks, nearly seven weeks. Has the Federal Council nothing to say in the presence of these events unfolding like a tragic film on the world screen?

The Federal Council had to reflect, anticipate, decide, and act, not discuss. We have all too much of a tendency to talk, which is not going to change the course of events at all.

If the council is addressing the Swiss people again today, it is because something very important has happened which is fraught with consequences and partially unpredictable.

France has just concluded a truce with Germany and Italy.

Whatever may be the sadness felt by all Christians before the ruin and accumulated sorrow, it is for us Swiss a matter of great relief to know that our three great neighbors are on the road to peace. These neighbors with which we have such close intellectual and economic relations, these neighbors who join together in spirit at the peak of our Alps—near the sky—and whose civilizations have enriched us for centuries, as the rivers coming down from the Gotthard have nourished their plains.

This appeasement—is that not the word?—is natural and human, especially for the modest neutrals who have been spared up to now in every respect. However, that must not deceive us. It would be dangerous to allow ourselves the illusions of uninformed contentment. The present we have just lived through carries too heavy a future for us to fall softly back into the past.

Whoever speaks of armistice does not yet speak of peace, and our continent remains in a state of alert.

Certainly, because war will no longer rage at our frontiers, we can soon envisage a partial and gradual demobilization of our army. But this demobilization in itself will pose delicate problems for our national economy, which has been deeply changed. International collaboration, so necessary for the prosperity of peoples, is far from being reestablished. The British Empire is proclaiming its firm resolve to fight on by land, sea, and air. Before resuming its progress, Europe must find a new equilibrium, so different from before, which will undoubtedly be grounded on other foundations than those which the League of Nations was unable to establish, despite its vain efforts.

Everywhere, in all fields, spiritual and material, economic and political, an indispensable realignment will need strenuous efforts that will have to be applied beyond outdated formulas if they are to have any effect. This cannot be done without giving up a good deal and without painful sacrifices.

Think of our trade, our industry, and our agriculture as concrete examples. How hard it will be for them to adapt to the new circumstances! They will need to overcome obstacles which would have seemed unsurmountable less than a year ago, in order to assure everyone bread to nourish the body and work to comfort the soul; this is a fundamental duty.

Some major decisions will be needed to achieve this result, a meager one perhaps in the eyes of the indifferent, but of capital importance for the country's well-being. These are not decisions that have been extensively debated, discussed, and weighed. What good would they be in face of the powerful and swift flow of events that can be anticipated? We need decisions that are at once considered, swift, and authoritative.

Yes, I do mean authoritative. Make no mistake, the times we are living in will destroy many of our old, comfortable, and lazy attitudes. I dare not call them superstitions, but that is what I think. No matter—let us not confuse routine and ossified habits with tradition, the nourishing sap which rises from the roots of history. Tradition, on the contrary, must be renewed because it does not intend to stand around, but to march intelligently from the past into the future. This is no time to look back sadly, but to look resolutely forward, to contribute all our modest but useful strength to the restoration of a dislocated world.

The Federal Council has promised you the truth. It will tell you the unvarnished truth without fear.

The time has come for a renaissance of self. Each of us must put off his old self.

That means:
Do not mince words, create ideas.
Do not discuss, work.
Do not play, produce.
Do not ask, give.

Certainly this cannot be done without psychological and material pain.

Let us not mince words — we must restrain ourselves. Before thinking of ourselves alone, think of others — inside and outside the family — of the disinherited, the weak, the miserable.

This does not mean giving charity from surplus; we will be called on to share what we had thought of before as our necessities. This will not be charity from the rich, but from a widow's mite. The Gospel always lifts up creatures in adversity.

There is no doubt we will have to give up many conveniences and commodities we hold to because they are an unconscious manifestation of our egotism. Far from impoverishing us, this will enrich us.

We will resume the salutary usage of enduring a good deal of pain for a modest result, when we had been lulled with the hope of little effort for a large result. As if the effort alone were not enough to make us happy! Ask the athletes; they have always known this!

Rather than thinking of ourselves and our comforts, we will think of others and their basic needs. That is where true solidarity lies, the solidarity of acts, not of words and processions. That is what builds up our national community in confidence and unity, by work and by order, these two great creative forces.

Work: the Federal Council will provide it to the Swiss people, no matter what it costs.

Order: it is innate in us, and I am persuaded that it will be maintained without difficulty with the support of all good citizens.

They will understand that the government must act. Conscious of its responsibilities, it will take them on fully; outside of and above political parties, in the service of all the Swiss, sons of the same earth, citizens of the same country. It is up to you, Swiss citizens, to follow it, as a sure and devoted guide who will not always be able to explain, comment on, or justify its decisions. Events are unrolling swiftly. We must adopt their rhythm. It is thus and only thus that we will safeguard our future.

Individual, regional, and partisan differences will disappear in the melting pot of national interest, the supreme law.

Line up behind the Federal Council. Keep calm as it does. Become firm as it is. Have confidence as it does. Heaven will extend its protection if we will deserve it.

Courage and resolution, a spirit of sacrifice, sure of itself — these are your saving virtues. Through them our free, humane, understanding, welcoming country will continue its fraternal mission, which will inspire the great European civilizations.

Swiss citizens, my brothers worthy of the past, let us go boldly forward into the future. May God watch over us.

Edgar Bonjour, in the original German edition of his *Geschichte der Schweizerischen Neutralität* (volume IV, 117–20), gives only the French text of the address delivered by Pilet and states in a note that the German version had been adapted in order to eliminate a small number of expressions that could be considered as superfluous rhetorical flourishes. He remarks that at certain points, the German text used terminology that "dangerously" approached National Socialist jargon. He lay responsibility for the address, with its ambiguity and lack of firmness, exclusively at Pilet's door.

Now we have seen that according to Bonjour himself, the substance of the speech had been discussed in common until late in the night of June 24 by the Confederation president, Federal Councilors Etter and Minger, and National Councilor Théodore Gut, who had originally proposed the idea. By all indications, the French text reflects the literary mannerisms of Pilet. But Etter did not confine himself to a passive reading of a text translated by his staff. If it is true that he received the speech barely an hour before delivering it and made only a few stylistic corrections, these "stylistic corrections," Bonjour assures us, could harden the tone of the speech in the mind of a well-read person with any stated political convictions.

As a loyal colleague, Etter admitted that there was some collective responsibility when he stated in 1966, according to Bonjour, that he had asked if the Federal Council had found the right words. Everything had been carefully considered. "But we were not sufficiently concerned at the effect the speech would have on the people; and who could guarantee that in his haste he never made mistakes?"[2]

It cannot be denied that the "stylistic corrections," not to speak of the differences, introduced into the German translation altered the tone of the speech in German, which the airwaves and the press delivered to three-quarters of the Swiss people. Erwin Bucher, in *Zwischen General und Bundesrat,* ascribes more importance than Bonjour does to these differences. He notes that the relatively literal German translation allows the style of the French to come through. "It does not sound very Swiss," one might have said. But it also happened that the translation changed the meaning: "authoritative decisions made" indicates only one direction of intent, not the new jurisdiction. The more exact term *Machtbefugnis* (authority, power) calls to mind extraordinary powers. The contribution to the "restoration of a dislocated world" is limited to a finding of disorder. The collaboration in the *Wiederherstellung der in Umbruch Begriffenen Welt* (the recovery of a world in total upheaval) implies participation in a transformation already underway. Finally, "the sure and devoted guide," which the Federal Council pledged in the French text that it would be, becomes the *führer* in German, not less "sure and devoted," but which could not fail to be compared with the führer raging beyond the Rhine.

According to an interview by Werner Rings, Enrico Celio, who took charge of the speech in Italian, recognized that Etter had made some changes in the text. However, Etter, as usual, expressed himself in a tone of solemn gravity that made an impression on his German listeners. This was confirmed by National Councilor Hans Konrad Sonderegger, in the *Demokrat* of June 29, 1940: "What happened that he addressed the people in so solemn and moving a way? With his sepulchral voice, Etter gave the impression that an unexpected catastrophe was threatening." In fact, the threat was real and more serious than the Federal Council thought at the time, since it was announcing a partial demobilization. But the theatrical tone appeared out of place, because people were so unaware of how real the immediate danger was. The speech hammered out in the harshly accented dialectical language of the federal councilor from Zug, and charged with understandable emotion, inevitably took on a more disquieting tone than that of the fluid and embellished prose of the magistrate from Vaud, which was closer to evangelical preaching than to patriotic exaltation.

Even though there was no formal difference in a text that had been drawn up in common, clearly the German version incited the most negative reactions. This did not stop the historical rumor from assigning all the responsibility to Pilet. It could be said, not without some truth, that Switzerland was a country where people listened well because they understood so badly. The fog of different languages and difficulties in translation could also cause misunderstandings and deplorable divisions. This partially explains the different, generally unfavorable interpretations given to the address of June 25, 1940.

Was it a speech or a sermon? Not with convincing arguments or by developing a detailed government program, this text moved its hearers as an eloquent sermon addressed more to the heart than to reason. Pilet addressed the listener, involved the listener personally, tried to seduce with literary imagery, of unequal quality but traditional and reassuring as when, for example, he referred to the peaks of the Alps near heaven, to the Gotthard from whence the rivers fertilize Europe, to the bread which nourishes the body, "the work that comforts the soul." As in a Sunday sermon, he first brought out as a confessing sinner, our well-being, our "illusions about uninformed contentment" to call on us thereafter to be converted again, to make amends, to make sacrifices which, under the guidance of the Federal Council and with the help of providence, would lead us to salvation through redemption. The elegant vivacity of the phrase, the flowery images, the frequent reference to Biblical memories, makes it a moving text on rereading it.

But was it decisive? In any case, it was scarcely decisive in the sense that its evocative imagery and its appeal to moral rejuvenation did not provide an interpretation of the political situation or any exact idea of what concrete steps were envisaged. Was this perhaps deliberate? What were the purposes of the speech? The interpretation of the situation had to be prudent. No matter how obvious it was, the overthrow of European equilibrium had to be evoked, but without value judgments, without celebrating the Axis victory, without deploring the defeat of the democracies, and without reassuring the Swiss people too quickly on the return of peace, when the disquieting weight of the tanks bearing down on our frontiers was well known and would have been unbearable to bring up. "Whoever speaks of armistice does not yet speak of peace and our continent remains in a state of alert. . . . Collaboration among the peoples is far from being reestablished. . . . The British Empire," and not just England, " is proclaiming its firm resolve to continue the struggle on land, sea and air." In any event, there was nothing in the speech that could be interpreted as predicting an Axis victory and resignation to German domination, in spite of Bonjour's assumptions. These ideas, taken separately, could even pass for a challenge in the eyes of a conqueror still flush with his victory, who believed he had remade Europe for 1000 years. But it is true that they were clothed by the evocation of a "new equilibrium that is very different from the former one and which will undoubtedly be grounded on other foundations than those which the League of Nations has not been able to establish, in spite of its vain attempts." This rejection of the former international order, obvious to public opinion which did not much regret it at the time, was appropriate for appeasing the Third Reich. But on the other hand, it did not mean adherence to the "New Order." The speech was carefully drafted to avoid defining its nature and principles and to refrain from celebrating its triumphant grandeur, which the great majority of Swiss were far from accepting. In spite of the restraint and ambiguity of the idea, the Third Reich believed it had found an announcement of deep changes in Swiss policy in this statement of a new equilibrium. This was the interpretation given rather quickly by the German minister at Bern and the Nazi propaganda services.[3]

After sketching the provisional situation in Europe, the next objective of the speech was to define what the Federal Council expected from the growing awareness of the Swiss and their acceptance of their responsibilities. Certainly they would have to adapt, even though the word was a dangerous one to use. It did not mean to adapt to an imported political regime that had been imposed from abroad, but to adapt to the gravity of the "new circumstances," to an indispensable effort to work in agriculture, industry, and commerce, to an effort at rearranging, and solidarity which "cannot be done without giving up a great deal or without painful sacrifices." Pilet stressed the government's desire to provide work "whatever it costs," which implied an intervention in the economy that the unions could like. Switzerland must find the force for this realignment "in itself, by shedding a number of old, comfortable, and indolent attitudes" from the bog of routine, by finding the force of "tradition, the life blood that arises from the very depth of history . . . which needs renewal because it does not intend to stand around in place, but to march intelligently from the past into the future." It is in this sense that "the former must be stripped away," and the country regenerated in its moral and traditional values of order and work. Without conceding a thing to National Socialist or fascist ideology, the speech prefigured the return to "the moral order," which was also to be Marshal Pétain's essential theme at that time.

Then, in its third element, the speech took up the exercise of power, which implied swift decisions and confidence in authority. "Not decisions that have been extensively debated, discussed, and weighed. What good would they be in the face of the swift and powerful flow of events to be anticipated? We need decisions that are at once considered, swift, and authoritative. Yes, I said authoritative."

Did these authoritative decisions "without always explaining, commenting on, or justifying them," announce a basic reform of institutions by restricting their democratic character? The literal translation of the mission of the *guide sûr* which the French text ascribed to the Federal Council as *führer* could, to tell the truth, make shivers run up people's spines. It evoked the evil dictatorship of our neighbors, especially since the speech did not specify either the subject or the nature of the "decisions made authoritatively."

One would undoubtedly be hard put to imagine some demonic führer taking into his hands the destiny of the Confederation, but it must be said that the French defeat imperiled democracy, even in its Swiss form. The image of Pétain, the venerable conqueror at Verdun, then untainted, "making a gift of his person to France," restoring the moral order and national discipline, could at that moment give ideas to many Swiss, as it did then to the great majority of French. The name of Philippe Etter, with his Roman profile and made into a *Landamann de Suisse*, could run clandestinely without Etter himself, or much less Pilet, getting lost in fantasies.

What fundamental revision in the institutions could Pilet and his colleagues have been contemplating? "Do not mince words, create ideas." However, the speech had no specific indication about these innovative concepts. It limited itself to marking a rhetorical indication—interior renewal, effort, solidarity, order, authority. "The government, aware of its responsibilities, will assume them fully." This was certainly the least of its duties, but it did not imply a new definition of these responsibilities, which had already been sharply increased by the full powers given it. At the least, this vibrant declaration of intent should have also articulated a precise plan.

The Federal Council does not appear to have thought of any plan. It is true that on September 10, 1940, at the request of the Full Powers Committee of the National Council, it discussed the broad lines of government policy on the basis of an outline prepared by the Department of the Interior. As to the institutions, the council admitted the need of a total revision of the Constitution, a vow that was piously renewed periodically but constantly postponed for lack of agreement. But the contradictory diversity of the propositions advanced was supplemented by the fact that there was less urgency for a full-scale debate on the law of the land than the country's political and economic survival. One of the requests was for an increase in executive power. This request was fulfilled by the full powers given it. It was therefore not necessary to increase its authority. The Federal Council firmly intended to use these full powers to the extent that that would be useful for the country's interest, but no further. The debate the following day in the Full Powers Committee does not appear to have reached any other conclusions.[4]

Neither Pilet nor his colleagues ever considered an alignment, whether imposed or spontaneous, with the authoritarian regimes which were then flourishing in Europe. On September 12, 1940, at the *Comptoir suisse de Lausanne* he stated on this issue, "The institutions are secondary. They are worth the use made of them. Ours are not as bad as some are claiming. Oh, I would be the last to deny that they have undergone what I might call demagogic degeneration which must be resolutely combated. We must make use of the experience of others. But when they are wisely used, without confusion of powers, without dispersion of authority and responsibility—with each in his place to accomplish the task assigned him—without a multiplicity of instances, their principles are sound."[5]

The Federal Council, in its cohesion and in close touch with the committees in Parliament, inspired by a common and firm will to defend the political independence and democratic institutions of the country without effusions for the press, showed itself in action to be more effective than phantasms of "muscular democracy," the mirages of corporatist structure, or the abstractions of law professors.

Further, public opinion, the press, and the political parties focused their interest less on the institutional aspects of the speech than on the Federal Council's activities directed toward saving independence and the emphasis the council had placed or had abstained from placing in the speech. In this regard, it may appear astonishing that neither the will to resist nor the merits of the frontier guards, the half-million men mobilized over the past ten months, nor the effort going into arming and fortification were evoked. Pilet defended himself from this badly by stating that it was a matter for General Guisan. But perhaps, after the very terse statements of April 18 and May 10 from the Federal Council, he was not inclined to sound the clarion call at that moment when the unleashing of an attack was hanging by a hair, on a caprice of the führer, or to increase confusion in the country by confirming an immediate threat with which we are familiar today in all its gravity.

In the context of the dramatic uncertainty of the future, it was both dangerous and presumptuous to pour out heroic proclamations and engage in definitive statements. Instead, it would be better, in view of the gravity of the circumstances, to appeal in general terms to renew hearts and spirits and have confidence in Heaven and the Federal Council.

But this reckoned without a good many critical spirits who, through simple civic curiosity or by political ill will, attempted to break loose from an idea that was more moral than political, more intuitive than rational, and even sibylline, to a process going so far as to provoke the suspicion of alignment.

In the first days, the principal press organs greeted the speech favorably, to the great unhappiness of Bonjour. They viewed it as an appeal to take account of our responsibility at a turning point of history. They congratulated the Federal Council for demonstrating an innovating state of mind and encouraged public opinion to rally to the principles of moral regeneration that would allow Switzerland to deal with events as it affirmed itself, "free, humane, and understanding, in building up the community in confidence and union, for work and for order."[6]

Bonjour countered the broadcast of June 25 with a confidential circular for the press from the Federal Council from the pen of Théodore Gut, who had participated on the 24th in drawing up the text of the presidential address.

"We are not living through the first disruption of Europe that our country has had to undergo, but certainly it is the most dangerous. This does not justify pessimism or confusion. We must fight energetically against a pessimistic attitude. We must oppose to it an awareness of the realities and our will to face them. To refuse to recognize these realities would be to lack courage. But concern for our dignity, courage, and confidence in the future must be placed at the same level."[7]

This confidential circular in no way contradicted the official address. This text brought out what was essential in a concise, firm manner, better, in these highly critical circumstances, than the oratorical prose of the speech could have done. Prudence toward foreign powers inevitably imposed ambiguities and the need to reassure public opinion, even while preparing it for indispensable efforts and sacrifices.

NOTES

1. On the speech in general, see *Documents Diplomatiques*, vol. 13, 76–62; Edgar Bonjour, *Neutralité*, vol. IV, 107–29; and Erwin Bucher, *Zwischen Bundesrat und General*, 536–47.

2. Edgar Bonjour, *Neutralité*, 116 (note).

3. Daniel Bourgeois, *L'Image Allemande de Pilet-Golaz 1940–44*, 77–78; see also a passage of the *Wehrmacht-Propaganda-Lagebericht* of July 8, 1940, as well as the further allusions of German Minister Köcher in Bern.

4. *Documents Diplomatiques*, vol. 13, 918–27.

5. Erwin Bucher, *Zwischen Bimdesrat*, 525.

6. Edgar Bonjour, *Neutralité*, 116–17.

7. Edgar Bonjour, *Neutralité*, 129.

Chapter Six

Reactions to the Speech of June 25, 1940

On June 26, Pilet-Golaz met with the Full Powers Committee of the National Council. This meeting gave him an opportunity to take the political temperature and to respond to the criticisms arising from his address of the previous day.[1] The federal president began by giving his understanding of the situation, discussing the position of the military forces after the two armistices. He was not aware of, or said nothing about, what we now know: the Germans were concentrating on our borders, and plans were being prepared for an attack on Switzerland. From there, he continued to state that the probability of Swiss territory being invaded was limited. The economy's needs justified some, but only partial, demobilization. He noted his country's de facto break, at least temporarily, in economic relations with France and England.

In response to a question by National Councilor Grimm on the neutrality policy and the consequences of recent events, Pilet noted with satisfaction the agreement that had been reached with Italy. Discussions with Germany were underway, but it was obvious that relations with the neighbor to the north were to become much more important. We were totally dependent on Germany for coal, and the Germans were certainly not going to make a gift of any. Given the circumstances, and in the face of an uncertain and agitated future, Pilet suggested that "Our efforts should be directed at avoiding subjection to any one economic bloc. We need to establish counterweights to certain economic pressures that could be brought to bear on us from the north, the south, and the west." This refusal to allow Switzerland to be integrated into an economic alliance bears witness to the desire for independence.

There was no way to minimize the difficulties of the situation. The Federal Council established a plan to provide work for demobilized soldiers, because the dangers of unemployment and its political consequences seemed for the moment more serious than those of military invasion.

45

In the ensuing review, which lasted into the following day, National Councilor Roman Abt of the Agrarian Party expressed his satisfaction with the speech of the 25th and hoped for the demobilization of at least two-thirds of the army, mindful as he was of the needs of agriculture in particular. He took issue strongly with the Swiss press, which in his view was ignoring the obvious and refusing to recognize that Germany had imposed its superiority on the continent. The British were heavily responsible. They pushed others into the conflict and especially dragged in the neutrals, without themselves taking the trouble to make the necessary preparations. Recognizing Germany's dominant position did not mean aligning with it but adapting to it.

This brought a vigorous reply from Gottlieb Duttweiler, according to whom Abt was preaching a defeatism more serious than the activity of a fifth column. The leader of the Independents and patron of the Migros denounced the speed with which certain business circles tried to adapt to the new situation. They were wrong. Germany understood clear and firm language. We should not proceed at a crawl. Although his preliminary reaction to the Federal Council's speech on the previous day was enthusiastic—"finally some new language"—Duttweiler warned the government against concessions, even minimal ones, and urged firmness. Political foresight was ultimately more important than economic adaptation. He questioned the potential results of government intervention. Only a free economy would make it possible to give work to the people.

Of the comments offered by the Socialists, one may note the concern of Perret from Neuchâtel for unemployment and the fate of Swiss exports. Oprecht was disappointed at certain ambiguities and protested certain debatable points in the speech, especially in the German text. Did the Swiss government think itself weak because France succumbed? That would lend a hand too easily to the Third Reich. We should harbor no illusions about Germany's feelings toward us. The peril had not passed; it would be dangerous to demobilize too much. Robert Grimm stressed the value of Switzerland's democratic vocation and the need to maintain and defend it. He warned against the danger of infiltration and stressed the need of a spiritual defense.

The Lucerne radical Meyer warned against a uselessly provocative attitude that could unleash a conflict, while the conservative Dollfuss from Ticino, who was also the adjutant general of the army, stated that the army was motivated by a desire to defend itself to extreme limits. Work was proceeding on a national breviary, and each day, unit commanders were enjoined to motivate their troops with the will to resist. Gorgerat, a liberal from Vaud, cast doubt on the illusion of security. Germany had not given up its desire to unite all the peoples that spoke its language. His fellow councilor from Vaud, the radical Vallotton, confirmed the danger of the Third Reich's ambitions and the strong

German concentrations on the Jura. He deplored the fact that the speech had not devoted a word to the soldiers and hoped that the Federal Council and the army would do their duty if conditions incompatible with the country's independence and honor were imposed. Thus, the great majority of the comments warned against concessions and stressed the need for political independence and firmness in defending Switzerland.

In his reply, Pilet brought out the distortions of certain ideas in the speech. There was no question of total demobilization, but only of a partial and gradual one whose economic consequences for the time being needed to be understood. He drew his listeners' attention to the fact that the armistice was not peace and that the military danger persisted. There could be no doubt that our country would have to be defended against any attack or intolerable demand from abroad. But it had to be defended intelligently; defensive deployments had to be adopted. There was no question of keeping only the unemployed in the army. There had to be troops ready and able to defend the country.

The danger from Germany was still present, but means other than weapons had to be used against it. The economic danger had to be fended off; the people had to be given not just bread but employment.

Pilet was reproached for not having said a word about democracy. He responded that "[i]t does not sit well to constantly bring up external matters, which are outside the discussion. I have carefully avoided any discussion of dictatorship, but I did speak of authority and of important decisions, without getting bogged down in interminable discussions in committees. It was not without good reason, furthermore, that I spoke of a free country. But we need a certain confidence in the government to keep it that way, without wasting our energy in vain verbiage and long accounts."

Why did he not address a special salute to our army? "The moment was not right for that. Today General Guisan will address the army; then the government will speak to the people to convey its thanks to the army after demobilization. Now it is under the banners." In addition, Pilet stated that "[w]e will have to undergo difficult privations and make sacrifices if we want to retain our position and our mission in the world."

One may credit the president with a desire to be effective in supporting democracy, independence, and defense, which Pilet clearly did. But the explanation he gave of his failure to deliver a message to the army was a bit abrupt. The army is not a separate institution. It must be closely tied to foreign policy, for which the government assumed responsibility and management. The army had a right to gratitude, encouragement, and a public confirmation of its mission.

It is only fair, however, to note that on July 5, 1940, President Pilet conveyed to the soldiers the gratitude of the Federal Council and the country for fulfilling their duty. They would be sent home the following day; a good number of them had also guarded our borders in 1914–18. Pilet's detractors scarcely mentioned this at all. Yet he said this: "Our most precious possession is our national independence, which the sacrifices and military qualities of our fathers have maintained. A people having confidence in itself has always had the right to exist. However, this confidence needs to be based on the people's will and strength to assert itself. The soldiers are the ones who take on this task. We rely on you, on the example you set, for your commitment to our small but beautiful country. You can count on the recognition of the country."[2]

At first, the press had favorably accepted the "sermon" of June 25, which annoyed Edgar Bonjour. He did not conceal his disappointment at seeing newspapers which had declared themselves to be the sworn enemies of National Socialism celebrating a new policy orientation. Gradually, however, testifying to an unusual adaptability, the tone of the press altered, opening the way to critical commentaries. The *Bund*, the *Neue Zürcher Zeitung*, and the *Basler Nachtrichten* expressed concern at what the hypocritical reform bloc might be concealing. The *Journal de Genève* deplored the sibylline nature of the speech and praised the democratic system in such a way as to criticize it: "It is not because democracy—or rather a certain form of democracy—has contributed to France's misfortune that ours is to be condemned. The two systems are different and their operation has nothing in common. . . . We would do well to refrain from a certain defeatism that is an abdication of the spirit." Clearly, there was suspicion of a drift to an authoritarian regime.[3]

"The speech came within a hair of a cold coup!" a fearful National Councilor Feldmann exclaimed similarly in a letter to General Guisan.[4] The Socialist press was bluntly critical. The *Sentinelle* of Neuchâtel certainly intended to save the ship's pilot when the storm was blowing, but the *Volksrecht* and the *Tagwacht* did not blunt their attacks; the terms in the speech were not in the Swiss vocabulary. Adaptation would not safeguard Switzerland's democracy and independence; they were unconditionally tied together.

Nevertheless, overall the biblical eloquence of the speech was sufficiently noble and extensive that everyone could find support in it for their sometimes contradictory convictions. It appeared that the speech was criticized less by the average Swiss than by a minority of the elite, partisans and politicians who were jealous to some extent of the competence they were compelled to recognize in Pilet and irritated by his attitude of derisive and distant superiority. Philippe Marguerat, seeking to balance in a simplistic and inequitable Manichaeanism the contrasting images of the two men who bore the weight of our destiny, came up with an original view of the speech. "If the external effect of Pilet's words—in Germany—was satisfactory, the domestic effect on Swiss public opinion appears much less negative than has long been believed. Without discounting the latent spirit of resistance in public opinion, the speech contributed positively to appeasing the Reich by catching German diplomats in the snare of its equivocations. It constituted a sort of smoke-screen, a screen behind which the Swiss army, surprised by the French military collapse, could reorganize . . . that is, draw up and adopt a new plan for better military defense and stronger dissuasion of the potential adversary."[5] This should have led to the conclusion that the two policies, expressed in the speech and General Guisan's remarks on July 25 at the Rütli, were complementary. However, Marguerat did not go that far.

The German consul general in Zurich stated in a report to Minister Köcher that opinions were divided on the day after the speech. He recorded a desire to adapt to new circumstances and to end long-winded discussions and a certain authoritarian bent, but in truth he displayed a satisfaction full of hesitation and reserve. The economic future caused concern, and bank activity was slowing down.[6]

In *La Suisse des Années Sombres*, André Lasserre mentioned the weekly analyses of public opinion drafted by the psychologists for the press and radio division of the army adjutant's office and also of the Interior and Justice Departments.[7] He brought out the order mentioned above, which was distributed in confidence to the newspapers. It laid special stress on the will to resist, which the speech had deliberately omitted.

The state of public opinion in the week following the speech showed a generally positive reaction but also great diversity of views. The authors of the weekly report noted that it was impossible to determine whether the majority of responses were positive or negative. "The greatest number of positive responses come from circles that are aware of the defects in the parliamentary system as it is practiced. . . . Thus, there are political groups that have long demanded a reinforcement of government powers and they see today the justification of their view. These include many conservatives, young liberals, and independents. However, it is impossible to generalize because these same circles criticized the form of the speech or various expressions in it. Overall, it may be said that young people approved the speech more than the older generations." The single word "renovation" can suffice here, whatever the substance may have been. Did public opinion among French-speaking Swiss reproach the speech for its pro-Pétain tone? There is reason to doubt that, because the democracy of the Third Republic was not then in favor, and Marshal Pétain enjoyed respect. On the other hand, the French speakers felt the threat of dictatorship less viscerally. Certainly the profascist frontists never enjoyed great success there, nor was there any surrender to anxiety. The nearly congenital antifascism of the majority in Italian-speaking Ticino kept them far from any thought of adaptation. As for the people of Basel, "their general antitotalitarianism led to a rejection of the speech: they neither closed ranks behind Germany nor conformed to the government."

The Axis press noted a change. Unable to interpret its significance, it recorded it as a step toward the new European order. But this was not without irony or reserve. It doubted—wrongly—the sincerity of this gesture. "The Swiss have quickly put off the old Adam." The press in Switzerland had known its "twilight of the gods," a terrible awakening as it lived through a night of a turning point in history. However, Swiss journalists should not imagine that this strategic retreat was being interpreted in Germany as the sign of better understanding. "We have not forgotten anything and we will not forget anything. Your pretentious self-sufficiency will learn the necessary humiliation. You will have nothing to say in the new Europe and you will have to pay for the windows you have broken." The appeasement policy the Federal Council had sought with the speech of June 25 was ill repaid in the German press, even if the official world expressed its satisfaction. As to the announcement of institutional reforms in the sense of a reinforcement of executive power, Minister Köcher doubted these reforms would be carried out. In view of the complications of the referendum procedure, it was doubtful whether they would be popular enough to be ratified.[8] Elsewhere, he proposed collaboration to Pilet without defining its nature or its limits.

Within the army, the speech elicited varied and contradictory reactions. Troops on active duty did not seem to have paid much attention to it. I do not remember personally having heard it or even having read it. The battalion to which I belonged in December 1939 had come down on foot from the Combremont Plateau to Lausanne to serve as honor guard at a reception for President Pilet, then newly elected. After a meal that was at least dietetic and an uncomfortable night in the straw, the honor guard resumed its march in nailed shoes in the snow and cold, without taking to heart the undying memory of the chief magistrate. The speech as I remember it neither lit the flame of patriotism nor led to indignation. Political eloquence was far and away the least of our cares.

If indifference predominated in the ranks—although some found it more favorably received among the young than the old—many officers registered their surprise or indignation at the fact that the only mention of the army was to announce "a gradual and partial demobilization." It appears this was not discussed at General Guisan's table, but people were thinking about it nevertheless. Among the officers on the general's personal staff, there was irritation at Minger's failure to protest against the speech which he had helped to draft and at "being ashamed for the first time of being Swiss." In his anger, Captain Alfred Ernst of the General Staff, assigned to the intelligence service and a future corps commander, threw his helmet to the ground, feeling betrayed. Twenty years later, time and experience would lead him to believe that the speech was less reprehensible than he had thought at the time. "An interpretation of the speech must take account of the tension then prevailing. Its negative effect was more from what he did not say than what he did."[9]

Meanwhile, in consternation at the speech and at the defeatism of many people, and undoubtedly influenced by the establishment of a Gotthard League on June 22 in Zurich on the initiative of Denis de Rougemont and Professor Théophile Spörri designed to fortify the people's spirit of resistance, Ernst and about thirty of his comrades, mostly captains, one lieutenant colonel, and a corporal who later became an ambassador, set up what was called the "officers' conspiracy."[10] Its purpose was to organize the necessary preparations "for appealing to the army to fight in case the Federal Council or even the general would be ready to surrender under the political or military pressure of the Third Reich." Even though the army's general orders called for resistance in all circumstances, they received political and military encouragement in their preventive rebellion. But their plans remained vague, according to the presently available documentation and historical criticism. The plot of the "young Turks," as Pilet called them, was not appropriate for either democratic institutions or military discipline. An investigation was opened and "the plotters," in view of the patriotism of their intentions, were given only benign disciplinary action that did not harm their careers and even earned them the good will of the high command. Pilet would have liked to have had them excluded from the Army General Staff "for having become involved in the country's domestic and foreign politics." At a time when the authorities appeared insufficiently conscious of the country's independence, it would always be difficult to set a boundary between the rules of formal discipline and, in times of imminent danger, the citizen's duty in conscience to resist in spite of that discipline.

Parallel to the "officers' plot," a national resistance movement, *Aktion nationaler Wiederstand* (National Resistance Action), had been developing since the end of summer 1940, inspired notably by Captain Hans Hausamann, who headed a private information service that worked with the Army Intelligence Service, among others.[11] This secret organization whose hundreds of members, in principle, did not know each other, had as its purpose to defend national independence, to fight against defeatism and the defeatists, and to prepare a clandestine struggle in case of war or excessive concessions by the political authorities. Politicians from all parties, industrialists and union leaders, officers, men of the church, and journalists rallied to the movement, which undoubtedly contributed to reinforcing the will to defend Switzerland. However, the organization also cultivated a methodical mistrust of the government in general and Pilet in particular, to which

Hausamann was certainly no stranger. As Bonjour noted, "Because of its activism, Action, more than other movements, entered into conflict with the authorities they were supposed to be supporting." The Federal Council countered with its policies, and this methodical mistrust which could otherwise have given rise to a serious division in the country gradually dwindled. Action was to die out, it seemed, after the summer of 1941.

Although some young captains, acting at the limits of discipline, had courageously recalled the will to resist and certainly encouraged it, other groups of older and more senior officers had conversely contemplated a policy of extensive and rapid demobilization even before June 25. Pilet was surely aware of this. This was the view of those whom Philippe Marguerat called the "pro-German technicians," and General Guisan termed the "triumvirate of the envious," referring especially to Corps Commanders Labhart, Wille, and Miescher. The idea of concentrating forces in the alpine redoubt was gaining ground. These three general officers wanted this regrouping to be as complete and rapid as possible, while maintaining only a minimum coverage at the border. This solution, which required fewer troops while maintaining at least the symbol of eventual resistance, would have allowed a significant demobilization, suitable for reassuring Germany on the score of Swiss aggressiveness—however unlikely—but especially "to put the Swiss economy more at the service of German policy." "We must hope that our economy will be able to fulfill Germany's industrial orders, in order to participate in this way in the Axis's new economic policy."[12]

This theory of collaboration, of an economic alignment with the Axis, would have meant giving up neutrality. The speech of June 25 had evoked "solidarity . . . which builds up our national community in confidence and unity, by work and by order" but not by alignment.

In spite of the rule of silence he had imposed on himself, Pilet would come back to the speech of June 25, 1940 two or three times later. On November 8, 1944, in the presence of his colleagues Kobelt and von Steiger and before a delegation of Socialist leaders, he said, "In placing oneself in the atmosphere of that time one soon realizes that the entire speech was inspired by the conviction that England would win the war, as strange as that may seem. And the English knew that." Neither the Socialist leaders nor, more to the point, the historian Bonjour were convinced by this assertion. Deducing from Pilet's ideas and attitude, Bonjour was even certain that "Pilet took a final German victory to be likely not only in 1940, but more so in 1941 and 1942."[13]

As we have already noted, the June 25 speech did not celebrate the German victory. Such flattery could have facilitated the difficult negotiations then underway with the Reich, which was all-powerful at that time. The war was not over. Minger and General Guisan were talking of a "cessation of hostilities."

Pilet corrected them; it was a "suspension of arms" between France, Germany, and Italy, as was stated in the speech. "International collaboration . . . is far from being reestablished." "The British Empire, and not just England, is proclaiming its firm resolve to fight on by land, sea, and air." This confirmed that total victory had not been assured, at the risk of defying German triumphalism. The former European equilibrium, based on the League of Nations, was destroyed. This did not mean that the new equilibrium, with other foundations, would be assured by the "New Order" which Germany would impose.[14]

Let us grant that the tone of the speech was muffled and its ideas sibylline. Could it have been anything else in that situation with its immediate threat and a formidable imbalance of forces? Pilet expressed neither his desires nor certitude of a final German victory, not so much because he would have provoked a reaction among the Swiss people as because he did not believe in it himself. But the reason he could not say so publicly is that it would have unleashed Hitler's forces. He could not even say so in friendly conversations among colleagues and friends since he knew by experience that they would not keep the secret and that the publicity would be all the more assured, diffused, and amplified. Even the secrets of the government were not safe from chattering vanity, attested by the "reliable source" in the *Café Fédéral* or the *Bar du Bellevue*.

Pilet, who was functionally prudent, naturally distant, and not inclined to conviviality, had one reliable, modest, and faithful friend in whom he could confide so as not to be alone and who would later be a witness for him. This was the journalist Georges Perrin, who wrote in the *Journal de Genève* of February 2, 1970, that "[a]t the end of September 1940, when I was walking with Pilet-Golaz, he confided to me, 'M. Perrin, the Germans are not going to win the war, but it will be a long one. If Hitler does not attack Russia, the hostilities could go on for fifteen years. If Germany turns against the Soviet Union, the war may last five years, but the Germans will not be the ones to win it.' His voice carried the accents of conviction. And I am as sure of it today as I was then that Mr. Pilet-Golaz did not believe in the final victory of the Axis." Perrin, whom I knew in Bern and for whom I have the highest esteem, explicitly confirmed this account to me.[15]

Perrin recalled two sentences in Pilet's speech of June 25, 1940: "Whoever says armistice is not yet saying peace," and "The British Empire proclaims its resolve to pursue the struggle by land, sea, and air." He added,

Pilet-Golaz always said that these two sentences in his speech expressed his deepest thoughts, if one could read them. If one were to say that it was difficult to see the certainty of a British victory under these formulas, Pilet would retort, 'Excuse me, I was not only president of the Confederation, but also head of the Political Department,' i.e., the Foreign Ministry. There was the diplomat, weighing his words, expressing himself. 'Rest assured that the Germans understood me.' Was he so sure of that? The art of diplomacy skillfully cultivates equivocation, and it may be admitted that Pilet's language could have left some with illusions. 'Since I couldn't be a lion, I forced myself to be a fox.'

It is obvious that, with his clear-thinking intelligence, Pilet could also show signs of pessimism. However, the fact that in 1936 he expressed to the French military attaché his disapproval of France's foreign policy and the responsibility of the Allies for the coming war for which they had not prepared does not mean that he espoused Germany's cause. That on one occasion he formulated justifiably critical observations on the democracies' policies obviously did not make him a zealot of National Socialism. That he expressed disappointment toward the end of the war at the expansion of Communism did not lead him to wish for a victory of the Third Reich. But there were allusions — certainly prudent ones — where he expressed his skepticism concerning the success of the Axis and stressed the need for Switzerland to save its independence in its neutrality.[16] When he stated to the Full Powers Committee on June 26, 1940 that the Swiss Confederation should not allow itself to be taken into an economic bloc, what did he mean by that if not the German-Italian alliance? On July 2, before the Foreign Affairs Committee of the National Council, he noted, "the Axis hegemony; but what military power will come to break it up now? America? Periods of hegemony are always dangerous for us. But the future belongs to God alone and equilibrium will be reestablished in the end." On July 29, the situation became critical because of the collapse of European equilibrium, "at least for the next few years."

On July 31, Pilet confided to the French ambassador his doubts about the success of an invasion of England. He believed that the German government "would not ask more than an arrangement with the British. The Reich cannot allow itself a defeat, nor even a half-success, and an offensive against the British Isles is an unknown quantity." In January 1941, when the German minister, asked against whom an order of the day from the commander in chief urging the Swiss to defend their country was directed if not the Axis countries, "your only neighbors currently?" Pilet answered, "Are you quite sure that we will always have only the Italians south of the Alps?"

Without claiming to be a prophet, his predictions turned out to be perceptive, more so than those of military intelligence. Erwin Bucher provides an example. In July 1940 Pilet announced to the French ambassador that the beginning of operations against England would be in the middle of the following month; it was on August 15 that the aerial offensive was unleashed. On

September 17, 1941, when the United States had not yet entered the war and the Germans were pursuing their blitzkrieg in the USSR, Pilet stated to the Foreign Affairs Committee of the National Council that, "[a]fter two years of war, the Axis has conquered Europe, but the Anglo-Saxons have encircled Europe." Before the same committee in May 1942, he said, "[o]n the continent, German hegemony has been defeated in the breach by Russia. Germany has seen the supremacy that it had acquired disappear." The conditions for opening a second front in Europe, however, had not yet been achieved, but one could see a southern front opening up—a prediction of the Anglo-American landing in North Africa in November 1942. In September of that year, Pilet noted that the German successes in Russia were not significant, that Russian resistance had not slackened, and that the entire Soviet front, from Kharkov to Murmansk, would soon be in motion.

When Bonjour stated that Pilet considered a final German victory "not only still possible but likely," even after the Anglo-American landing in 1942, it is probable that the author had taken into account neither the minutes of the committee meetings, nor Pilet's personal papers. But it is true that Pilet, even during the confidential discussions in committee, had to exercise the utmost prudence to keep from "letting the cat out of the bag," in spite of urging from the deputies. However, if he legitimately had feared it for a brief period, he never believed in Germany's final victory.

Pilet would comment further on his June 25 speech in the draft of a letter to Pierre Béguin dated December 22, 1948, which Béguin assured me he never received but which Bonjour published.[17] Pilet wrote:

We would need to know by whom and why, under those conditions, this speech was requested, how it was written, the modifications suggested to me after it was reviewed, and the sentences that were taken out. The manuscript demonstrates this and gives it its real meaning, perhaps a little too clearly and even imprudently in the situation in which we found ourselves; the fears we suffered which were not in the least those of the population; especially the diametrically opposed interpretation of the future that awaited us. This profound difference in conception and prediction explains the interpretation given, which falsified its meaning.

He had foreseen the swift defeat of the Allies in the campaign in France in 1940. But, contrary to public opinion, he intended to state that the war was not over, that it would be long and difficult for Switzerland before an Allied victory was reached, which he never doubted. "But how many Swiss read the speech? The Third Reich, on the other hand, had only too thoroughly discerned the true basis of my reflection. It led me to think that it needed us more than we needed them. My silent struggle with it during the summer of 1940 and throughout 1941, like my 'kid glove' efforts to hold off those of us who wanted rapprochement and cooperation, could not be disclosed—that would take a personal tone, not for myself, but for many others who were always there; we had to wait. They in turn confirmed the meaning of the speech and its profound conviction, although masked by the source of its inspiration."

It is easy for the historian wishing to paint a heroic fresco to condemn, in the quiet of his study fifteen years after restoration of peace, in the name of moral rigor and intransigent patriotism, a speech delivered by those politically responsible in the heat of events. The flames of war were threatening to engulf Switzerland; the aggressive army was on an operative footing and invasion plans were being hastily drawn up. The very fact that "the cloudy and troubling words that could be interpreted in different ways," as Bonjour puts it, had inspired a surge in their spirit of resistance in many who had not always supported the country's defense shows a felicitous awareness after all. But because it was delivered by the *government*, a proclamation of aggressive patriotism could easily have unleashed the avalanche amidst the hesitations of Germany's masters. The Federal Council was already taking serious—and necessary—risks by not celebrating the Axis victory in any way, and not lining up with a totalitarian Europe but instead simply urging patience, hard work, and solidarity for its people.

The speech, as Pilet admitted, failed in its effect. It brought confidence to some people but also the irritated hostility of politicians and military men, disappointment to some, and the indifference of many. He did not succeed in reestablishing the warm unity of the country in hope and cohesion. Certainly he did not approach capitulation, but rather a "kid glove" resistance that was also firm, as he in fact conducted it. This speech, awkward overall because of its ambiguities and interpreted with malice by his adversaries, was to place a heavy and lasting burden on the credit of Pilet-Golaz.

NOTES

1. *Documents Diplomatiques*, vol. 13, 763–68; and Edgar Bonjour, *Neutralité*, vol. IV, 112–16.

2. Erwin Bucher, *Zwischen Bundesrat und General*, 124.

3. Bonjour, *Neutralité*, vol. IV, 117–20.

4. Willi Gautschi, *Le Général Guisan*, 213.

5. Philippe Marguerat, *La Suisse Face au IIIᵉ Reich*, 23.

6. Bonjour, *Neutralité*, vol. IV, 121–22.

7. André Lasserre, *La Suisse des Années Sombres*, 32–34, 88–90; and Gautschi, *Le Général Guisan*, 211–12.

8. Bonjour, *Neutralité*, vol. IV, 122–23.

9. Gautschi, *Le Général Guisan*, 212.

10. On the Gotthard League, see Christian Gasser, *Der Gothardbund* (Bern, 1984); on the officers' plot: Bonjour, *Neutralité*, vol. IV, 172–86; Gautschi, *Le Général Guisan*, 227–57, 330; and Bucher, *Zwischen Bundesrat*, 244–51.

11. On National Resistance Action, see Bonjour, *Neutralité*, 212–17; and Bucher, *Zwischen Buhdesrat*, 465–71.

12. *Documents Diplomatiques,* vol. 13, 751–60; Gautschi, *Le Général Guisan*, 289–95; and Marguerat, *La Suisse*, 17–23.

13. Bonjour, *Neutralité*, vol. IV, 124.

14. Bucher, *Zwischen Bundesrat*, 516.

15. Jean-Philippe Rau, *Pilet-Golaz*, 37; and *Journal de Genève*, February 27, 1970.

16. Bucher, *Zwischen Bundesrat*, 516–19.

17. Bonjour, *Neutralité*, vol. IV, 124–26.

Chapter Seven

The Will to Resist

The omission of defense and the army from President Pilet-Golaz's address of June 25, probably deliberate but certainly unfortunate, cast doubt on the Federal Council's will to defend Switzerland. Some sporadic concessions likewise contributed to raising doubts, including the return of German planes and pilots interned for having violated neutral Swiss airspace and a partial demobilization, which was of dubious value when considerable German troops were on a war footing on the Jura border. But the harvest needed to be brought in!

Given the gravity of Switzerland's situation and the prevailing uncertainty and concern, rumors circulated questioning the government's commitment to resistance. David V. Kelly, Great Britain's representative in Bern, readily echoed these rumors in his reports to the Foreign Office.[1] Earlier, in a report of May 3, 1940, the diplomat had expressed concern at the possibility that the Swiss government would allow German troops to pass through Switzerland without resistance, when nothing in the attitude of the Federal Council, General Guisan, or public opinion gave the slightest indication that this would happen. On May 20, Kelly participated in a meeting with President Pilet. The latter saw no immediate danger for Switzerland; however, there would be a risk if the French abandoned the Jura border and Italy entered the war. Italy certainly did not want to see Germany intervene in Switzerland. Pilet renewed assurances that Switzerland would defend its neutrality. Kelly noted that "I was happy to hear all defeatism refuted."

However, an even more pessimistic, although quite vague, note arrived in London from Kelly on June 15. He discussed the possibility of a coup d'état by the army, which would confirm the impression that the army was more prepared to resist than was the government. In effect, it seemed to Kelly that the morale of the federal councilors was lower than that of the army and that a surrender to German pressure concerning Swiss neutrality was possible at any moment. On August 5 Kelly had a long conversation with a pessimistic Pilet, who did not conceal the difficulties of resistance. However, Pilet reaffirmed that Switzerland would fight against invasion. This, Kelly noted, contradicted the rumor of disagreement between the government and the army command.

The Federal Council and General Guisan continued to affirm the will to defend the country, in spite of the considerable risk from the partial demobilization early in July, the excessively long operational uncertainties, the two-month-long strategic void caused by the transfer of some of the partially demobilized army line to the plateau, and the regrouping of most of the divisions in the redoubt. The rumors of defeatism or a coup that Kelly had mentioned should be attributed to the suspicious mistrust of the resistance fundamentalists or to the fantasies of Hans Hausamann, a doubtful information source for the British Legation.[2]

On May 30, 1940, when the situation was clearly turning to the Reich's advantage in Flanders and throughout northern France, and the fortunes of war clearly pointed to an Axis victory in the near future, the Foreign Affairs Committee of the National Council met under the chairmanship of Henry Vallotton of Vaud to proceed, in the presence of Pilet, to examine the situation as a whole. Although we do not have the text of Pilet's extensive introductory presentation—he was parsimonious with written texts both through personal style and because of the need for confidentiality—he left a detailed outline of the main points.[3]

Pilet realistically analyzed the overall military situation, which was dangerous for Europe because of the inequality in military strength, economic resources, and popular morale. The German adversary's strength in materiel, tactics, and discipline had been underestimated. Germany's attitude with respect to our country could be qualified as "correct," with no indication of a change of behavior. (It seemed then, wrongly, that there was no plan to invade Switzerland.) Italy's attitude was "good" and was expected to remain so, even if that country, as was likely, were to enter the war. (In fact, between June 7 and 10 the Italians began drawing up plans to invade Switzerland.)[4] France had other concerns, and England "remains what it is." The United States was sympathetic but far away.

President Pilet continued, "In this new, topsy-turvy Europe, expect anything, prepare for everything. However, invasion is not inevitable. *Strict neutrality.* A feeling that our national interests are prized above all others. A will for unquestioned neutrality. Military realism. A calm and dignified manner, carefully thought out and prudent; criticism of foreign propaganda. *Active neutrality*: Red Cross. Prisoners, the wounded, sacrifices. No trading. Brave and generous."

Summing up its activities, the Foreign Affairs Committee concluded in its communiqué: "There can be no doubt concerning Switzerland's will to defend its independence against all aggression of whatever kind and from whatever source." Because nothing indicated then that Swiss neutrality was threatened, the committee took favorable note of the Federal Council's intention to facilitate prisoner exchanges to the fullest and to engage in further humanitarian activities to relieve the suffering that war had caused the belligerents.

In this period, the army command took pains to give the soldiers a feeling for their responsibilities and confidence in their resources. The June 3 order of the day recalled that our terrain was not similar to that where the battles of the last few weeks had taken place in France and offered advantages that the will to fight could put to use.[5] "Be ready to sacrifice your life, do not allow yourself to be deterred from your mission or to be distracted by tank infiltration or parachute landings; bring in the mobile reserves. Hold the line like St. Jacques at the Birse."

The order was to be read to the troops "in a vigorous manner." Unit commanders were to be infused with the meaning and spirit of the order and to train the troops according to these principles.

At the same time there were some disturbing elements, which President Pilet discussed on July 3, 1940, before the Foreign Affairs Committee.[6] As with the previous session, we do not have the text of his speech, but we do have the notes he drew up beforehand, which bring out the points he stressed. He evoked the tension and excess of work. Obrecht's health was irrevocably compromised (he no longer attended meetings of the council and died on August 21). Pilet's own health was threatened; there was no vice president and the burden of difficult commercial negotiations was added to his diplomatic tasks. He was forced to be discreet in this emotionally trying period, but he could not conceal the truth. "In spite of the defeat of France, the foreign situation is increasingly confused. Anglo-German relations? German-Russian relations? The Reich's brilliant victory has created German-Italian hegemony on the continent. It is difficult to see who could break it. These are dangerous times for Switzerland. The situation calls for the emplacement of a new military deployment, which does not concern him. But the economic situation is grave; we are surrounded and our neighbors control our food supply. Risk of unemployment."

"Little or no good will among our partners. The English—who broke with the French after the aggression at Mers el Kebir—are thinking only of themselves. What will happen to France, its colonies, the Mediterranean? Italy is very friendly, but has no raw materials and depends economically on Germany. Relations with Germany are not very good. The Germans know that the attitude of the Swiss favors the Allies. Our press is plain for them to see. The troubles stemming from internment—maintain decency in dealing with them." (Pilet recalled the delirious welcome given the French and the Poles of Daille's army corps who were received as conquerors, while Germany and Italy were booed by the population of the Jura.) "The air incidents: international law is hesitant and some of our aircraft could have crossed the border. It is difficult to discuss this matter with an adversary that has overwhelming superiority (according to whether you are powerful or miserable, the judgments of the court)." But Pilet evoked the unpredictable movement of history.

"The present is dark. The future is in God's hands." Pilet recalled the Napoleonic epic: "Rome-Madrid-Berlin-Vienna-Moscow. Then France retreated back into its borders; Russia emerged from the period expanded; Austria made policy; Italy prepared its unity. Do not despair. See clearly. Act quickly. Have confidence in those who assume responsibility. Personal confidence: intelligence, realism, adaptability. Perhaps peace is not so far off. But cohesion-union-discipline."

Although they are only hasty notes, Pilet's reflections are worthy of mention in illustrating not only his realistic lucidity but also the difficult role that Switzerland would have to play as it adapted itself to the situation without aligning itself with the "New Order." Written at a time when the outcome of the French campaign and its consequences for Switzerland were already foreseeable, these notes corrected the toned-down impression of the June 25 speech. However, they remained confidential and were directed to a small number of political leaders.

Weapons were displayed at our borders. Switzerland was completely surrounded by Axis military forces, which dominated Western Europe with the exception of Sweden and the Iberian Peninsula. The chances for British resistance appeared problematic. The Soviet empire was the ally of the Third Reich. America was still very far off. Patriots were demoralized by the defeat of the democracies, but were resigned to an apparently uncontrollable fate. Realists evaluated the inequality of the forces in play. Swiss fascist zealots were more agitated than numerous, and businessmen weighed the profits of collaboration. All thought the war was over and demobilization certain.

This was not the view of those with political and military responsibilities, who, however, did not clearly perceive the gravity of the immediate threat, which the documents would reveal to us only later. The armistice was not peace, and the war went on elsewhere. Equilibrium in Europe and international collaboration were far from established. Only a partial, gradual demobilization could be imagined.

On June 25 Guisan, presenting a plan for the limited demobilization requested by the government, called the Federal Council's attention to two urgent matters: the new deployment that would authorize the reduction of our resources and the new defense plan to be adopted in case of war.[7]

He also requested the government "in case of need, to confirm or specify the mission assigned to the army" by the Federal Council's instructions to the commander in chief of August 31, 1939. On June 24, 1940, Guisan had conveyed the country's appreciation to the troops, announced a partial demobilization, and praised the still necessary spirit of resistance. On July 2 he issued a stronger order, at a time when some of the troops were to be released and returned to civilian life, in which he doubtless specified that the threat was immediate.[8] With most of the troops remaining under arms, Guisan warned the army against the dangers facing it both at home and abroad. The first danger was excessive confidence in the international situation. "The war continues; it could break out in other countries, approach us, and threaten our territory." The second was "our lack of confidence in our ability to resist," defeatism and doubt concerning our mission. Instead, he noted that "[w]e possess one of the most effective means of defense: our terrain." He elaborated: the steep slopes and gorges, our forests, and our mountains were obstacles impassable to tanks and served as a protection against air attacks. "We will fight for our territory foot by foot, and we will save the honor of army and country." With this he brought up the theme of the redoubt, which was then being planned. In quickly giving him its total support, the Federal Council confirmed the instructions issued to General Guisan in August 1939 and reaffirmed its desire for independence and resistance.

This order to resist, together with periodic reports on the international situation and the country's problems, would be the subject of orientation to the troop commanders and lectures to the soldiers by the army command's organization, Army and Home, and would play an essential role in maintaining national cohesion.

NOTES

1. Edgar Bonjour, *England und der Schweizerische Widerstandswille 1939–1940* (RSH, 1981), 3, 332–35; and Erwin Bucher, *Pilet-Golaz im Urteil des Englischen Gesandten* (RSH, 1981), 4, 492–94.

2. Erwin Bucher, *Zwischen Bundesrat und General*, 231–32.

3. *Documents Diplomatiques*, vol. 13, 700–702.

4. Alberto Rovighi, *Un Secolo di Relazioni Militari tra Italia e Svizzera 1861–1961*, Documents de l'Etat-Major Italien (Rome, 1987), 524–30.

5. *Documents Diplomatiques*, vol. 13, 705–6.

6. *Documents Diplomatiques*, vol. 13, 791–96.

7. *Documents Diplomatiques*, vol. 13, 750.

8. *Documents Diplomatiques*, vol. 13, 788.

Chapter Eight

Planning and Deciding
on the Redoubt

"The national redoubt had the impact and weight of myth," wrote the Neuchâtel historian Philippe Marguerat, who took on the task of narrating in detail its difficult elaboration, its contradictions and ambiguities,[1] without belittling the deterrence it contributed to maintaining Switzerland's political independence in a Europe that had largely passed to the somber colors of the Nazis and fascists.

It is well known that strategic planning has an unfortunate tendency to replay the previous war. The war games of 1927 in Switzerland foresaw that in mountainous terrain, without much likelihood of penetration or encirclement, the army could hold vast fronts. On more open terrain—the greater part of the Swiss plateau, where a close-in defense had less of a chance, success had to be sought in mobility, which would allow a better concentration of resources.[2]

These principles, which recalled Marshal Foch and the Allied offensives of 1918, were carried out in Swiss maneuvers between the wars. In their articles, exercises, maneuvers, marches, and countermarches, along roads and through woods and fields, in the conquest of the Combremont Plateau or the Vaulruz Gap, strategic thinkers gave free rein to their combative temperament. Military thinking was traditional and conformist, while information on new strategies and techniques was late and out-of-date. In this army which generally retained the same resources it had in 1918, there was a tendency to prefer the horse over the engine, in spite of the warnings from General Wille, commander in chief from 1914 to 1918. The clatter of spurs was the prestigious mark of authority for the officers, with their hereditary love of barracks life. The stiffness of quick-time marching, which the French Swiss were the first to give up during the war, got in the way of close combat. There was more close inspection of the precision with which weapons were handled in drill than of the mine launchers or antitank firing. The tanks themselves were a few old, rattling prototypes known only in the newsreels, while the writings of von Seeckt, de Gaulle, and Guderian were unknown. From 1920 to 1939 one could lightheartedly devote maneuvers and exercises to fantasies of a fresh and joyous war of movement, without marking time in unspectacular defensive and static combat.

It is true that in 1937 Colonel Däniker, a well-regarded technician who commanded the Walenstadt infantry school, had broken the taboo by showing that in the current state of our resources, only a defensive posture was conceivable. We had neither the mechanized forces, the air force, the artillery, the troop instruction, nor the officers needed for war of movement. These critical remarks on the capabilities of the Swiss army reflected the views generally presented by foreign officers in the immediate prewar period, as brought out by Hans Senn in his work on the Swiss General Staff.[3] According to Colonel La Forest-Divonne, French military attaché in 1935: "The statements of Colonel Guisan express the firm and tenacious desire of the Swiss people to defend themselves, contrary to the still numerous observers who are inclined to believe that when faced with Hitler's Germany, which is becoming more threatening every day and is interfering more and more in the country's affairs, a frightened Switzerland will be content to put up a pro forma resistance to a German invasion and retire its army to the mountains." In 1936 La Forest-Divonne noted, "The policy of armed neutrality, which continues to be regarded as one of the main trump cards of the Swiss army, condemns it by forcing it to face the enemy on all fronts, causing a premature and excessive expenditure of troops, limiting the possibility of maneuver . . . ready to act in totality if necessary at the threatened point. . . . The Swiss army regards itself as a flank guard against the great power, but it is actually regarded as a target throughout its territory by this aggressor." In 1937 he pointed out the delays in weaponry and in aviation; he reported on risky combined firing exercises; in 1938 he had a low opinion of a defense in a retreat to the Gotthard, a timeworn plan, and wished rather for a withdrawal to the Jura with French assistance. All in all, he saw a"precarious situation, which will continue for two or three more years, for national defense."

Concerning public opinion, the report by the French generals Touchon and Boucherie in 1934 notes that the federal and cantonal governments were deeply imbued with two viewpoints: an ardent patriotism and an absolute desire to assure neutrality, especially with respect to Germany. Their characterization of Swiss leaders ascribed to Pilet a pro-French inclination, although the French efforts at a rapprochement with the USSR "brought the wolf into the sheepfold." The French report feared the influence the German General Staff was trying to exercise on its Swiss counterpart, especially on "General"

Wille (then a division commander, a future corps commander, and the son of a World War I general). Mr. Minger was a "peasant from Bern" and proud of it. He was crafty, with the appearance of a good fellow, sure of himself, resolute, stubborn, and certainly authoritarian. He was very popular and knew well how to maintain his popularity.

Among the military leaders, Corps Commander Guisan was thought of as young—he was then sixty years old—cheerful, lively, and brilliant. He showed sincere admiration for all that was French. His military knowledge was extensive and his authority in the army well established. His popularity was unquestioned even among the German Swiss. "Corps Commander Wille . . . is more German than French in appearance. He is very learned, expresses himself clearly, and has a forceful personality and a good deal of authority. For some he should be the designated commander in chief. . . . He is said to be very much subject to German influence; he does not conceal his relationships beyond the Rhine at all. . . . He has been especially friendly with the French delegation. . . . He gives the impression of a loyal chief who remains 'Swiss before anything else,' in spite of his preferences and his relationships."

The deployment, weaponry, and combat preparations justified some critical remarks by French officers that echoed those of Colonel Däniker. "Troops well instructed, disciplined, and trained; cadres are intelligent, conscientious, and intent on their role." There was extensive praise for the troops. But French General Schweisguth noted in 1935 that, "[t]he troops have all the defects of an army that has not been in combat and finds some difficulty in adapting to modern conditions of offensive combat." "The cadres are truly admirable, if it were only the physical, intellectual, and moral qualities that make leaders," said General de Lannurien in 1936. "However, they would be capable of leading their troops into a catastrophe if they overestimated themselves. In spite of their total lack of experience and a technique that is perforce insufficient, they still think themselves capable, when the day comes, of conducting a war of mobility. They are not at all trained for this, and it corresponds neither to the natural characteristics of their country nor its needs. Instead, they should hold more modestly to a static defense of their borders where, if they are provided with the necessary defensive means, their troops would naturally excel." He continued: "If the officers in the Federal Army pursue their claim to conduct a war of movement before an adversary like the Germans, they will inevitably be led to defeat and slaughter."

The French officers were happy with the organization of the border defenses, then being organized and strengthened. "The Swiss army represents an undeniable resistance force, capable, if not of erecting an insurmountable barrier . . . at least of slowing the enemy's advance until we ourselves are able to reinforce it. In our own interests, that is very much what we could desire: the Swiss army on the Rhine from Basel to Schaffhausen, the forward line of French defenses."

From 1934 on, German officers noted the Swiss hostility to the Nazi regime, but they accepted the Swiss attachment to neutrality. Certain senior officers among the Swiss did not conceal their preference for Germany, but the French influence seemed to predominate, through the training many of them received at the French War College in Paris. The value of the Swiss army was noted in its discipline and service spirit, but the short period of service in the militia brought out a certain inexperience and lack of familiarity with combat, especially among the cadres. Although the army's combined firing was impressive, General Muff, the German military attaché in Bern since 1933, judged the 1936 divisional maneuvers severely. "The troops and their leaders are inspired by the best of good will. But their training has not given them a valid military education. War will bring them severe disappointments, all the more because the Swiss people, and even their officers on many occasions, do not seem aware of the weakness of their militia army. You can tell that they have not gone to war in more than 100 years."

Overall, a picture emerges from the critical reports of visiting military attachés and foreign officers of troops and officers that were motivated, disciplined, and hardy. But, in spite of the improvements made since 1933 and the border fortifications then under construction, their aircraft equipment, antiaircraft, artillery, and infantry weaponry were all insufficient. One sees that the total absence of tanks, the low mobility of the infantry still tethered to the harnesses of its horse-drawn vehicles, the insufficient training of officers and troops and senior officers' training for command left much to be desired.

The most pointed criticism was that of the French General de Lannurien in 1936. He disagreed strongly with the Swiss preference for "direct combat" and a war of mobility. "It would be desirable for Switzerland itself and for us" (since the French willingly looked on the Swiss army as the flank guard for their Maginot line) "for the high command to give up the war of mobility and hold to the study of a static defense of its territory devoted to preparing most, if not all, of its assets for it. This is not the place for a war of mobility seen in all the maneuvers, but for establishing a barrage of fire and obstacles, the only form of war that really lies within their possibilities and their needs" (and also in the interests of France).

In less flowery language, the Italian military attaché compared "the Swiss officers to children amusing themselves by imitating great men while they play at war, but they know nothing about it." Did he borrow this sarcasm from the judgments of his future German allies concerning the Italian army?

In spite of the attraction of direct combat and a war of mobility prevailing in the Swiss maneuvers, the army command essentially adopted a static defensive solution beginning in September 1939, based on the military organization that entered into force in 1938, at least for the northern front. Eight brigades would assume a forcibly held linear defense and neutrality on the eastern borders, the north, and the Jura to the west. Three brigades and one mountain division would assume defenses in the Alps to the south. The main effort was marked by an army line from the fortress at Sargans to the Gempen Plateau south of Basel, passing through Zurich and the Limmat and Aare rivers, where four divisions were stationed and country fortifications were being actively constructed. To the west, two divisions without an established defensive line were prepared to reinforce the border troops. Two divisions between Bern and Langenthal remained as the army reserve; three light cavalry brigades and some motorized elements constituted the rest of the deployment.[4]

From the end of May, the rapid progress of the campaign in France and the strong concentration of German troops behind the Jura led to the hasty fortification, dangerous and of dubious value as a deterrent, of a defensive line between Lake Neuchâtel and Lake Geneva, on the Mentue, and the forests of the Jorat. But it was obvious that the strategic and political reversal led to a fundamental review of our defenses, once the will to resist had been affirmed. Were we to fight in place, on the army lines of the plateau, weak and relatively close to the frontier, or shift the main resistance to the alpine redoubt where the reinforced and well-guarded natural obstacles would win out over armored and motorized vehicles?

The idea of a redoubt to which an army withdraws, if possible to the shelter of a natural barrier, when it no longer has hope of winning a battle in open country and where it can safeguard the country's entire territory, belongs to strategic thinking of all times. It was in his entrenched redoubt on Alesia Hill that Vercingetorix hoped to defeat Caesar. Above the Dead Sea, the rock with its steep slopes at Masada was the bastion of Jewish resistance to the Romans in the first century. The idea of a Breton redoubt, or more widely, of a withdrawal to the colonies, occurred fleetingly to planners in France in May–June 1940. Whether a withdrawal to a redoubt under enemy pressure was contemplated, or whether the retrenchment was immediately planned for the Alps as the main line of defense, the idea of a redoubt appeared sporadically in the nineteenth century as a natural element in Swiss strategy.

The encirclement of 1940 and the regrettable lack of tanks and antitank weapons made this the only possible defensive solution if we were to avoid a rapid collapse on the plateau. In 1945, General Guisan recalled the redoubt in a talk given at the Zofingue Society. "The idea of the redoubt is certainly not the work of a genius. It was a common-sense solution, and I believe more and more that it was the only solution. It did not require great intellectual effort; what it required most of all was courage—make no bones about it—to impose certain sacrifices on a country that had barely conceived of them. But courage comes from audacity, just as fear comes from hesitation!"[5]

If the idea arose naturally, its birth was difficult, and the ways it could be carried out gave rise to extensive controversies between strategists in combat boots and offices. After the operational exercise of spring 1939, the possibility of a withdrawal and a retrenchment in a "central porcupine" of mountains was drawn up.[6] In November of that year Corps Commander Labhart, who was still chief of the General Staff, presided over a discussion on the value of the alpine fortresses and their reinforcement. "The Gotthard acquired even greater importance as a redoubt for the Swiss army in the heart of the Alps." In mid-December 1939, Labhart proposed tightening the deployment, especially on the southern front. General Guisan remained wedded to a primary defense on the plateau, giving the possibility of resisting at a greater depth. When Division Commander Huber replaced Labhart at the head of the General Staff after the latter was transferred to command of the Fourth Corps, he supported the plateau defense, as did Lieutenant Colonel Gonard, an influential advisor of General Guisan on his own staff.

The gradual encirclement of Switzerland by the Axis armies, the experiences of the campaign in Flanders and France, and the methods of massive use of armor and aviation made the redoubt problem ever more urgent.

In the middle of May 1940 General Guisan received a general staff study directed by Colonel Germann, a professor at Basel, who envisaged a withdrawal into the Alps in case of a breakdown of the front at the Limmat River. The report was not convincing to Huber, but Guisan admitted that a withdrawal around the Gotthard Pass was a way out that would save the national honor in case of enemy invasion. Germann saw a more lasting mission there. The German advance into France strengthened this idea and on June 13, Germann resubmitted his project, *Festung Alpen* (Fortress Alps), to the commander in chief.

On June 22, Guisan called a meeting of his direct subordinates (the chief of the General Staff, the four corps commanders, and the chief of training) to an unofficial council of war.[7] He showed a certain optimism as he stated that a German attack was unlikely any time soon and led off the discussion by analyzing the situation. He sketched three solutions:

1. Maintain the army's front lines, even though exterior assistance could no longer be counted on;
2. Maintain the army's present lines in its fortified elements on the northern front, from Sargans to Hauhenstein in Soleur, but withdrawing the west

wing from the dangerous line of Neuchâtel Lake-Jorat-Lake Geneva to a line Lake Morat-Gruyères that was not fortified and would be based at Saint Moritz, in more difficult terrain; or

3. Withdraw the army into a central redoubt south of a line Lakes of Zurich and of the Four Cantons-Napf-Thoune-Saint Maurice. The advantage there would lie in the strength of the terrain, but nearly three-quarters of the country would be sacrificed, and there would be the problem of the food and munitions that would have to be moved. Guisan expressed his preference for the second solution. On that basis, the discussion was carried out and two diametrically opposed conceptions were presented.

Corps Commanders Prisi (Second Corps) and Lardelli (First Corps), generally supported by Chief of the General Staff Huber, stated that a stand should be taken at the army position from Lake Zurich to Lake Geneva, which had the advantage that it was already in place and had been heavily fortified. The three other general officers, Miescher (Third Corps), Labhart (Fourth Corps) who generally opposed Guisan's ideas, and Wille, frustrated in his ambitions and dynamism and champing at the bit as chief of training, were partisans of maximum concentration of the army in the redoubt. Philippe Marguerat called these officers the "Germanophile technicians," and attributed far higher strategic imagination to them. While maintaining the protective cordon at the border, they totally renounced the forward army position to reassemble most of the troops where the terrain would impede the enemy's deployment and its massive use of tanks. To the strategic arguments brought forward by the partisans of the "pure redoubt," Wille added, as we have seen, a politico economic argument that shed particular light on a plan that, under a pretext of defense, went clearly against neutrality. In effect, the reductions in manpower achieved by this solution would pacify Germany, which was carefully studying our troop strength. Further, the Third Reich was requiring France to resume work on joining the economic effort required for the war against England. Orders to Swiss industries whose forces were intact could associate Switzerland with the new European policy of the Axis.[8]

It was up to Guisan to decide between these two views. Philippe Marguerat smoothly assigned definitive and contrasting qualifications to him: "A remarkable leader, an engaging personality, the general shows a weak strategic sense. . . . He does not succeed in asserting himself and instinctively heads toward compromise solutions to which everyone can adhere. . . . Actually it was Wille who dominated the strategic discussions because of the originality and relevance of his ideas. He had an impressive intellectual authority and was supported by the sharp and farseeing Labhart and Miescher." Labhart and Wille had long had tense relationships with the Swiss French Guisan, who had come up from the militia. Less of a strategist and rather pro-French, Guisan occupied the high position to which they would willingly have seen themselves appointed. Further, it is rare indeed when the upper military hierarchy of any country—this applies to other elite corps—cultivates effusions of solidarity and cordial collegiality at the summit. The strategic disagreements ill concealed some settling of accounts based less on deep reflection than on personal, petty, tenacious, and reciprocal vanity. These military leaders were used to ordering their subordinates about without being contradicted, which may explain the difficulties they had in agreeing with their peers.

Incidentally, the value of a decision is judged by its effectiveness more than by the brilliance of the invention and the Cartesian dialectic leading to it which made its defense feasible. It is easy to count points after the matter is over. A decision must be more pragmatic than abstractly logical; it must take account of realities, multiple resistance, and obvious lapses in logic, proceeding from a definitive synthesis that is more intuitive than doctrinaire and academic. It must benefit chiefly from the unforeseeable decrees of providence, the whims of chance that "no throw of the dice will abolish" and the personal reflection of that leader who could arbitrarily discountenance the most infallible operational and rational research and make great men more than their own superior intelligence could.

Neither General Guisan nor those minds "impressive with intellectual authority, farseeing, and sharp" conducted triumphal campaigns nor left to history a strategic breviary worthy of Clausewitz or Jomini. Guisan was a pragmatic, prudent man who hardly wrote anything. He did not proceed by inspiration but had the intelligence to hesitate, sometimes at length. He listened without permitting permanent equivocation, compared and weighed matters before deciding, and then acted firmly once a decision had been made. Compromise can be deplorable if it seeks to conciliate opposites while playing for time. But it is wise if it derives from the most extensive synthesis of strategic, logistic, political, and economic factors, if it seeks to go beyond unilateral parity. The men Guisan chose did not show themselves to be up to it, said Marguerat. If Prisi and Lardelli, at the head of their army corps, could give the impression of the "old guard" or the "ranger sentries" faithful to their post, Chief of the General Staff Huber, though more cooperative than Labhart had been and would be as head of the Fourth Corps, was no less well prepared; he was a good organizer who was not afraid to enter into controversy with the commander in chief and to become irritated at the excessive role played by Guisan's personal staff.[9] In addition to his training responsibilities, Wille was called on for important definitions of combat doctrine and drafting the army's plans. Finally, on the private staff was Barbey, constantly accompanying Guisan's reflection. He was sophisticated, wrote elegantly and copiously, and was intelligent and imaginative. He too would be a competent general staff officer. Gonard, chief of Guisan's personal staff and later chief of the operations sections of the General Staff, was destined to senior appointments and knowing it, combined audacity of action with a passion for ideas and an abrasive critical lucidity.

Gonard would write in 1959 of the redoubt that, "[t]he situation was characterized by the continuity of the successive strategic provisions. . . . There was no break in the progress of these decisions; quite the contrary, the passage from one arrangement to another—no matter how different they were— was always done progressively so as to allow the army to be ready for combat at all times with at least a minimum of forces."[10]

These considerations refuted Marguerat's reproaches of a "strategic void, a stupid deployment," and the "hesitation of the Swiss strategies, their groping, empirical progress directed to focusing the potential enemy in an obsolete image that is not much of a deterrent." If there was a strategic void, the choice of the redoubt was not part of it. Operations Order No. 12 in July provided for a judicious transition, but because of the uncertainty that prevailed from the end of June to August 1940, a half-demobilized and unmotivated army was spread out on the plateau, "awaiting orders." It faced a mechanized concentration ready to cross the Jura whose importance had been underestimated and which presaged intentions and threat. Hans Senn noted this forthrightly, as Division Commander Bircher had done in 1941, in a report to the Federal Council.[11] The delays in decisionmaking were as much the fault of the government, which did not urge it on more forcefully, as it was of the high command.

At the "war council" of June 22, the army corps commanders did not come up with a unanimous choice—far from it. As time was pressing, Guisan and the General Staff continued studying the different solutions. But before making his decision, Guisan wanted the view of the Federal Council. He did not request approval for a new concept of defense that he was not yet in a position to formulate, but set store by assuring his freedom of maneuver.

On June 25 he sent to the government, through the chief of the Military Department, a letter in which he confirmed the orders he had given, at the request of the Federal Council, for a partial demobilization (which could be considered premature in view of the German concentrations on the border).[12] But it was important to focus on two matters of prime importance: the new provision authorizing the reduction of resources and the new defense plan that had to be adopted in case of a threat of war.

To this end, Guisan requested the Federal Council to "confirm or specify in case of need, the mission assigned to the army by the instructions issued on August 31 to the commander in chief, especially point two: 'safeguard the country's independence and maintain the integrity of the territory with the use of all appropriate means.'" He added, "We take note with interest of the instructions you propose to issue in order to adapt our own measures of safeguarding the country's independence to the present situation, and we request that you inform us on this subject in good time."

This text would astonish some. It did not have the tone of a subordinate who "was awaiting orders." The phrase, "We take note with interest of the instructions you propose to issue," may verge upon a certain literary casualness, as the general was requesting instructions equivalent to orders on the basis of which he would prepare the measures to be taken. The accent on independence and neutrality is surprising; these principles seemed obvious. On the very day of the Federal Council's memorable but deliberately ambiguous address, did Guisan wish to cast doubt on the government's firmness and the continuity of its policy? Did this constitute a bend in the policy of neutrality? Or was it to reaffirm belief in neutrality and inspire its defense?[13] Guisan, by raising in some way the question of confidence, sought to obtain from the government a general agreement to the new defense concept that was still being drafted but whose principles and variations the Federal Council could not ignore, although it had not been officially informed.

The Federal Council's reply, dated July 2, was brief and unequivocal.[14] "We believe that the suspension of hostilities among our neighbors does not require a modification of these instructions, for the moment." In other words, the war was still going on; the threat was still there; and the mission was confirmed. There was no preliminary reserve, for example, on the integrity of Swiss territory to be defended; the government did not disavow in advance the measures the general was preparing, but it wanted to know what they were, not to say that it wanted to be able to pronounce on them.

The importance of operational changes justified this requirement. The plan involved abandoning a decisive fight on the plateau, the concentration of most of the forces in the alpine redoubt, and abandoning to the enemy without major resistance the most populated and most productive part of the country. The political aspect of the problem superseded the strategic option. Alfred Ernst, who reminds us that every great strategic problem has a political impact, stressed it here, in his study of the Swiss high command. "So serious a decision could not have been made without the consent of the Federal Council, without causing a crisis. . . . Even in strategic questions the last word belonged to the Federal Council."[15]

With his orders confirmed, the general, who had also met with Minger on July 4, held a new "council of war" on July 6, where disagreements were aired for four hours.[16]

The triumvirate of Wille, Labhart, and Miescher forcefully resumed their argument for an immediate and total redoubt, the abandonment of the army position, and the refusal of any compromise measures. Prisi held firmly to the Jura sector of his Second Corps. "To send the army to safety in a refuge in the heart of the Alps is simply absurd. . . . To defend the glaciers and the massifs does not make sense while the plateau, with all its economic wealth, as well as the greater part of the population, is delivered to the enemy. The army will lose its morale." Miescher contradicted this view, seeing in the new idea of the redoubt the best way to remedy a spreading and disturbing defeatism. Dollfus, the adjutant general who took part in the council, expressed astonishment at this reaction and concluded that the army should be better oriented to our possibilities of resistance. The countries that succumbed—with the exception of Finland—did not fight well. Air Force Commander Bandi called attention to the small number of airports in the Alps. The antiaircraft units should follow the troops partially, covering the locations on the plateau, which would have to take their own measures. Huber, who had been unconditionally wedded to retaining the army position two weeks previously, was easing into an intermediate position after his discussions with Guisan, Gonard, Barbey, and Germann. He replied to Prisi that there would doubtless be no sense in defending the rocks and the glaciers but that the country would be more seriously and more rapidly lost if the army position, weak in its terrain, were to be overrun. An entrenched position in the Alps would afford the country a long period of resistance.

It was in this sense that the commander in chief, who limited himself on July 6 to summing up the differing opinions, would specify his decision with the concurrence of the chief of staff, his collaborators, and his personal staff. After having persuaded Prisi to give up his fundamental position but maintain for the moment an advanced army position from the Limmat River to the Jura, he decided on July 10 to regroup in the redoubt, south of a curved line Sargans-Lucerne-Bulle-Saint Moritz, four divisions from the army position which would rejoin in the Alps the units already holding them. Eight brigades were providing linear coverage of the frontier from the Rhine to the Jura. Four infantry divisions and a large light unit were still holding the army position or providing mobile defense from Lake Bienne to Bulle.

General Guisan thus chose an intermediate solution, a withdrawal in two stages to the redoubt, because, in the summer of 1941, the four divisions of the former army position were to return to the Alps. The triumvirate claimed that this halfway measure indicated the hesitation of the high command. Marguerat supported this view: "From June 10, 1940 to the fall of 1941, Switzerland lived through a 'strategic void.' The deployment of July 10, 1940 cannot and does not serve as a deterrent." In any event, in principle or in its modalities, in its excesses and deficiencies, this revolutionary defense could not be dissociated from intelligent hesitation. Gonard, like Guisan whose closest advisor he was, did not escape criticism of the plan, either at the time or long afterward.

However, if there was a "strategic void," as we have seen this was not in the decision finally made, but in the delay in arriving at it.

Three factors merit discussion in support of extending the operation in time and space. This first is psychological: the abrupt abandonment of the most densely populated towns and regions would arouse emotions, a negative shock. A postponement was needed for public opinion to understand and accept both the need for defense and the condition for deterrence: the prospect of lasting resistance in mountainous terrain.

The second factor was military, strategic, and logistic. Strategically, it was difficult to conceive, when strong German mechanized concentrations were at the border from the Black Forest to the Jura, and the invasion plans were being drawn up in the general staffs of the potential enemy, to set the whole army in motion and to redeploy it suddenly in the redoubt. The rapid and massive withdrawal and the inevitable confusion it could not fail to engender would be an invitation to the enemy to precipitate invasion. Logistically, it was necessary to move rapidly all the reserves of munitions and foot supplies, to prepare the barrages, the depots, the billeting, the hospitals, and the connections.

The final factor in favor of the redoubt was that of deterrence. This was borne out by changes in the Axis invasion plans between June 1940 and 1941. The German generals thought they would end the resistance on the permeable lines of the plateau in a few days, no matter how strong it was. As the German and Italian general staffs became aware of the reality and the development of the redoubt, they reviewed their troops and timing. Siege warfare in difficult terrain would be needed to gain possession of the alpine passages and tunnels, which would be an essential goal of the invasion. "The alpine redoubt makes a blitzkrieg improbable," said Minister Frölicher in Berlin.[17] The period of the redoubt also gained time for developing fortifications, equipment with new weapons, training, and physical and moral preparations of the troops for war in mountainous conditions and at the same time contributed to reenforcing esprit de corps in the units.

Having made his decision on July 9, Guisan informed the Federal Council by a letter he sent through the chief of the Military Department.[18] In this document dated July 12, Guisan referred to the instructions that had recently been confirmed for him. He recalled the plan made in September 1939 covering the frontier, an army position Sargans-Limmat-Jura-Mentue-Lake Geneva and the probable assistance from one of the belligerents in case of an attack by the other.

The collapse of French resistance and Italy's entry into the war changed the situation completely. From then on, Switzerland was completely encircled by Axis forces, which could exercise political, economic, and military pressure on Switzerland to assure control over the transport routes passing through its territory. Guisan noted that, "[t]hus, the German demands could sooner or later become such as to be irreconcilable with our independence and national honor. Switzerland could not escape from the threat of a direct German attack unless the German high command calculated that a war against us would be long and costly, that it would encourage a struggle in the center of Europe uselessly or dangerously and would interfere with the execution of its plans."

"From now on, the object and principle of our national defense is to show that this war would be long and costly. If we have to be dragged into the struggle, it will be a matter of selling ourselves as dearly as possible."

The general then described the new defensive articulation in three echelons:

- The frontier troops in their present deployments;
- An advanced position on the present army line where four divisions and one light division will fight a delaying action; and
- An alpine position or national redoubt held by five divisions and three mountain brigades, supported by the fortresses of Sargans, Gotthard, and Saint Moritz, to be held with no thought of withdrawal and with provisions for a maximum stay.

The deployment could be executed at the beginning of August. The command post of the army would probably be transferred to Altdorf, and the general suggested Kandersteg for the Federal Council in case of hostilities.

The general informed the Federal Council of this new deployment, which was already underway since three divisions in the advanced position had already received the order to move toward the Pre-Alps. This did not require the explicit approval of the government. However, the latter could not limit itself to "taking note" of this new deployment, which involved the nation's existence and whose economic, political, social, and psychological consequences were more important than the strategic justification.

There is no doubt that the general's note did not surprise the government. After the middle of June, either from the chief of the military department in direct contact and with reciprocal trust with Guisan and through other unofficial or personal channels, it could not disregard the clashing propositions within the high command—the status quo on the plateau, the exclusive hard and pure redoubt, or the redoubt in sections and by stages. It is obvious even in the absence of minutes or personal notes that it was discussed collegially, at the margins of the order of the day as in an exchange of personal opinions. It seemed certain that the renewal of the instructions could not be decided on in ignorance of the intentions of the commander, who could not engage himself in an operation as fundamental as this without concerning himself with political views. Guisan had certainly exchanged views animatedly with as many different opinions on the modalities of the operation as there were general officers. What was not said was that the proposals on the table and the confidential conversations played as important a role as the reports in the archives of this historic event.

In its meeting of July 16, the Federal Council took account of the deployment in the redoubt drawn up by the high command and gave its agreement, by the report Pilet had Minger submit that same day. Basically this was the culmination of a consensus procedure on both the plan by the high command and that of the government, even though the general assumed sole responsibility by Operations Order No. 12.

Obrecht, who was very ill and had resigned, was absent. Minger, a faithful supporter of Guisan, suffered from an indisposition that probably had nothing to do with a diplomatic illness. Pilet's critical spirit was well known; he exercised it occasionally at the expense of the general, and he constantly emphasized the prerogatives of political authority. He presided at the meeting and introduced discussion of the new army deployment. It appears that no opposition in principle was raised, in contrast to the instructions renewed on July 2.

"The Federal Council declared its agreement," wrote Pilet in a letter to the chief of the Military Department.[19] However, he made four remarks that Minger would transmit to the general. He did not agree with establishing the army command post at Altdorf and the headquarters of the Federal Council at Kandersteg. This distance was decidedly too great, and communications would be problematical. He wanted fewer troops in the intermediate position and stressed the need for relief by rotation. He believed it indispensable to introduce the troops to the maintenance of order. Wetter insisted on the economic importance of relieving the troops.

There was nothing in the observations transmitted to Minger that showed the government's overall skepticism, which Willy Gautschi believed he could find. He cited only two examples in support of his impression.[20] First, Gautschi cited Walther Stampfli, who while carrying the heavy burden of watching over the country's economic survival and assuming with Pilet the task of commercial relations with the powers, and though thoroughly patriotic, would note some irritation at the army's requirements and some frustration at the deeds and plans of his chief. In November 1940, in a letter to Heinrich Walther, he voiced his opposition to the redoubt, which increased more than it diminished the danger to the country and took up hundreds of millions in expenditures that one did not dare to criticize under penalty of being branded as a defeatist.[21] Let us leave him with the responsibility for his ideas, noting mainly that he did not attend the July 16 meeting because he was not yet a federal councilor.

According to Gautschi, Pilet reproached the concept of the redoubt for its rigidity. This criticism, which was perfectly valid, did not concern the principle of the concept. And Pilet, in 1946, rendered the redoubt concept the homage of close experience. "If the solution was cruel from the viewpoint of the country and the population, it was proper for the military plan and was very useful politically."

NOTES

1. Philippe Marguerat, *La Suisse Face au IIIe Reich*, 13–83.

2. Alfred Ernst, *Die Konzeption der Schweizerichen Landenverteidigung 1815–1966*, 135ff; and General Henri Guisan, *Entretiens Accordés à Raymond Gafner* (Lausanne, 1953, Frauenfeld, 1971), 124–26.

3. Hans Senn, *Erhaltung und Verstärkung, Etat-Major VI*, 426–67.

4. Hans Senn, *Dissuasionsstrategie, Etat-Major VII*, 88–104.

5. Edouard Chapuisat, *Le Général Guisan* (Lausanne, 1949), 125.

6. Willy Gautschi, *Le Général Guisan*, 284–317.

7. *Documents Diplomatiques*, vol. 13, 71–60; Philippe Marguerat, *La Suisse Face*, 45–83, especially 79; and Hans Senn, *Erhaltung und Verstärkung, Etat-Major VI*, 305–19.

8. *Documents Diplomatiques*, vol. 13, 758.

9. Karl J. Walde, *Generalstabschef Jakob Huber* (Aarau, 1983), 50–75.

10. Samuel Gonard, *Die Strategische Probleme der Schweiz im Zweiten Weltkrieg* (Thoune, 1959), 41, and cited by Marguerat, *La Suisse Face*, 66–69.

11. Hans Senn, *Dissuasionsstrategie*, vol. VII, 348–49; and Eugène Bircher, *Rapport au Conseil Fédérale du 1.08.1941*, cited by Bonjour, *Neutralité*, vol. IV, 69.

12. *Documents Diplomatiques*, vol. 13, 750.

13. Bernard Barbey, *PC du Général*, 26–28.

14. *Documents Diplomatiques*, vol. 13, 750.

15. Alfred Ernst, *Die Ordnung des Militärischen Oberbefehls im Schweizerischen Bundestaat* (Basel, 1948), 125–30.

16. Edgar Bonjour, *Neutralität*, vol. IX, 379–92.

17. Hans Frölicher, *Meine Aufgabe in Berlin*, 41.

18. *Documents Diplomatiques*, vol. 13, 826–29, the general's note.

19. *Documents Diplomatiques*, vol. 13, 825–26, letter from Pilet to Minger.

20. Willy Gautschi, *Le Général Guisan*, 314.

21. Hafner, *Bundesrat Stampfli 1884–1965* (Olten, 1986), 224.

Chapter Nine

The Rütli

The concentration of most of the troops in the redoubt, which would be completed in 1941 with the abandonment of the army position on the plateau, had a strategic justification. It meant concentrating resources at the strongest point, imposing a lasting resistance offering all possible deterrent value against a potential enemy. However, it also required moral force—the conviction that invasion would not be accepted without a fight and that there would be no surrender with resignation. The existence, independence, and liberties of the nation would be defended.

The watchword was still to be given out. The army and the public had to be convinced, and the country's morale needed to be bolstered after the shock of France's collapse and Switzerland's encirclement by the totalitarian powers. The military command showed itself more talkative and persuasive than the political authorities, who were required to be more prudent in the negotiations they had to undertake in order to ensure the survival of the country's economy. But the country's will and capacity to resist were also an essential trump card in the conduct of negotiations. As Pilet-Golaz observed in 1945 in his *Summary of the Dangers to which Switzerland was Exposed during the 1939–45 World War,* which he delivered to his successor, Max Petitpierre concerning 1944 in an observation that is valid for a more extensive period: "Our army, perhaps unknowingly, was one of the cards in our diplomacy, and not the least of them."[1]

General Guisan missed no opportunity to recall the necessity of defense to the army and the people. We have seen this in the army order of June 3, 1940, calling for "the unwavering will to fight to the very end."[2] Then, in the order of July 2, when part of the army was being demobilized, giving rather quickly the impression that the threat had gone, the general declared that the war was not over, that it could still affect us, and that there was no question of giving in to defeatism. "In our hands, our terrain will amount to a formidable defense, if we keep in good spirits and have a stout heart."

This was a prelude to the Redoubt. Guisan solemnly noted the impending change in strategy by convoking all the troop commanders from battalion level and above at the historic meadow of the Rütli, above the Lake of the Four Cantons, to convey to them instructions for vigilance. Because it was not recorded at the time, and the text was not preserved but only partially reconstituted later by Guisan, the address by the commander in chief has given rise to commentaries and suppositions.[3] What did he say and what did he not say? Oscar Gauye, then the director of the Federal Archives, published in 1984 a speech drawn up on Guisan's orders, probably drafted by Barbey, but about which the most certain thing was that this speech was not delivered. It was too long, and the general was not used to giving long harangues, preferring rapid, concise, and frequently improvised language. Further, the prepared text contained political allusions and a severe criticism of National Councilor Grimm, who had written a violent diatribe against fascism. The draft also contained a spirited attack against the leaders of the Swiss extreme left. It continued with an allusion to changing the Constitution, appealing to "national renovation," evoking the decadence (!) of the parties. These political ideas, inspired more by the declarations of Marshal Pétain than the Swiss democratic tradition, were certainly not those of Guisan. The survivors of the convocation at the Rütli gave many assurances to this effect. If Guisan had held these views, that would have justly provoked a heated controversy, in spite of the confidential nature of the meeting.

This text was clearly drafted by a member of the general's personal staff. Did Barbey, with his agile pen and vivid imagination, translate the general's deepest thoughts? Certainly Guisan was conservative and held Pétain in high esteem at the time, as did a majority of the French and Swiss, but not to the extent of expressing that esteem in political propositions. What did he say? After reading some letters he received from civilians and soldiers expressing disappointment, he is said to have countered with the spirit of resistance before a lasting threat and the necessary struggle against defeatism. He noted the current regrouping of the Swiss divisions in the Alps, which gave increasing credibility to our defense. The army order distributed and published that day summed up his views and informed public opinion:[4]

General H. Guisan to All Members of the Army
Army Order

1/8/VU   No. 11900   Rütli, July 25, 1940

Secrecy is one of the measures of national defense. Keeping secrets is one aspect of a disciplined army.

I have recently ordered important modifications in the deployment of our forces. Many became aware of this when their unit was transferred. They asked why the work done seemed to have had no purpose; why the army was still mobilized.

I know that you will carry out my orders, even if you cannot understand the reasons behind them from your place in the ranks.

But there is one reason I can give you, which I propose to do.

On August 29, 1939, the Federal Council ordered the mobilization of the border troops, followed immediately afterwards by a general mobilization. It entrusted the army with the mission of safeguarding our centuries-old independence. Our neighbors have respected this independence up to now. We will make it respected to the end.

Recent historic events have not in the least diminished our obligation to remain constantly on guard. At this point, there are more troops outside our borders than there have ever been. And they are excellent troops. We could be attacked on all fronts at once, which was scarcely imaginable only a few weeks ago.

The army has to adapt to this new situation and assume a position that allows it to hold on all fronts. It will fulfill its historic mission, which will not change.

This is the reason for the redeployment in which your unit participated. That is what you need to know and that is sufficient.

As long as millions of men in Europe are under arms and large forces can attack us from one minute to the next, the army has to be ready. Whatever happens, the work you have done has lost none of its value; our sacrifices have never been made in vain, for we are always masters of our destiny.

Do not listen to those who are not well informed or whose intentions are evil. They are the ones who through ignorance or vested interest will make you have doubts. Have confidence not only that right is on our side, but also have confidence in our forces and, if everyone does his part, in making our resistance effective.

Soldiers of August First, 1940, the new assignments I have given you are those where your courage and your weapons will best serve the nation in these new circumstances.

Today, on the meadow of Rütli, the cradle of our liberty, I have summoned your commanders to give them their orders, and I will have them passed on to you.

Courage and confidence—the country is counting on you.

There were a few blasé colonels who regretted being made to travel so far to be told so little. Some of them—among the most important ones—did not conceal their disapproval and regarded the speech as a provocation of Germany. The great majority, however, considered the speech and Guisan's firm resolve to resist as an essential solemn and symbolic act.

The commanders transmitted the watchword to their troops. As a young lieutenant at that time, I felt a reinvigorating breeze pass over the company which had been demoralized by the disappointment of the French defeat, by the inaction in which it had been held for more than a month, and by a defeatist propaganda systematically communicated by the extreme left. The march to the redoubt, the arrival in Gruyère, the bivouac in the mountains, and the work on fortifications reestablished confidence and morale. Was this improvement general? Hausamann doubts it. He stated on July 20 that the Rütli meeting failed in its purpose and that the majority of public opinion, deprived of firmness and character, was inclined to integrate into the new European system. Was this simply the pessimism of an ambiguous person?[5]

It is true that Willi Gautschi noted that the effect of the Rütli meeting was neither immediate nor general and that doubt persisted for some time in certain units. He did not believe that the meeting of July 25 and the ideas presented there "constituted the event that allowed the army to emerge from a deep crisis." The Rütli meeting "led to a radical change in the motivation of most of the army and the population. Tranquil resolve to oppose any aggressor, to a degree of fanaticism in some, followed defeatism and resignation." From that moment on, General Guisan truly represented the country's will to resist.

Although (or perhaps because) the Rütli meeting had a positive influence overall on the country's morale and reanimated its will to defend itself, it was not well received by the Axis powers. Anticipating this reaction, the head of the Political Department, who had experienced more diplomatic fears than patriotic enthusiasm from the general's ideas, judged it necessary to send the text of the order of the day of July 25 to the Swiss minister in Berlin. Foreign Affairs Division Head Bonna urged Minister Frölicher to put it in context, in view of the "fantastic notions" and various rumors that had sprung up. The meeting of the troop commanders at the Rütli and the general's brief address in French were only a symbolic commemoration, an encouragement of the troops to be patient.[6]

The task then became to "mitigate the ill humor that had been displayed" in the German and Italian legations in Bern. In any event, the speech was not against "the countries that surround us." It was not possible for the moment to proceed to a general demobilization for economic reasons, including the fear of a swift rise in unemployment. The soldiers would have to be persuaded to be patient and to be reminded of their patriotic duty. Domestic political considerations could also explain keeping part of the troops in the army.

The reactions of the two Axis governments were identical and were not long in coming.[7] On August 3 the Swiss Legation in Berlin announced the German reaction, the situation having been aggravated by the discovery of documents compromising Switzerland. "There is great irritation at the recent army order, which is thought to be directed against Germany. Await a démarche." The telegram added this information that was disturbing in its vagueness: "Discovery in France of documents implicating the army command."

On August 9, Frölicher confirmed that the démarche had taken place that State Secretary von Weizsäcker had said was coming. "This move did not question the mobilization, but the justification that the general gave for it." As a friend of Switzerland, he advised us not to react too violently. However, he would not conceal from our diplomat the fact that he took the "pronouncements" of Guisan very poorly. Unpleasant consequences could be expected.

On August 13, in the absence of Pilet, Etter, as substitute head of the Political Department, received German Minister Köcher, who delivered the note dated August 10.[8] The latter acknowledged the assembly's relationship to the historic tradition dating back to 1291. It then cited some terms in the order of the day: "Our neighbors have respected this independence up to now. We will make it respected. . . . As long as thousands of men in Europe can attack us from one minute to the next. . . . Do not give in to defeatism. . . . Believe in our force. . . . A firm will will assure the success of the resistance. . . . The new deployment of the Army will allow our weapons and our courage to validate the country's interests."

The German government was unpleasantly surprised by these statements, in which it saw only the intention to mobilize Swiss public opinion against Germany and Italy. If it was desired to move the Axis powers from the policy they had been applying to Switzerland, the unfortunate ideas of General Guisan could well contribute to it. The German government recalled its interventions against the hostility shown to Germany and its expatriate citizens living in Switzerland. It would hold the Swiss government responsible from then on for all inconvenience that could result from the official statements of the commander in chief.

Federal Councilor Etter immediately explained that he was not in a position to comment on the substance of the note. There was clearly a misunderstanding in the significance of the general's ideas. Guisan had not intended to stir up hostility against the Axis powers. It had been a watchword of the commander calling on his troops to do their duty whatever might happen to the country's independence.

Köcher thought that Etter's statements disassociating the general's ideas from any hostile intent to Germany would be well received in Berlin. But the general had actually spoken of a chance of aggression at any time. At that moment the threat of aggression could come only from the Axis powers, so that his ideas were inciting public opinion against them. German citizens living in Switzerland had felt the effects. Etter countered by noting in addition that the German troop movements near the border had caused disquiet. Köcher assured him that the troops had to be located somewhere.

That same day, Etter received Italian Minister Tamaro in Bern, who delivered a note analogous to the German one. Tamaro stated that he reacted immediately to the general's entourage, encouraging the officers to urge the commander in chief to show more reserve and prudence in the future. The potential aggressor, for the moment, could only be one of the Axis powers. Etter replied that Guisan had only done his duty as a soldier, and Tamaro concluded that if the general had spoken only of independence instead of a "danger of an attack at any moment," there would be nothing to reproach him for. In shaking Etter's hand, the Italian minister gave him to understand that his démarche should not be overly dramatized. This comforted the federal councilor a little, but he nevertheless concluded his report on the conversation by stating how much he had to surpress his pride as a man and an officer as he courteously accepted, in the name of the Federal Council, the unjustified reproaches of foreign powers concerning the general's order of the day.

In the absence of Pilet, who was still in Baden, the reply to the German note was drafted by Etter, Minger, and Colonel Logoz, the army's legal officer. General Guisan was consulted. The absence of the head of the Political Department (Switzerland's Foreign Ministry) cannot be imputed to the relative enthusiasm Pilet felt for the speech at Rütli; he feared repercussions from it. But it was preferable after all for the Axis powers' "remonstrances" to be received not by the president of the Confederation but by one of the federal councilors. Pilet loyally played the game thereafter and covered the general on August 26 by delivering the official response to Minister Köcher and commenting on it.[9]

The Swiss response was brief. It conveyed the desire of the Federal Council to maintain the warmest relations with the German government and set great store by not disturbing these good relations. The general had stated to the Federal Council that the sense of the speech at Rütli and the orders it transmitted did not correspond to the interpretation that had been made of it. It was far from his purpose to single out Germany as the possible aggressor or to incite public opinion against that country. The only purpose of the speech and the order of the day had been to recall officers and men to the fulfillment of their duty.[10]

At the meeting, Köcher expressed astonishment at the even partial continuance of mobilization and wondered why Switzerland had to remain under arms. Pilet stated that this was not directed at Germany, but that the situation in free France still caused concern. For the moment, Pétain's government was still capable of maintaining some order. However, there was no telling what would happen in the fall and winter, when the shortage of food and coal would be more serious. The Bolshevik current was getting stronger, and waves of it could be expected in Switzerland. Nicole and Schneider, extreme left Socialists, would let no opportunity go by to raise the colors of Communism. Pilet recalled the 1918 strike in Switzerland and his own memories of it. The fear of social unrest prevented total demobilization. Köcher retorted that keeping the troops under arms could also favor subversive propaganda if they were kept inactive. Pilet replied by noting the leave given the troops in rotation, which allowed the soldiers to keep in contact with their families and thereby mitigate the effect of propaganda.

What was the real basis of these propositions? It is true—I was a witness to it—that in 1940 there was significant Communist and defeatist propaganda among the troops. Did that in itself justify the maintenance of several divisions under arms, especially since the disorders in France had rapidly provoked an Axis reaction? Pilet might just as well have brought out the danger of aggression coming from Liechtenstein. Köcher did not allow himself to be convinced any more than the German leaders did. While justifying the maintenance of troops, Pilet could not help waxing ironic about "certain speeches that might seem superfluous and infelicitous." The Rütli speech had the further effect of causing the German government to refuse to receive a delegation of Swiss officers. The general had proposed this move for study and information purposes. Unofficially delivered by the Political Department, the request was refused. The attitude of Switzerland and especially the events of July 25 made this visit undesirable, according to Hitler himself. As it happened, the Rütli meeting saved Switzerland from the obvious faux pas of making this mission to the German army.[11]

On August 1, President Pilet-Golaz and General Guisan each delivered speeches conveying the same patriotic message.[12] Guisan demonstrated the need to defend ourselves and the effectiveness of defense in simple, energetic, categoric, and direct terms. Pilet was perhaps not felicitous as he raised in his habitual oratorical and rhetorical style the glorious defeats of the Swiss at Saint Jacques on the Birse, at Marignan, and at the Tuileries in 1792 to show that one must resist even when victory is not certain. This courage, however realistic it was, passed for defeatism.

It was perhaps this realism that explained why the American minister in Bern wrote in a dispatch to the secretary of state that "the Swiss army is more determined than the Federal Council to resist aggression."[13]

NOTES

1. Georges-André Chevallaz, *Le Défi de la Neutralité*, 420.

2. *Documents Diplomatiques*, vol. 13, 705–6, 788.

3. Oscar Gauye, *Au Rütli*, July 25, 1940, see "The general's speech: new aspects, studies, and sources from the Federal Archives", 5–56; General Henri Guisan, *Entretiens Ac-*

cordés à Raymond Gafner (Lausanne, 1953), 126–28; Willi Gautschi, *Le Général Guisan,* 258–83; Edgar Bonjour, *Neutralité,* vol. IV, 144–60; and Erwin Bucher, *Zwischen Bundesrat und General,* 420–38.

4. *Documents Diplomatiques,* vol. 13, 863–64.

5. Erwin Bucher, *Zwischen Bundesrat,* 427–30; and Willi Gautschi, *Le Général Guisan,* 280–83.

6. *Documents Diplomatiques,* vol. 13, 862–72.

7. *Documents Diplomatiques,* 870.

8. *Documents Diplomatiques,* vol. 13, a) German note of August 10, 1940, b) Etter's report on the conversation with Köcher, 882–85.

9. Erwin Bucher, *Zwischen Bundesrat,* 430–36.

10. Daniel Bourgeois, *L'Image Allemande de Pilet-Golaz,* 80–82.

11. *Documents Diplomatiques,* vol. 13, 900–901.

12. Erwin Bucher, *Zwischen Bundesrat,* 437–38.

13. Edgar Bonjour, *Neutralité,* vol. IV, 160.

Chapter Ten

The Charité-sur-Loire Documents

The matter of the French papers discovered by the Germans at La Charité-sur-Loire and Dijon was more serious than the storm around the differing interpretations of General Guisan's speech. The documents could have served as a pretext for a German attack, and they caused tensions to mount still further. A telegram of August 3, 1940 from the Swiss Legation in Berlin announced the matter in veiled language. In addition, it was difficult to discover to what extent these documents belonging to the French general staff implicated the Swiss army command. It was not a violation of neutrality for the army command, acting on the always public assumption of an attack on Switzerland by one of the belligerents, to make contact with a general staff of the other side to discuss possible cooperation. This had been done in 1917–18, under the command of General Wille, with the French general staff of General Foch. There had also been contacts with the staffs of the Central Powers, but no agreement sanctioned by the governments was reached.[1]

The documents the French had abandoned, which were discovered in mid-June 1940 at La Charité-sur-Loire, and the papers of the Eighth French Army whose mission was to intervene in Switzerland that were discovered later near Dijon, showed that there had been secret contacts between France and Switzerland since 1939, which were pursued more intensively in the winter of 1939–40. The documents defined precisely the terms of collaboration in case of an attack from the north. According to Hans Senn, these papers indicated contacts at the general staff or command level but did not formulate a plan for a political alliance or a military convention. The German officers who analyzed the papers compiled two reports for Hitler. If there had been a flagrant violation of neutrality, the reaction would have been immediate and grim. The file of papers was kept in readiness for any eventuality.

Georg Kreis, in his work on the La Charité affair, concurs with Erwin Bucher in his interpretation of the contacts. The collapse of the French defense could not have been foreseen, at least if one based one's estimates on the relative perspicacity of the Swiss intelligence services. The neutrality argument could not be invoked against Switzerland; the French commitment would be effective only if Germany violated Swiss neutrality. Actually, neutrality is not an end in itself; it is only a means for safeguarding independence. Maintaining independence, the supreme goal of our country, is the criterion by which one should judge these agreements, which do not exclude the rights of neutrals.

Hans Senn notes that the French did not seek to cover the Swiss plateau but intended to reinforce their own defenses in the Jura.[2] He notes that France would have crossed the border in any event if Germany were to attack our country. All that remained for us was to adjust to how they would do so. We even had the right to ask whether a violation of Swiss neutrality by the German armed forces would not have been the occasion for a French offensive in the direction of southern Germany.

The Federal Council, or at least Rudolf Minger, head of the Military Department and President Pilet, were partially informed of the démarches. Minger had been involved perhaps since before the war. On January 31, 1940, Pilet participated in discussing a planned agreement.[3] According to Barbey, officer of the personal staff of General Guisan, he appears to have been informed beforehand. However, if the operation had to be prepared, the president insisted that the Swiss government should retain complete freedom of action and that the French intervention should not be automatic but rather requested in proper form. He confirmed this several times to German Minister Köcher on April 15 and May 14 and 25 but denied that there was an agreement. Perhaps there was a gray area here. The French—as shown by certain premature movements—were ready to "march with the cannon" and Guisan spoke twice after the fact in July 1940, when he was still talking of "assistance from those of the belligerents who would automatically become our ally in case of aggression." Pilet, however, noted dryly on the general's letter that, "[t]here was never any question. Quite the contrary." Further exchanges on this matter between the two men lacked both clarity and courtesy.[4]

Had Guisan committed himself to the French more than he should have, in a military convention that called for an automatic engagement, without the consent of the Federal Council? Willy Gautschi, who appears to be convinced of it, stated concerning the affair that: "[i]n normal circumstances, such an attitude of the army commander in chief with respect to the president of the Confederation would be beyond the bounds of duty and loyalty as they were understood."[5] But perhaps the common background of these two men from

Canton Vaud, who tolerated each other more than they understood each other, prevented a sensation that would have caused the country great harm.

If General Guisan (and this is far from proven) had signed a convention calling for the automatic and immediate intervention of the French army—something Guisan constantly denied—he would have been guilty of grave insubordination, even if the procedures for this intervention had allowed for a swift and effective reply. However, the situation being what it was, if he had signed, it would have been even more serious than he stated, since it would have led to a severe crisis in relations with Germany and another crisis in the conduct of Swiss policy. Whether signed or not, the hypothetical agreement for an automatic intervention was not subject to an acid test. General Daille's unfortunate army corps and its Polish division would have been only a weak reinforcement to the Swiss army in case of a German attack.

Paradoxically, the La Charité affair caused less of a stir on the German side than among the Swiss. The German Legation in Bern received instructions from Berlin to ignore the documents. The matter seems to have been filed away for the moment in order to save it in case of conflict. But according to Gautschi, it also appears that in Germany some persons, in spite of their senior responsibilities, secretly pursued a policy of opposition to the Nazi dictatorship and held pro-Swiss sympathies. Admiral Wilhelm Canaris, head of counterespionage; General Oster; Hans Gisevius, former vice consul at Zurich; General von Ilsemann, the military attaché in Bern; and even Foreign Secretary von Weizsäcker made arrangements to put the La Charité file in a safe place and later had it destroyed, perhaps by SS General Schellenberg.

In Switzerland, on the other hand, certain officers sought to use the documents discovered in France to bring about a change in command and bend policy toward closer cooperation with Germany. We will not go into the details of this lamentable plot, which has been fully described by Edgar Bonjour and Willi Gautschi. Without insisting on the names of those who do not deserve the honor of being mentioned, we will note that some general officers, whose undoubted competence was not equal to the basic hostility they felt for General Guisan and the admiration they had for the German army, tried to take advantage of the situation. German Minister Köcher, in his reports to Berlin, noted that at the end of September one of them came to him and suggested that he use the documents discovered at La Charité-sur-Loire to cause the resignation of Guisan and general demobilization.[6] Köcher noted that it would be difficult for him to make any more use of documents of which he had only heard, but he did pass on the message.

Again in December another senior officer, based on information obtained in Berlin directly from the Franco-Swiss documents, proposed in a report to President Pilet that the consequences of the affair must be faced and that

Guisan must be relieved of his command, either by demobilizing the army, putting him on leave, or firing him. Swiss Minister Frölicher in Berlin made similar recommendations.[7] The accusation was so serious that Pilet transmitted the report to the auditor general and summoned the general for a tense meeting on the problems arising from the Franco-Swiss agreement.[8] In this meeting of December 31, 1940 between the president and the general, Guisan assured Pilet that he had not reached a military agreement with any foreign power, and he submitted written confirmation that same day. "This was an evasive and crafty reply," in Gautschi's view. But the commander in chief was not put at risk. National Councilor Meili, who had inappropriately brought up the responsibility in this matter of Lieutenant Colonel Gonard, a close collaborator of the general, was obliged to retract.[9] On January 31, 1941, when the auditor general asked whether he should request further information from the Germans (!), Pilet concluded in the Federal Council: "Do we have any interest in asking questions of Germany? No. That's the end of the matter."[10]

The General Staff, however, returned to the problem, seeking in vain in the spring of 1941 to find out which papers had fallen into the hands of the Germans.[11] Pilet wrote about this to his successor, Petitpierre, on February 9, 1946, that "[t]his search, which the army ordered and carried out, was dangerous. It could be interpreted as an admission. You do not look for something you know does not exist." The inquiry, incidentally, was addressed to the authorities in Vichy. Informed by Minister Stucki of this unfortunate démarche, Pilet conferred with him to stop the inquiry or at least limit it to information which the minister could obtain discreetly. Bonjour notes that in the French diplomatic correspondence there is no mention of these planned consultations between general staffs. There is only a proposal by the French Embassy in Bern of January 6, 1940, on what interest there would be in a meeting of Generals Gamelin and Guisan, which would provide an opportunity to discuss the delivery of the Oerlikon cannons that had been ordered before the war: "The meeting could take up more important matters."

The matter, to which the Federal Council had put an end, was not over for the cabal of pro-German officers. They contributed suggestions in publications and in interventions at the German Legation or with responsible German officials, advocating changes at the head of the army, inciting demobilization, allowing closer collaboration with the Third Reich, and gaining Switzerland a place in the new Europe. The German victories in Russia in 1941 encouraged their cause.

At the beginning of 1941, Karl Kobelt, an engineer from St. Gallen, had replaced Rudolf Minger as head of the Military Department. Kobelt was chief of the General Staff of the Fourth Army Corps commanded by Labhart, whom Guisan had transferred from his position as chief of the Army General Staff.

A not very communicative technician with a reserved temperament, Kobelt did not hold for General Guisan the same fraternal feelings as the robust Bern peasant Minger. Guisan imprudently expressed his reservations on Kobelt's candidacy for the Federal Council. It was with Minger's approval that Guisan, after a long interval of patience, sent to meditate in retirement the most active of the band of his opponents who had gone far beyond the boundaries of insubordination in their proposals and writings.[12]

In conclusion, the Franco-Swiss negotiations, which were justifiable before the war, continued uninterruptedly during the winter of 1939–40, conducted by the young turks of the general's personal staff, on the fringes, as often occurs, of the General Staff. Preparations for collaboration and intervention were carried out down to the level of the French troops, to the point that in May 1940 some French detachments were preparing to cross the border, prematurely applying the orders drawn up in advance. Was there an agreement calling for automatic engagement? The Federal Council, especially Pilet-Golaz, had often stated its desire to remain in control of the decision. The head of the Military Department and the president of the Confederation were informed of the existence of these contacts, and they did not disavow them, but they were probably not familiar with them in detail, and they certainly were not called on to ratify an agreement that was military as well as political. Was an agreement entered into between the military men? Pilet, who had issued a proper warning, was mistrustful. The general denied it. There is no text attesting to it. If the Germans had discovered the proof they would not have limited themselves to keeping it in reserve, as they did with other documents they had discovered.

However, in Switzerland these contacts contributed to the attempt to unseat Guisan. The Federal Council did not yield, even though the general could appear to have imprudently stepped over the line of his authority, due to the zeal of his eager collaborators.

NOTES

1. Willi Gautschi, *Le Général Guisan*, 355–78, 379–406; Edgar Bonjour, *Neutralität*, vol. II, 217–25, *Neutralité*, vol. V, 9–41; Hans Senn, *Dissuasionsstrategie, Etat-Major VII*, 119–44, 149–63; Hans Senn, "Militärische Eventualabkommen der Schweiz mit Frankreich 1939–1940," in *Neue Zurcher Zeitung*, August 2, 1988; Erwin Bucher, *Zwischen Bundesrat und General*, 403–13; and Georg Kreis, *Auf den Spuren von La Charité* (Basel, 1976).

2. Hans Senn, *Dissuasionsstrategie*, 161–63; *Militärische Eventualabkommen*.

3. Bernard Barbey, *Aller et Retour, Mon Journal après la Drôle de Guerre 1939–1940*, (Neuchâtel, 1967), 95–97.

4. *Documents Diplomatiques,* vol. 13, 826–27.
5. Willi Gautschi, *Le Général Guisan*, 138–40, 370–78.
6. Willi Gautschi, *Le Général Gusian*, 359–60.
7. Willi Gautschi, *Le Général Guisan*, 365–66.
8. Hans Frölicher, *Meine Aufgabe in Berlin*, 42.
9. Willy Gautschi, *Le Général Guisan*, 367–70.
10. Erwin Bucher, *Zwischen Bundesrat*, 412.
11. Edgar Bonjour, *Neutralität*, vol. V, 29 note.
12. Willy Gautschi, *Le Général Guisan*, 473–80.

Chapter Eleven

Reception of the
National Movement's Delegation

A series of domestic political incidents aggravated the tension of conducting foreign policy under the pressure of events and the permanent threat. These incidents attracted more attention through exaggeration, often false interpretations, and exploitation by the media and politicians, and they caused more domestic tension and concern than the essential problems did. Pilet-Golaz was not spared these problems, as for instance when three emissaries from the Swiss National Movement were unfortunately received, arriving by the service stairway, in itself an aggravating circumstance.

Nazi activism became especially active in Switzerland in the summer of 1940, in accordance with the tactics defined by the leaders of this Hitlerian party and in view of the progressive deterioration of the Swiss domestic situation, aided by the collapse of France. The activation of a relatively numerous German colony of 30,000 persons was noted, as was the zeal of the personnel in the German legation and consulates, and the encouragement given to profascist groups reactivated by cast-offs from the "fronts." These fronts had enjoyed relative favor until 1935. They won a few seats in cantonal councils and one in the National Council. But the *Kristallnacht*, the unleashed anti-Semitic and authoritarian violence by the Nazi regime, later dimmed their enthusiasm. German military victories, however, restored some of their attractiveness.

The most important of these groups was the Swiss National Movement, whose French and German names were *Mouvement National Suisse* (MNS) and Nationale Bewegung der Schweiz (NBS). The group was constituted in June 1940 from the remnants of the National Front, the Eidgenössische Soziale Arbeiterpartei (ESAP) and the Bund treuer Eidgenossen nationalsozialistischer Weltanschauung (BTE), terminology difficult to translate both in its letter and spirit.[1]

The movement calling itself "national" had a democratic and legal facade, but its true nature was not difficult to discern. Its terminology was identified with that of German National Socialism. It preached liberation "from the chains of capitalism," a trial for the politicians who had "been losing Switzerland for several years," the spirit of new times, and other revolutionary stereotypes of every variety. The choice, which they claimed to be a more important one than routine elections, they said, was between isolation or belonging to the spiritual community of the "new Europe." The bylaws identified themselves, in their authoritarian rigor, with those of the German National Socialist Party.

It could well be judged unusual and out of place for the president of the Confederation to receive three delegates of the movement, Max Leo Keller and Ernst Hoffmann, escorted as an intellectual and moral chaperon by the well-known Swiss poet Jakob Schaffner, once a Communist sympathizer and converted since 1936 to National Socialist lyricism, especially since Pilet was to see Max Leo Keller separately a few days later. These men, especially Schaffner, had long been trying to make contact with the president. Pilet, who was also head of the Political Department, had at first refused to grant an audience and had only agreed to a meeting at the urging of his colleague Ernst Wetter, and that after having informed the Federal Council. What could anyone expect from such an interview? As far as relations with Germany were concerned, the situation was tense. Carl Burckhardt had informed Etter through Gonzague de Reynold that Germany planned to intervene in Swiss domestic affairs. At the beginning of September, Etter informed the political press commission of Germany's strong irritation at the overflight of Switzerland by British aircraft. Dramatic developments could be expected from one minute to the next. This was what made the contact useful, at least for information purposes, as the attorney general of the Confederation had recommended.

These frontists were undoubtedly counting on the meeting as a kind of recognition, both in Switzerland and by the Nazi leaders. They hastened to publish a communiqué without its terms having been agreed by President Pilet. They presented, they said, their political and social program, and the meeting would be a first step toward easing political conditions in Switzerland. Schaffner later pressed in vain for an audience with the führer. Obtaining only a limited talk with State Secretary von Weizsäcker, Keller, whose imagination was fertile and whose veracity was doubtful, did manage to meet Rudolf Hess and claimed to serve as intermediary between the two countries. He earned no more credence with the führer's deputy than he did with Pilet.

What was Pilet's intention in receiving the delegation? He explained that and other matters in a letter of December 22, 1950 to Pierre Béguin, citing Edgar Bonjour.[2]

Meeting with the frontists? Remember that they were Swiss and that after that we met with many people much more dangerous. . . . I had refused several times to see them. I would have much preferred not to. However, that was not the view of some of my colleagues. . . . The situation was very tense, not just with Germany, but also with Italy . . . (nearly nightly overflights of British aircraft). We were in very great danger then . . . that was the period when some very important people were constantly recommending "a break in diplomatic relations with England." Naturally that was out of the question for me. In short, after I consulted the Federal Council, I invited the three frontists, as it were, to defend myself. Should I have seen them in the presence of a third party? Some said so. I think that was wrong. My only interest in meeting them was to know "what their gut feeling was." You had to let them speak freely in order to get to know them. . . . Immediately after the meeting I drew up a report for the Federal Council. In fact, the frontists appeared inoffensive except for one (that must have been Keller) who, since then has been condemned for treason by the Federal Tribunal and who was the only one who seemed dangerous to me.

Why did Pilet not explain that publicly at the time? He went on:

When the agitation you are familiar with had taken over the country, it would have been easy for me to explain. But that would have aggravated our relations with the Axis, which were already critical. Before the committees in closed session? On one hand, that would not have done much good because it would have been in secret. On the other, I learned that secrets are not always kept. (Other federal councilors after him were to have the same experience.) After I had spoken, some committee members hastened to inform the German or British legations, misrepresenting what had occurred. It got to the point that I was explaining to the British minister, with whom I had a trusting relationship, what I was going to tell the committees and why, so that his government would not be informed secondhand and tendentiously, concerning our real views. Thank God we were good friends and I could talk with him in all frankness and confidence.

The encouragements he had received and the usefulness of being informed had led Pilet to receive the delegation. It was not an ordinary favor for the movement, which was banned two months later by the Federal Council. Pilet also anticipated that easier relations could be established with the Third Reich with the aid of these activists. The "mission" he was said to have entrusted to Max Leo Keller, whom he wrongly received one more time doubtless at Keller's insistence, seemed completely unlikely, even if the Federal Tribunal at Keller's trial in 1948 focused more attention on the defendant's assertions about certain points—although it did condemn him—than to the testimony of the former president of the Confederation. At first, Pilet was intelligent and prudent enough not to entrust a quasi-diplomatic mission to the first emissary to appear, all the more so if the first one to come was the founder of a political group whose loyalty was dubious at best and which was later was to provide evidence for his condemnation. It is not surprising that Keller used his meeting with Pilet to curry favor with the Nazi leaders and to support his claim that he was charged with an unofficial démarche. This person whom Pilet refused to see on his return from Germany never gave him an account of the mission he claimed to have been given.

President Pilet asserted his right—which could be contested—to receive anyone he liked, even "the devil himself" if he thought it fitting. His reason was both to inform himself and to encourage the National Movement to respect democratic legality. There was no question of his giving pledges to the new European order or to any kind of annexation. If he had, the three cronies in the movement would have set an entirely different tone in their communiqué celebrating their victory.

Pilet wrote an account of the meeting for the Federal Council that very evening. Two days later he was attacked by nearly all the members of the Full Powers Committee of the National Council. Some of them, like many Swiss at the time who were more English than the English themselves, were already disappointed at the criticisms of England that Pilet had pronounced the previous evening: "It defends its interests and does not intend to concern itself with anything else. A proof of that is the casualness with which its aircraft have violated our neutrality. . . . It has no concern for our rights. It is the eternal play of the great powers with respect to the small countries." The publication of the unilateral communiqué by the Swiss National Movement lent fuel to their fire. More often charged with the acrimony of an old partisan conflict, the criticisms of these purposes were directed at Pilet as minister of foreign affairs, with only one exception. His colleague Phillip Etter firmly defended him. The Federal Council had refused several times to hear the Swiss National Movement, judging it unsuitable at this time to receive its representatives and allow them to explain their purposes. Falling prey to some illusions about the sincerity of the democratically reformist intentions of the movement, the Federal Council, in its "guidelines" of September 10, declared to Parliament that the prohibition was inappropriate in virtue of the freedom of association on one hand, and on the other, the fact that it would be easier to control them as a legal organization than if they went underground.

The Federal Council published a communiqué three days after the meeting. Some of Pilet's colleagues reproached him for his imprudence, even after they had approved the move. One courageously desired Pilet to defend himself. However, the council did have the loyalty to assume its collegial responsibilities, which was not automatic. Its communiqué reported the meeting, which had been organized with the consent of the Federal Council and the head of the Political Department, with three delegates from the Swiss National Movement. The latter explained the group's purposes and presented its requests. They desired to remain in favor of a free and independent Switzerland. They received neither funds nor instructions from abroad and respected the laws. The frontists confirmed this in a written memorandum a few days later. It was agreed that they would publish a communiqué after the meeting, limiting themselves to stating that they were received and had presented their point of view. However, they did not keep their word and did not submit their text to Pilet. The president kept the Federal Council fully informed of the substance of the meeting and the memorandum delivered by the movement.

"Naturally, the Federal Council, both before and after that meeting, held to the policies it had defined, in its solemn declarations of August 30, 1939 and September 11, 1940 in the explanations of the president of the Confederation before the Full Powers Committee of the National Council and in Pilet's public speech of September 12 in Vaud. This policy calls for the inflexible desire for independence and liberty, strict observance of neutrality, and cordial relations with all countries. Domestically, it called for order, discipline, union, and solidarity in the framework of our centuries-old institutions, the tried and true principles of democracy and federalism."

"Having confirmed and stated its policies there, the Federal Council is convinced that it is in full agreement with Swiss public opinion. Therefore, it can have confidence in the future, with the support of Parliament."[3]

Some have found a compromise in this text between the differing views expressed within the government. If that had been the case, the disagreements would not have appeared at all. Pilet could see no disavowal in it: the government admitted to having accepted the meeting in principle. Pilet denounced the bad faith of his interlocutors and, far from disavowing what he had done as head of the Political Department, he cited his own ideas for confirming Switzerland's desire for independence in neutrality, with order and discipline domestically.

With the passage of time, and in no way seconding the ensuing harsh criticism, it must be said that Pilet, and implicitly the Federal Council as well, were tricked. It was not reasonable for the country's first magistrate to receive these three leaders of a faction whose bylaws, based on Nazi texts, went against their patriotic protestations and their statements—and to receive them without any witnesses. The disinformation in their communiqué, which was published in bad faith, and the favor they would try to obtain with their Nazi patrons from the meeting (without much success) showed the maneuver for what it was. It was understandable that the reaction of public opinion, the press, and Parliament was energetic and severe. It was useful that it presented an opportunity to refuse alignment, to stress the desire for independence and resistence, and to show both the Federal Council in general and Pilet in particular that they should confirm these policies.[4]

Some members of Parliament would have liked to force Pilet to resign. He did consider it, if one can judge from a draft letter taken from his personal files. The allegedly relevant case of Federal Councilor Hoffmann was cited, obliged to resign in 1917 for having supported an attempt, with the Socialist Robert Grimm, at a separate peace between revolutionary Russia and the Central Powers. But the two cases were not comparable. An error of judgment, in the absence of collusion, could not condemn a policy whose prudence did not exclude firmness in admittedly trying circumstances.

It is true that Otto Köcher, the German minister, who was undoubtedly in touch with the activists in the Swiss National Movement, interpreted the meeting and its tumultuous effects on public opinion as a move on Pilet's part toward a rapprochement. But Köcher also noted: "The controversy brought on by the meetings with the delegates of the Swiss National Movement has not reinforced Pilet's authority, strictly speaking."[5] And Pilet did not resign.

Germany was to intensify its propaganda and subversion campaign in Switzerland. The program which SS Brigade Leader Heinz Jost developed on October 21, 1940 was cited in a letter to a senior official in the Foreign Ministry:[6] "We should use the very favorable atmosphere in this general upheaval to achieve an annexation which if not formal, is at least spiritual, economic, and cultural and assure the spread of the Reich's ideology." But Switzerland, in spite of all the military and economic threats bearing down on it, would meet the challenge. With the aid of the press, the Federal Council would show the necessary firmness in resisting ideological subversion by word and deed, without departing from prudence as interpreted diplomatically by the head of the Political Department.

The tone of diplomatic relations with the Reich was to harden after the end of 1940. The conclusions that Köcher, the German press, and the Nazi activists had thought they could draw from Pilet's ambiguous speech of June 25, the severe reproaches of Pilet against England, and the arbitrary interpretation by Max Leo Keller of the contacts between the Swiss National Movement and the president were not long in changing. In his report to the Foreign Ministry of November 19, Köcher asked whether "the speech of June 25," which opened a new line in Swiss policy as he interpreted it, "was not premature. In any event, the success of that policy has not been observed."[7]

On that same day, November 19, the Federal Council banned the Swiss National Movement, "by an act which was not lacking in courage," as Daniel Bourgeois noted. Rumors coming from Hausamann's dubious agency—he was systematically hostile to Pilet—claimed that Pilet had opposed the ban. This was not the case. The decision was unanimous, and three days later, Pilet firmly explained to the German diplomat that a ban had been pronounced by the Federal Council against the Swiss National Movement.[8] The illusions that might have been harbored in September had been followed by more accurate information on the activity of the "reformers" and on their relations with the Nazi organizations, especially the Germanic Working Group in Stuttgart, which was trying to coordinate the extreme right forces in Switzerland in the Swiss National Movement, considered as the only representative of national and social renewal in the country. The movement then had between 2,000 and 3,000 members. There could be no further doubt about its National Socialist nature, anti-Semitism, subversive intentions, and authoritarian tendencies, all of which the *Neue Zürcher Zeitung,* the *Bund*, and the *Volksrecht* were publicizing. In addition to banning the Swiss National Movement, the Federal Council also banned its newspaper, *L'Action Nationale* and had its offices searched. On November 26, it also banned the communists and their associates, after the Confederation's attorney general had established some singular connection between the two movements. Was not Hitler's Germany then the ally of Stalin's USSR, for the moment? Needless to say, the justification for this step which Pilet gave on November 22 to the German minister did not stress the close relations between the Nazi organizations and the Swiss National Movement and their probable collusion with the communists.

Further, Pilet stated that these people, acting in bad faith, had not aided the desirable easing of relations between the two countries. But he invoked the danger that the movement, which had also been infiltrated by communist elements, placed the country in peril, because of its subversive organizations. Köcher replied—in a telling but necessary statement—that this step must be considered a measure against Germany and against those sympathetic to it who were close to the National Socialist philosophy. He doubted that the movement represented a danger for Switzerland. Not wanting to say anything further on the banning of the Swiss National Movement, he could assure Pilet that the Reich would not forget this and would recall it at the proper time.

On June 10, 1941, the Federal police arrested 126 persons, 90 of whom were detained. Five were of German origin; two were even in the German Consular Service. They were accused of espionage or membership in so-called sporting organizations on the SS model. This led to virulent attacks on Switzerland in the *Stuttgarter Neues Tageblatt,* reproaching the Swiss attorney general and part of the Army General Staff for pursuing friends of the Reich in this country, which it termed a bastion of hostility to Germany. The "world's oldest democracy" had, according to the paper, become the refuge of Freemasons, Marxists, Jews, and emigrants spewing hatred and anger against the National Socialist Reich. The Army General Staff and the federal police had entered a new phase: "the wave of arrests shows that Switzerland has not understood developments in our time."[9]

Pilet justified these measures in an animated discussion with Köcher. Espionage must be repressed. But these subversive political maneuvers were intolerable, and he regretted that Germany was associating with people as dubious as Max Leo Keller. Pilet noted that the measures were taken in a framework of legal procedures whose appropriateness could be debated but which he could not influence in a country that still respected the separation of powers.

These events in June and July 1941 and the heated controversy between Köcher and Pilet "confirmed to the Germans," as Bourgeois observed, "that the Pilet-Golaz who they thought was ready to make overtures to the Swiss Nazis in September 1940 had truly ceased to exist, without there being any question of his general attitude, which was still thought to be favorable to Germany."

However, this positive impression, as Bourgeois recognizes, was far from unanimous in Germany, as was borne out by the reactions in the official German press to Pilet's speech to the Council of States (the upper house of Parliament) on June 4, 1941, which it judged too favorable to England.[10] On this point Köcher tried hard to find excuses for Pilet. If he had not faced the problem of integrating Switzerland into the new European order, as head of the Political Department, it was because he did not intend to compromise his position in domestic politics. Once more Köcher tried to maintain an image of a Pilet who was accessible to the Reich's interests.

NOTES

1. In general: Walter Wolf, *Faschismus in der Schweiz* (Zurich, 1981), 81ff; Edgar Bonjour, *Neutralité*, vol. IV, 316–40; Daniel Bourgeois, *Le IIIe Reich*, 246–52; and Erwin Bucher, *Zwischen Bundesrat und General*, 557–74.

2. Edgar Bonjour, *Neutralité*, 339–40.

3. Edgar Bonjour, *Neutralité*, 330–31.

4. Daniel Bourgeois, *L'Image Allemande de Pilet-Golaz,* 83–87.

5. Edgar Bonjour, *Neutralité*, 337.

6. Daniel Bourgeois, *Le IIIe Reich*, 153–54.

7. Daniel Bourgeois, *L'Image Allemande de Pilet Golaz*, 79.

8. Daniel Bourgeois, *Le IIIe Reich*, 262–66; Edgar Bonjour, *Neutralité*, 385–97; and Erwin Bucher, *Zwischen Bundesrat*, 486–87.

9. Edgar Bonjour, *Neutralität*, vol. VIII, 313–20; Daniel Bourgeois, *Le IIIe Reich*, 270ff.

10. Daniel Bourgeois, *L'image allemande de Pilet-Golaz*, 89–96.

Chapter Twelve

Pleading for Alignment

Some Swiss continued to be concerned at the liberties taken by the press, which censorship was tempering only moderately. Thus, as we have seen, Swiss Minister Hans Frölicher in Berlin readily allowed his pessimism to favor an accommodation with the Nazi regime. "Even if," he wrote in 1962, "my pessimism could have been excessive in light of how we see things today, my recommendations for prudence and encouragement of the best possible relations were not unjustified." On May 20, 1940, he recommended that some of the editors of the leading newspapers be replaced.[1] He was not the only one to be disturbed. General Guisan, who in 1942 had finally had the army relieved of the responsibility for controlling the press, was frequently worried that certain liberties of expression could endanger neutrality by fueling the aggressive campaigns of some in the German or Italian press. He even desired the establishment of prior censorship.[2]

Three members of the *Volksbund*, a self-styled alliance for independence — the historian Victor Ammann; the lawyer Wilhelm Frick of Zurich, active in extreme right movements; and Andreas von Sprecher — sent a telegram on July 27, 1940 to the Federal Council requesting Switzerland's immediate withdrawal from the League of Nations. That moribund institution was still operating amidst its political ruins in Geneva, but Switzerland, late to be sure, had withdrawn from what remained of its activities, while contributing financially to the institution out of respect for commitments previously made. The three *Volksbund* members asked for a meeting, which Pilet was requested by his colleagues to grant.[3]

Pilet met with them on August 1, 1940, without giving that anniversary date any symbolic meaning. He argued that it was not in Switzerland's interest to separate itself so crassly from the League and join the chain resignations encouraged by Germany. That would mean taking Germany's side, and

England could justly regard that as a hostile act. Switzerland thus intended to continue paying its dues. Pilet's interlocutors later complained in the presence of Robert Grimm, a national councilor and a state councilor for Bern Canton, a Socialist leader and later a very effective head of the heat and energy section of the war economy. They also insisted on intensifying economic and military contacts with the Axis countries.

The group, now four with the addition of the industrialist Caspar Jenny, next complained about some measures taken by the civilian and military police, which certain officers and citizens had had to undergo because of their pro-German views. They requested that an independent committee be charged with putting that procedure in order and desired that some heads should roll among the senior levels of the police and justice authorities.

Finally, the four *Volksbund* representatives complained against the press and articles that could irritate a victorious Germany. They were especially interested in the dismissal of the editors in chief of the main newspapers, who, they felt, were manipulating public opinion and compromising Switzerland's international situation more dangerously than certain extreme right organizations that had been banned. Their letter confirmed their concern, which they claimed that Pilet shared. They requested the Federal Council to act quickly and firmly to free Swiss public opinion from these evil spirits.

Pilet wanted to avoid a public controversy that could have increased domestic and foreign tensions. He insisted on keeping the meeting confidential and, if only to gain time, gave them to understand that he would be willing to resume contact with his interlocutors on any of the discussion points.

However, pressures were mounting for stricter controls on the press, whether in the ideas presented at a private meeting in the presence of Federal Councilor Wetter and Corps Commander Wille on August 29; in the alarming reports from Berlin in the Swiss Legation; or from warnings of private persons such as, as Bonjour records, "the frontist" Wilhelm Frick, who traveled to Germany at that time and made contact with many important people, especially some close to the entourage of Marshal Herman Goering. Frick, in a letter of September 21, informed Pilet of this.[4] He noted strong irritation against Switzerland. There were two such currents of opinion, the most violent of which came from the SS. That organization saw a provocation in the existence at the Reich's borders and in the middle of Axis-controlled territory of an independent state not at all in favor of its hegemony. The other current was more moderate and located in Goering's entourage and the army. The fate of Switzerland was at stake. Those who were ready to contribute to the Confederation's independence with their benevolent support proposed their fundamental conditions:

1. Information to be given the Swiss people on the reality of the German empire.
2. Hostile statements against Germany to be banned, especially in the press.
3. The right of exile to be refused to those hostile to the Reich and all anti-German activity by emigrants living in Switzerland to be banned.
4. A definition of neutrality in keeping with the present state of forces.

Specifically, the adaptation was to be carried out in the following areas:

1. Agreement on general economic questions;
2. Adaptation of Swiss industry to the needs of the German economy;
3. Construction of electric plants and the supply of current to Germany;
4. Joint study of transportation problems and adaptation of the Swiss transport system to the needs of the Axis; and
5. Cooperation in the study of a European currency.

According to Wilhelm Frick, these conditions would not endanger Switzerland's neutrality. Economic collaboration was necessary, since Switzerland had much to offer in this area. Contacts with leading figures in the Reich also needed to be intensified, and Switzerland should take advantage of the great prestige which former Federal Councilor Schulthess enjoyed in Germany.

Did these reflections, which were not offered in isolation—consider Frölicher's notes—have a great influence on Pilet as has been claimed, and did they confirm him in his pursuit of a policy which some have claimed to find in the speech of June 25, 1940? There is nothing to show that his attitude to the Third Reich was compliant. Wilhelm Frick's program went much further in its collaboration with the Axis. It is essential to know the Federal Council's policy as it was presented and defended specifically by the head of the Political Department, rather than relying on some ad hoc ideas, often distorted or exaggerated, or rumors and falsely ascribed views. As it happened, the government did not follow up either on the meeting of August 1 or Frick's letter.

A petition referred to as the petition of the 200—though there were only 173 signers—was submitted to the Federal Council on November 15, 1940. It originated in the same circles from which the interlocutors of the August 1 meeting had come. It opened by expressing the firm will of its signatories, Swiss citizens from all regions and different political backgrounds, to maintain patriotism and the country's liberty. But it also expressed their serious concern at the dangers threatening this small country, in its state of economic and cultural dependence on its neighbors, and the need of maintaining good relations with them and avoiding partisan positions in domestic controversies to preserve its neutral stance.[5]

The petition continued by claiming that some of the press, including some leading influential newspapers, had put our country in a dangerous position by their blind prejudices and limitless hostility with respect to one of the belligerents. They described events abroad with a single tone, concealing the realities of world politics from their readers and making it extremely difficult for our people to have a serene and objective approach to international events. Certainly the signatories declared themselves ready to fight to defend liberty. But they would like to do so in good conscience, believing that Switzerland had honestly fulfilled our obligations as a neutral. They requested that those permanently and notoriously employed in poisoning our foreign relations be immediately put in a position where they could do no further harm.

According to the petitioners, in these very dangerous times, the Swiss people had to be reminded of their vocation, guarded against foreign ideologies, and fortified against defeatism. It was a question of reestablishing relations of friendly trust with our neighbors. As to specific propositions, the petition requested:

1. Radio and press devoted to reconciliation of peoples in the spirit of the Swiss Confederation, the mother of the Red Cross;
2. Elimination of those responsible for steering the press in a direction fraught with consequences for Switzerland;
3. Liquidation of those press organs that were visibly in the service of foreign political ideologies;
4. Placing the Swiss Telegraphic Agency, whose attitude had given rise to criticism and which had a national responsibility with respect to foreign countries, under strict control;
5. Dismissal of those responsible persons whose political activity had clearly been contrary to our country's interests;
6. Purification of our public life by putting an end to the encroachments of the political police and restoration of the reputations of those affected by them and compelling those responsible to render accounts;
7. Development of cultural relations with all our neighbors to which we are tied by origin and history, within the diversity of our three cultures; and
8. Clarification of our foreign policy by the dissolution of our last ties to the League of Nations and the elimination of all foreign political agencies on our soil.

These propositions, as can be seen, were far less radical than the program of near integration defined by Frick in his August letter to Pilet. Nor did they tend, under a paradoxical affirmation of liberty, to put the press in a position to remove independent spirits from journalism and the political authorities by dubious means that were implicitly authoritarian, by placing the press under strict control. Nor did it contribute to intensifying "cultural" relations with the Axis countries at the same that it branded the universal democratic principle with the term "foreign ideologies" or to the struggle against defeatism by recommending alignment with our neighbors.

The Political Department and the commercial negotiators were in a position to understand the military and economic risk to which the country was subjected by the freedom of the press under a posteriori surveillance punctuated by some warnings, as was the army command, informed as it was by direct or private information sources such as Hausamann's agency. "It is difficult to evaluate in millions of francs what the senseless luxury of publishing phrases like the following samples will cost us at a time of commercial negotiations with Germany" wrote an employee of the Political Department. As for General Guisan, he had often voiced his concern and had informed one of the signatories of the petition of the importance he ascribed to the problem, without, however, approving the petition.[6]

Of course, the Federal Council did not intend to accept the petition's recommendations. However, it would act prudently. The attorney general and the Department of Justice and Police proposed an appropriately public rejection. But the government was afraid to provoke contradictory reactions in Switzerland and especially in our neighbors which could have increased tensions. The council therefore charged Federal Councilor von Steiger to inform one of the principal signatories of the concerns felt by the civil authorities and the army about the press but also the impossibility of granting the petition's specific requests. No administrative or criminal procedures were set in motion against the petitioners. The text and the list of signatories were not published until after the war. It would have been deplorable to make known while the war was on "how many respectable officers and how many respectable Swiss had affixed their signatures to such unsustainable recommendations."[7]

Edgar Bonjour concludes with the time-honored truth that it is easier to interpret the most controversial political events with the hindsight of history than in immediate proximity to the action, but he does not excuse the petition signers on the ground of the threat then weighing on the country. He hopes that descendants will look on errors and defeats with more indulgence than contemporaries did.

Proceeding more accurately in the same direction as the petitioners, the report which Colonel Gustav Däniker drafted in confidence in May 1941 led to sanctions from the Federal Council. This officer, who was highly qualified technically, commanded the Walenstadt miltary school. He had traveled privately to Germany at the beginning of the month and had made contacts in military and political circles in both the state and Nazi Party as well as among economic and university figures. He even met with an SS leader concerned with the center at Stuttgart which was recruiting Swiss—though not many joined—into Nazi military formations.[8]

Däniker's memorandum was supposed to remain confidential, but, as often happens with this sort of document, it soon had a wide audience. "The official document designated 'secret' became a mass article more or less deliberately," noted Gautschi. This manifesto was more political than military and had a European perspective: "If Switzerland is to play a role on the European continent, if it desires to be a truly useful member of Europe, it will have to join it. Such collaboration is not anti-Swiss. On the contrary, in view of our future and our nature, it respects our traditions. Collaboration with the new Europe does not contradict the idea of Switzerland; it merely discards some old and obsolete forms. One can be a good citizen of Switzerland while thinking in European terms and committing one's self to the new Europe. . . . What is incomprehensible is that we are proud of our stubborn determination to stay out."

Däniker noted strong tension between Switzerland and Germany for which the Swiss bore the main responsibility by their written and verbal aggressiveness. The war in fact was a struggle for the unity of Europe and we had to collaborate with it. Certainly our objective was to safeguard our identity and do everything to affirm it. There was no doubt that we had to defend ourselves if anyone were to notice it. But collaboration in Europe would not detract from our identity.

That is why we must silence the press that attacks Germany, the Axis, and the new Europe, Däniker went on. We should not ban political movements with the excuse that they come from abroad. Switzerland has often imported ideas. We should intensify our cultural and economic contacts. We do not want to live through these events day by day. "Let us not claim that the people does not want a new European order. That is wrong, first because the people are more reasonable than our press thinks. In addition, a democracy needs to know where it is going and proceed there courageously."

Däniker certainly did not encourage conscientious objection. He compared himself to Adrien de Bubenberg who entrenched himself in Morat at the head of a bold troop, even though he had advised against the Burgundy war. However, his memorandum encouraging integration into the new Europe over defense, independence, and the democratic liberties must be considered a breach of discipline coming as it did from a senior officer, all the more since Däniker was prolific in criticisms of the army and the way it was commanded. In several conversations with Guisan, he supported his views with a frankness that was honest but in all logic hard to reconcile with the exercise of high responsibility in the army. It took Guisan no less than a year, after a long investigation into the distribution and contents of the memorandum, to impose fifteen days of house arrest on Däniker, after which the Federal Council relieved him of his duties, allowing him to keep his pension. The new European order north of the Rhine was considerably less lenient with its undisciplined generals.

To say that relations between Guisan and Corps commander Wille were never truly good, as Willi Gautschi[9] notes, is truly a euphemism. Certainly with his intelligence and technical competence, the son of the commander in chief in the 1914–18 war had rendered precious services when he was chief of instruction in the army in drawing up the directives that adapted and intensified the military formations for combat and some draft orders of the day which Guisan had signed without any essential changes. But it was well-known that Wille felt marginalized in the teaching mission Guisan had assigned him to in September 1939 and would rather have been an active commander. His mission was galling further because of the gap that frequently developed between the principles and methods imparted by instruction and their application, which was altered if not made actually different by the commanders of the mobilized groups. To establish unity of doctrine and preparation, Wille had proposed an increase in his powers and the verification of the effects of the instruction among the troops, which Guisan had accepted in principle while retaining his authority and not delegating any of his powers.

However, controversy was not long in coming. Wille permitted himself some direct interventions at the General Staff, openly criticized Guisan's decisions, and deplored the role of his personal staff at the expense of the official hierarchy. After the development of the redoubt, he led the opposition by the triumvirate of the "pro-German technicians," as Philippe Marguerat called them, partisans of an immediate regrouping around the redoubt accompanied by a large demobilization. He want as far as to suggest to Germany through its minister in Bern to request the dismissal of the commander in chief because of the papers discovered at La Charité-sur-Loire. The Däniker affair brought the controversy to its height, with Wille taking the part of his subordinate and drafting some "reflections" that accused the chief auditor, who was responsible for the investigation; Guisan; and the Federal Council. Collaboration became increasingly difficult, but the commander in chief, at the advice of the government, waited for the transfers of the end of 1941 to retire the chief of instruction, who made it known that he had not asked to retire.

This shows that in an especially hectic period fraught with threats, the Federal Council, especially Pilet, kept their heads perfectly, however heavily criticized he had been. They were not swayed by diplomatic pressure from Minister Köcher, nor by the virulence of the German press, nor by the ideological, military, and business encouragement to align with the European order the

Third Reich meant to dictate. Stephen Halbrook, in *Target Switzerland*, quotes Goebbels in the magazine *Reich* for January 9, 1942 on Sweden and Switzerland:

> If these neutrals are not prepared to fight with us for the German victory, they should at least pray God for that victory. But they have not even enough sense for that. . . . Their political tendencies incline them toward bolshevism.[10]

Without worrying about German reactions, they did not lend an ear to these proposals. They banned subversive organizations—both communist and Nazi—and firmly but mildly punished those who broke the national discipline of resistance to the totalitarian order.

NOTES

1. Hans Frölicher, *Meine Aufgabe in Berlin*, 30–35.
2. Erwin Bucher, *Zwischen Bundesrat und General*, 373–76.
3. Edgar Bonjour, *Neutralité*, vol. IV, 341–75.
4. Edgar Bonjour, *Neutralité*, 346–47.
5. Marcel Pilet-Golaz.
6. Edgar Bonjour, *Neutralité*, 359–63. Gives the complete text.
7. Edgar Bonjour, *Neutralité*, 368–75.
8. Edgar Bonjour, *Neutralité*, vol. IV, 398–413; Willi Gautschi, *Le Général Guisan*, 379–406; and Edgar Bonjour, *Neutralität*, vol. VII, 261–72 (text of the memorandum).
9. Edgar Bonjour, *Neutralité*, vol. IV, 414–23; Willi Gautschi, *Le Général Guisan*, 462–81.
10. Stephen P. Halbrook, *Target Switzerland* (Rockville Center, NY: Sarpedon, 1998), 162–64.

Chapter Thirteen

Swiss Legation in Berlin

In the conclusion to his dissertation, *Le IIIe Reich et la Suisse de 1933 à 1941* (*The Third Reich and Switzerland 1933–1941*), Daniel Bourgeois observes: "The great lesson of this epoch is that politically, the audacity of our faith in Swiss constitutional principles and the announcement of our will to defend ourselves made a much greater impression on the adversary than did 'realistic' calculations. Certainly this audacity alone, or the Swiss military apparatus alone, would by no means have been enough, however, to dissuade the enemy, if foreign factors independent of Swiss behavior had not played a role."[1]

We can easily endorse this conclusion. The will to resist was expressed by the army, and generally affirmed by the press, public opinion, and in parliamentary committees where leaders could speak more freely than in public debate. Without the will to resist, the country ran the risk of being seduced by ideological propaganda or actually invaded, as is shown by the planning of foreign general staffs and the objectives of foreign political leaders. But this observation does not in the least detract from the distinguished role played by Swiss diplomacy under the most unequal of conditions: the overwhelming disproportion of military forces and Switzerland's strong dependence on the Axis, especially the German Reich which totally surrounded it, for its economic prosperity, provisions, survival, and international trade. Additionally, aggressive German and Italian nationalism in the press and in emigré organizations, plus the vivacity of certain Swiss views in spite of prescribed or spontaneous prudence, constantly provoked incidents that could have lead to an Axis intervention.

It was certainly to Pilet-Golaz's credit that he so ably conducted Switzerland's foreign policy while safeguarding its political independence, neutrality, and diplomatic and economic relations, without caring for—or even harming—his popularity. Traditions and circumstances did not then require direct diplomacy or direct contacts between leaders, which are practically constant today. Or, contacts such as the summit meetings at Berchtesgaden or Munich produced such lamentable results for the countries involved that Switzerland's foreign minister had no stomach for them. Nor was he inclined to put his trust in an "extraordinary ambassador" to put Switzerland into the problematic good graces of the führer or the Duce. This justifiable reserve reinforced the role of normal diplomatic liaison and the influence of the Swiss minister in Berlin, Hans Frölicher, and the German minister in Bern, Otto Köcher. The two diplomats were in fact the *ambassadors* of their countries.

Frölicher ended his career disgraced among historians and satirized by playwrights. Köcher died tragically by his own hand shortly after the war. For both, the formidable pressure from National Socialism's totalitarian policies, which left diplomats no room for critical reflection or maneuver, was often raised in their defense to rebut the accusations levied against them.

Had Frölicher not been cast into the infernal caldron of the Third Reich starting in 1938, he would have had the reputation of a prudent, reflective ambassador in the tradition of courtesy and good company, a good bridge player and musician. These qualities were not much good, however, to him in the circles of arrogant bullies who held Europe at their feet. Nevertheless, it is possible that a certain feeling for the authoritarian right (he had a tour as counselor of legation in Berlin from 1930 to 1934 and had ties to Franco's Spain) facilitated his appointment as minister in Berlin, especially with the *agrément,* the official approval of the German foreign ministry, on recommendation of Baron von Bibra, a trusted officer in the German Legation in Bern. "I will try," Frölicher wrote in his memoirs, "to settle the practical problems with those who wish us well"—the economy appeared to be the most important factor—"and to avoid potential problems with the others."[2]

Edgar Bonjour had reservations about the partiality of Switzerland's minister in Berlin and his naive bias toward the Nazi regime. He cites the future division commander Max Waibel, who was assigned just before the war to the German *Kriegsakademie* and frequented the Swiss Legation in Berlin, that "[t]he triumvirate of Frölicher, Kappeler (chargé d'affaires), and von Werdt (military attaché) is giving the Swiss mission its political line." Bonjour believed that the influence of these three men through their reporting was a constant threat to our independence during the war. "The tone of their reports led the Political Department [the Swiss Foreign Ministry] to underestimate the danger of National Socialism." Although this interpretation of the department's opinion is debatable, it is true that Frölicher did not function well in the German environment and was clearly under the influence of a small group of Swiss industrialists living in Germany or in contact with it who favored alignment with the Axis.

As his tour began, Frölicher certainly benefitted from the good will of Ernst von Weizsäcker, secretary of state for foreign affairs, whom he had known in Bern when he had been chief of the German Legation. This career diplomat had a benevolent attitude to Switzerland and was trying to moderate the adventurous course of German policy. He would reassure Frölicher on occasion concerning the impetuous reactions of men like Ribbentrop or Goering and would give him, and through him the Swiss government, good advice on how to respond without leading to an incident or aggravating tensions.

On the other hand, the Swiss diplomat scarcely ever obtained direct access to Foreign Minister Ribbentrop, much less to Hitler. However, it was to Hitler that he delivered his credentials in 1938 and from whom he heard some apparently reassuring words. Hitler rejoiced at the annexation of Austria but also expressed pleasure at the good relations existing between Switzerland and the Reich, stressing with satisfaction that our country had returned to complete neutrality. He repeated what he had said two years previously to former Federal Councilor Edmund Schulthess: "Germany will never question Switzerland's neutrality and independence." Frölicher attributed great importance to this declaration and stated that it had never been denied in spite of all the risks that had been run. Apart from a meeting where the Swiss diplomat was subjected to stern reproaches, he had but little contact with Ribbentrop. Frölicher recalled only the last reception the foreign minister gave for ambassadors from satellite and neutral countries in February 1945, held in the ruined Presidential Palace in the tragic mode of Wagner's *Twilight of the Gods*.[3]

Frölicher certainly did not see the conflict coming in the summer of 1939. In May, when Hitler announced the annexation of Czech territory and its transformation into the protectorate of Bohemia-Moravia, it appeared to him that Germany was still on a path of peaceful collaboration. On September 1, 1939, when Hitler was announcing at the Reichstag the invasion of Poland, Frölicher still believed that peace would prevail and was known as the only diplomat in Berlin who still did not understand that World War II had begun. However, he would soon slide from that optimism to an alarming disquiet. Impressed by the power and the expansionist dynamism of the Third Reich, he complained in unison with German diplomats about the liberties taken in the *Basler Nachrichten,* the *Bund*, and the *Neue Zürcher Zeitung* by the Oeris, the Schürchs, and the Bretschers, suggesting they be fired.

On September 17, 1940, Frölicher listed for the Political Department the matters about which he was concerned.[4] He noted the matter of the documents at La Charité-sur-Loire that had been "temporarily put aside for further use." The border at Alsace was closed on Ribbentrop's orders. Rail travel in

Savoy was limited, as were air connections from Switzerland to Munich. On his return from Germany, former Federal Councilor Musy brought back some unfavorable impressions. Lieutenant Colonel Ilsemann, the German military attaché in Bern, had just noted to Berlin the discontent in certain leading circles in Switzerland at their country's political and military direction. "We are coming to the end of our reserves. The divisions mobilized around the Gotthard are not making much of an impression. We need to seek a cooperative solution before we are forced to give way to force," Frölicher noted.

"The balance of forces that justified neutrality is no longer there; the principle has no substance. We must rally to the new Europe. We must welcome German students and send new press correspondents to Germany. Given the animosity against General Guisan," undoubtedly an echo of the intrigues about relieving him of his command and replacing him with an officer favorable to Germany, "we have to clean out his entourage."

Minister Frölicher approved the Federal Council's pragmatic policy. However, he was still waiting for an answer to his previous questions: the reception of German students and the dispatch of new press correspondents to Germany. And was it not time to cancel the diplomatic privileges of the representatives of Norway and Poland, who no longer represented actual governments? Frölicher hoped that the Federal Council would not let itself be influenced by the reactions of the Swiss press. "The same people who sabotaged Motta's intelligent policies are trying today to stave off, in the postwar period, the reasonable policies on which the existence of our country depends. We have to prevent this with all our strength."

Pilet verbally acknowledged Frölicher's note to the Federal Council of September 20, 1940. The reply was a vigorous correction to Frölicher's views. The head of the Foreign Affairs Division at the Political Department, Pierre Bonna, set things straight in a message on September 24 to the minister in Berlin.[5] Frölicher's note, said Bonna, showed that Berlin meant to make us understand our dependence on the German government's good will. Switzerland is expected to make one-way concessions; Bonna gave a list of favorable responses given to German requests and demonstrated that they had not been well reciprocated.

But Frölicher found it difficult to share this point of view. He responded: "Please try to understand us. We agree that our situation, faced as we are with the two Axis powers, implies a new direction in our foreign policy. This new direction is indispensable in economic policy; it has already had its concrete application. . . . But there is no question of giving up our traditional neutrality policy willingly. We would gain nothing in benevolence from the Axis powers if we were to hastily sacrifice our existence as a country by subordinating it to the good will of our large neighbors. This is the line we must press *strongly,* which the German government will not fail to understand."

Nevertheless, Frölicher pressed his point again on October 3.[6] He recommended that Switzerland withdraw from the League of Nations, "which is not neutral" and renewed his recommendations to close the official missions of Poland and Norway, "which no longer represent anything." He repeated his attacks on the journalists Schürch and Bretscher and requested that the government improve relations with Germany by controlling the press. Then he turned bluntly to the German threat, sarcastically referring to Bern's note of September 24: "We can *firmly* reject these contributions to an understanding and imagine that Germany will understand. As for me, I see the danger that our partner's demands can expand much further. . . . It is better to tolerate fewer concessions willingly than to be forced later to give up even more."

Pilet provided the elements for a reply. "We have done what is required to prevent the League of Nations from abandoning neutrality. That means that it does not exist, but it still obliges us to make do with what remains. The legations of Poland and Norway no longer represent much, but it would be against diplomatic tradition to close them. The departure of Messrs. Schürch and Bretscher is a private matter." Pilet also noted that Frölicher was more severe on Switzerland than was the German Legation in Bern, which had recognized an improvement in relations between the two countries.

On October 5, Bonna abruptly shut down the debate.[7] "Switzerland must recognize not only the new alignment of powers, but also the domestic and international facts which retain all their significance, and which Germany and Italy have recognized, in their necessity and in their own self-interest."

Still, on November 1, Frölicher again contacted Pilet: "In the present situation, we need to guard against negative behavior and declare ourselves ready to collaborate in the reconstruction of Europe, as France is about to do, and set about the functions and tasks which a politically and economically neutral Switzerland is able to fulfill in the new continental Europe." Frölicher stressed the contrast in practice between Swedish and Swiss neutrality. In his memoirs, the minister complained of the dangerously provocative attitude of the Swiss toward the Third Reich[8], expressed by public opinion, the press, and even the Federal Council in their spirit of resistance, for instance Pilet's having to justify to Parliament his meeting with representatives of the extreme right.

The German Legation was reproached for receiving persons favorable to the Third Reich. The Swiss National Socialist organizations were banned and sanctioned, even though their views were only slightly echoed, in spite of the French defeat. Control measures that socialist Sweden considered useless and that Frölicher's Swedish colleague judged to be provocations were current practice in Switzerland. The minister also pointed to a compliant Swedish attitude that allowed the transit of German soldiers, even the passage in 1941 of a German division with weapons and baggage from Norway to Finland. Frölicher recommended the designation of former Federal Councilor Schulthess as a special ambassador to the führer, as the Swedes had done with the explorer Sven Hedin. Schulthess had been received in 1937 by Hitler, who had stated his desire to respect Swiss neutrality (just as he had done for Belgium and the Netherlands!). The former federal councilor, who shared Frölicher's concerns, would have been ready to go on such a mission.[9]

Frölicher was not the only one to suggest an extraordinary mission to Berlin. The fear of a future loaded with threats that a more conciliatory policy could have turned away, the business interests, and the apparently incontrovertible domination of Germany over Europe led some responsible Swiss economic leaders, without giving allegiance to Hitler's regime, to attempt to seek pragmatic accommodations without sacrificing political independence. This trend was strengthened because certain leaders of the Reich seemed to offer this opportunity, in spite of the Nazi press's aggressive hostility.

The nephew of former Federal Councilor Schulthess had numerous contacts in German economic circles through the *Bodenkreditanstalt*, the German firm of which he was a director in Zurich. On October 17, at Frölicher's suggestion, he met with Bonna in his uncle's presence. Having just come from a trip to Germany, he noted the deterioration in German-Swiss relations. German critics stressed the hostility of the German-language press, the maintenance of a strong army at the ready, and the lack of zeal among the Swiss for intensifying their connections with the German economy. These complaints, said the younger Schulthess, were systematically exploited by Propaganda Minister Goebbels and had already alienated sympathy for Switzerland in the population and the army. Willy Schulthess's correspondents, who were well introduced in economic and political circles, judged that it was time to react against these misunderstandings and send to Berlin a person of great stature who could meet with the highly influential Marshal Goering and counteract the hostility of those such as Ribbentrop, Goebbels, and Himmler. The former federal councilor evaluated the difficulties of the mission and did not seek it but would have undertaken it if the Federal Council had judged it appropriate. At the beginning of November, he sent Pilet a memorandum on the issues he thought should be raised in Berlin.

The doors of the new Europe seemed to be opening just a crack. In his message of November 1, Frölicher noted a rumor of the "partition of Switzerland" that was circulating in Berlin but also reported a conversation with Ernst Weizsäcker, who brought out the role that an independent and neutral Switzerland could play in Europe in accordance with the Nazi victory, of which he had no doubt. This Europe would be essentially economic and would consist of a customs union without borders and would have only one monetary unit. The speeches of Economy Minister Walter Funk seemed to point in the same direction. The construction of Europe would be more empirical than doctrinaire and would take individual circumstances into account. Frölicher recommended that Switzerland not take a purely negative attitude but urged the Federal Council to contribute to building up Europe, as France had committed itself to do, and insisted that Switzerland would be assigned an economic and political role in the new organization of the continent.

General Guisan himself campaigned in favor of an extraordinary embassy to Berlin.[10] One may read this astonishing proposition in a letter confidentially addressed to Federal Councilor Minger on August 14, 1940. Apparently influenced by the alarmist information on Germany from Masson, his intelligence chief, and most probably relying on the alert and imaginative drafting of one of his collaborators, perhaps seasoned by the lyricism in the manner of Reynold, the commander in chief transmitted an overall reflection on changing the European equilibrium and on the unsuitability of Swiss diplomacy, "with its superannuated methods," for a new world. "We must begin a policy based on Swiss prestige and Swiss propaganda." Doubting that our minister in Berlin was effective, the letter suggested sending an extraordinary ambassador and recommended assigning the mission to Professor Carl Burckhardt, a former League of Nations commissioner at Danzig who had dealings with Hitler at the time and had just successfully completed a Red Cross mission in Berlin. Finally, as an afterthought, Guisan's letter outlined a project then belonging to his collaborators' intellectual fantasies of an Italo-American economic plan in which he believed Switzerland could find some advantage.

Minger forwarded to Pilet the letter Guisan had addressed to him on August 14. In what was at the least an unusual coincidence, President Pilet had received a letter two days previously from Corps Commander Wille making the same recommendation for a Burckhardt mission. The army was certainly showing a strange zeal for diplomacy. What did the Federal Council think? Pilet had briefly informed Frölicher that he shared his views on the need for a détente in relations with Germany but believed that "it would be harmful to provoke reactions in public opinion contrary to the end we are serving by taking shortcuts." He did not comment on the idea of a Burckhardt mission.

On November 9, General Guisan repeated his recommendation in a letter addressed to the head of the Political Department.[11] He based the letter on an alarming report Frölicher had just sent to the Federal Council, of which he had been informed. Guisan noted that certainly he was not in the "habit of becoming involved in political matters." But the report bolstered his opinion to the point that he no longer felt he had the duty to remain silent. He thought the choice of Schulthess appropriate for the extraordinary mission he had already suggested, but he insisted that Carl Burckhardt be sent, given his personal acquaintance with the Third Reich and its leaders as well as his activity with the Red Cross. Pilet reported this letter to the Federal Council, recommending that it not be followed up. Ernst Wetter, president of the Confederation for 1941, politely rejected a similar proposal from Guisan. The Federal Council did not intend to consider suggestions from the army commander that were not within his jurisdiction and which, moreover, seemed completely inappropriate.

The idea of an extraordinary ambassador to Berlin was therefore a dead letter. Had it not been interpreted by the Third Reich and by the diplomatic world in general as a sign of weakness, a denial of the policy previously pursued, and a first gesture of allegiance? The rumor was already spreading. People were talking about "political traveling salesmen," of a "Hacha mission," from the name of the unfortunate president of Czechoslovakia summoned to Berlin to sign his country's takeover, or the "pilgrimages to Berchtesgaden or Munich" during which so many heads of state or ministers had sacrificed their honor and their country to Hitler. By only one vote, the Full Powers Committee of Parliament rejected the idea, with one of the deputies equating it to treason.[12]

The discretion in the general's reply and a fortiori the publicly announced position of the Federal Council on this extraordinary mission to Berlin is easily explained. Germany had not proposed this mission, but the Swiss government's refusal to send it could rate as a discourteous gesture, if not an act of bravado, which would not have facilitated the permanent, inevitable course of practical negotiations between the countries.

Pilet, as head of the Political Department, reproached his representative in Berlin with failure to see the Third Reich's objectives clearly. They could be summed up as "Political collaboration, with Switzerland adhering to the Axis; its foreign policy would soon be directed by Berlin. For the prestige of the Axis, the oldest democracy in Europe itself would voluntarily adhere to the "New Order." The unity of the continent would be achieved against the claims to hegemony of the Anglo-Saxons. Economic collaboration: Swiss agriculture and industry (especially industry) put at the service of the Axis. Monetary collaboration: the gold stocks still in Switzerland would pass to the service of the Axis in exchange for its protection." Were we to become enmeshed in this machinery?[13]

Indeed, it was in *Germany's* interest that Switzerland should take the first step and willingly send a semiofficial ambassador to Berlin to discuss improved collaboration. Pilet stayed on his guard. He was aware that all the conquests of the Third Reich had begun with such meetings and with "cultural" agreements. Further, even to sound out Hitler's intentions presented a double danger. Accepting overtures that Hitler could make meant adhering to the Axis. Rejecting them would lead to a break with all its consequences.

With the same desire to proclaim its continued independence, the Federal Council rejected Swiss participation in several organizations or congresses that were outwardly nonpolitical but clearly under the thumb of the Axis powers, such as the International Film Chamber, the International Union against Tuberculosis, or the International Organization for Lodging and Urbanization.[14]

Without alluding to the idea of the problematic extraordinary mission, Pilet confirmed the will for neutrality to the National Council on December 1, 1940.[15] "A neutrality born of experience and wisdom several centuries old, guided by our interior structure and confirmed by the general interest. A sincere, loyal, and complete neutrality that calls for correct relations with all countries and makes these relations trusting and amicable, to the extent that it depends on us. This neutrality is specifically Swiss in the sense that no other country is similarly neutral. It is inspired by the needs and aspirations proper to Switzerland in the center of Europe . . . while maintaining the fundamental character of our country.

"We know that we cannot be isolated: Switzerland has always lived in close contact with the world and will live only by remaining in contact with it. Immobility would be a fatal mistake. In the great current of events . . . it must follow its own channel, certainly, but 'sail bravely to its destiny,' if I may be so bold as to use that expression, and not become stuck in some lateral and dormant port.

"The fact is that our vocation is to understand, to approach, and to unite by intelligence and the heart as much as by the technique of the large-scale material and spiritual activities of the continent. Our mission should be one of liaison and collaboration: we are born for it and will remain faithful to it."

These ideas concerning the will for neutrality, and the requirements it levies in the service of the world and Europe in the heart of a continent lined up by force, still retain all their validity in promoting courage and independence.

Pilet, as it happened, stuck to general principles and did not touch on current problems. After the war he justified the step taken, in a memorandum written as former head of the Political Department and presented before the Federal Court in 1948 during the treason trial of Max Leo Keller.[16] At the time several people, including not a few important ones, thought it would be useful to have closer contact with Germany and more personal connections with its leaders, proposing trips, meetings, and missions in fulfillment of that purpose.

Pilet was diametrically opposed, being familiar with Nazi tactics used in Austria and Czechoslovakia. He wanted to keep things strictly on the basis of official, correct, and traditional relations and not make commitments for the future. With prudence and precautions imposed on him by the circumstances of the time, but with a constancy that has never been forgotten, Pilet rejected these tendencies and refused to allow himself into a path he regarded as dangerous and false. For the entire second half of 1940 and a good part of 1941, he had to maneuver to avoid these undertakings or to keep them strictly within purely technical limits.

In 1948, he wrote in a letter to Pierre Béguin: "My deaf struggle (with the Third Reich) during the summer of 1940 and all of 1941, as well as my 'kid gloves' efforts to restrain those of us who wanted rapprochement or cooperation, cannot yet be revealed. That would make it too personal, not for me, but for many others who are still there. We will have to wait."

Bonjour concludes from this—and it mitigates the reproaches he had heaped on Pilet-Golaz—that "In that period of the war, the entire Federal Council was not lacking in courage as it defended the country's interests. Its policies were reserved and prudent but were not prepared to adapt, in the pejorative sense of the term. The council struggled to gain time without sparing words." This applies especially to Pilet, the one who was the most responsible for this policy, who directed it.[17]

As for the unfortunate Frölicher, with all the naive honesty of his conscience, his duties made him into a lightning rod for criticism. One can understand how, in his timid isolation in the heart of the threat, he played the role of Cassandra, learning from so many tragic precedents, trembling before Nazi insolence, and shaking with fear on reading the critical independence of the Swiss press. In the conclusion of *My Mission to Berlin*, he deplored the fact that the Political Department had taken his warning so lightly. "Motta would never have done that. He knew that dictators cannot stand criticism, and he had, in his policies, the habit of taking unfavorable events into account." This praise of Motta's policies in Frölicher's writings offers a sharp contrast to Pilet's steadfast firmness. Yet Frölicher considered that he did his duty in trying to avoid anything that would have provoked a deadly decision from the führer.[18]

Without approving the recommendations for concessions, or even for alignment, that Frölicher made, in reading his account, one can better appreciate the risks he ran and also the firmness and courage of the government that refused to fulfill them. Frölicher admits that, "History will show that the Federal Council did what it could in that critical period to adhere to a prudent line." But given the hostility Switzerland faced from the leading circles and the press of the Nazi regime, and the fact that it was constantly under sometimes brutal pressure, the diplomat had the burden of strong, attenuating circumstances. In the words of Homberger, a delegate for commercial agreements, who saw Frölicher up close in his difficulties. "It may be that Frölicher"—to whom Homberger attributes the qualities of a diplomat and patriot, plus the knowledge of Berlin circles—"had a rather accommodating character that was too much inclined to concessions. But in the circumstances of the Third Reich, it was rather a virtue to be appreciated in diplomatic circles. It would give a false interpretation of the role Frölicher had to play on the diplomatic scene to reproach him for having been subdued by the massive confrontation then in Berlin, as Bonjour does."[19]

With his attitude and the esteem he enjoyed, Frölicher facilitated the task of our economic delegations. But the unfortunate diplomat, on his return to Switzerland in 1945, received less recognition than bitter criticism at his excessively accommodating attitude to the Third Reich during the nearly impossible and thankless mission he had been given.

In his play *The Ambassador*, Thomas Hürlimann evokes in the character of Zwygart the interior drama through which Frölicher lived with talent and sensibility, taking the view opposite to common opinion and Bonjour's conclusion in particular. But without doubting the good conscience and patriotism of the diplomat, the documents also show that he did not "obey orders regularly sent from Bern" and that Pilet and his collaborator Bonna repeatedly opposed his insistent recommendations to collaborate. They were right in judging him too accommodating to the Third Reich.[20]

NOTES

1. Daniel Bourgeois, *Le IIIe Reich e la Suisse 1939–1941*, 301.

2. Edgar Bonjour, *Neutralité*, vol. IV, 239–56; Hans Frölicher, *Meine Aufgabe in Berlin*, 5–159; and Marcel Pilet-Golaz, *Le Défi de la Neutralité*.

3. Hans Frölicher, *Meine Aufgabe*, 143–59.

4. *Documents Diplomatiques*, vol. 13, 934–37.

5. *Documents Diplomatiques*, vol 13, 937–38.

6. *Documents Diplomatiques*, vol. 13, 963–64.

7. *Documents Diplomatiques*, vol 13, 964; and Edgar Bonjour, *Neutralität*, vol VIII, 61.

8. Edgar Bonjour, *Neutralité*, vol. IV, 229; and Hans Frölicher, *Meine Aufgabe*, 43–45.

9. *Documents Diplomatiques*, vol. 13, 991–94.

10. Edgar Bonjour, *Neutralité*, vol. IV, 220–24.

11. *Documents Diplomatiques*, vol. 13, 1000–1001; and Edgar Bonjour, *Neutralité*, vol. IV, 233–34.

12. Edgar Bonjour, *Neutralité*, vol. IV, 225–26.

13. Edgar Bonjour, *Neutralité*, 233–34.

14. Edgar Bonjour, *Neutralité*, 197–98.

15. Edgar Bonjour, *Neutralité*, 200.

16. Edgar Bonjour, *Neutralité*, 232–33.
17. Edgar Bonjour, *Neutralité*, 200–201.
18. Hans Frölicher, *Meine Aufgabe*, 154.
19. Heinrich Homberger, *La Politique Commerciale de la Suisse durant la 2ᵉ Guerre Mondiale* (Neuchâtel, 1972), 60–61.
20. Thomas Hürlimann, *L'Ambassadeur* (Lausanne, 1993).

Chapter Fourteen

German Delegation in Bern

Daniel Bourgeois derived Pilet-Golaz's "German image" principally from the reports that German Minister Otto Köcher sent to his Foreign Ministry.[1] The historian recognized at once the difficulty of the task. The relative abundance of German texts has no equivalent in the documents left by Pilet-Golaz, which have many gaps. Exploiting the extensive archives of the Political Department represents a great deal of work, despite the fact that the essential part was published in *Documents Diplomatiques Suisses*. On the other hand, one must appreciate the subjective character of the diplomat's reports, "the extent of agreement or distortion between Pilet's actual thoughts and what comes through in the German documents, between what he had in mind and what was reported." However, despite these reservations, the critical contribution and the interpretations of Pilet are a symmetrical foil to Swiss Minister Hans Frölicher's reports from Berlin.

Brought up in Basel and speaking the Basel dialect, Otto Köcher had several ties to Switzerland. "He had a Swiss heart," Gonzague de Reynold noted somewhat optimistically in his *Mémoires*. Although Nazi enthusiasts surrounded him, Köcher was ready to promote positive cooperation between the two countries, as opposed to brutal annexation, just as he was aware of the hostility of a great majority of the Swiss people and their will to resist the Third Reich. This would explain his tendency if not to distort, at least to embellish or attenuate what Pilet said and to interpret his subtle irony or frequent ambiguity in a sense favorable to Germany. If it is true that Köcher tangibly encouraged the Swiss National Movement in 1940, proposed a joint démarche by Italy and Germany after General Guisan's speech at Rütli, and suggested requiring the dismissal of the general over the La Charité-sur-Loire papers—at Swiss instigation, alas!—he later provided a moderating influence against Nazi activism and defended the cause of Swiss neutrality. Finally, it was understandable that Köcher was concerned to improve his own standing by showing the effectiveness of his mission and by assuring his foreign minister that he enjoyed influence and good relations with Swiss government leaders, especially the head of the Foreign Ministry.[2]

Although he regretted the departure of Giuseppe Motta from the leadership of the Political Department at the beginning of 1940, Köcher looked favorably on his successor, Pilet-Golaz. The latter appeared to be a credible defender of neutrality and, by affirming the primacy of civilian political power, he compensated for the bias of Guisan, whom he judged to be pro-French. Pilet, however, replied firmly to Köcher's complaints about the attitude of the Swiss press. According to Bourgeois, he gave "the impression of a man anxious to assure Germany on the credibility of Swiss neutrality, whether at the price of ideas unfriendly to the powers on the other side and in some way disposed to consider the German viewpoint, but also to indicate its limits. The distance between the way that public opinion and the head of the Political Department looked on events appears clearly in the German minister's reports, as well as the reserve Pilet imposed, even at the risk of duplicity."[3]

Could Pilet have acted differently and if so, should he have? He was a responsible official whose duty was to assure that his country remained independent and at peace. At the risk of unleashing a war and threatened by combat-ready, armed concentrations and the pressures of an aggressive nationalism, he could not afford the luxury of serene judgment in the comfortable distance of elapsed time, such as a theoretician of public law or a Manichaean historian separating the just from the unjust in an absolute sense could permit himself. Justice, especially in a period of crisis, was necessarily subject to variable geometry.

The diplomat and politician could not be the docile medium of public opinion in his country or express popular views in all their impulsiveness, versatility, and diversity, however legitimate they might be. He needed to weigh the risks to which his plans subjected him as well as other people. He had to try to compromise, even if his temperament, the circumstances, and his feeling of being in the right impelled him to go to the heart of the matter. He had, without giving up the essentials, in this case his country's independence, to reassure and not disturb, to gain people's confidence, even by deceit if necessary, and not to provoke the susceptibility of a pathologically irascible leader who was unpredictable in his rages.

The picture Köcher painted of Pilet was equally subject to change, according to how the situation developed, and equally susceptible to the interpretations each of them made independently. This has led Bourgeois to distinguish several phases in their relations.

Köcher obtained a good impression of Pilet from his first meeting on March 21, 1940 with the new head of the Political Department. The German Foreign Ministry even gained the impression from Köcher's report that Pilet, as a French-speaking Swiss, could more easily pursue a policy favorable to the Reich than could a Swiss from the German linguistic area. Pilet's assertion of the primacy of civilian political authority over the army was reassuring to Köcher, who shared the general German concern for the pro-French sympathies of the Swiss army command. Pilet replied that if there had been contacts, they did not exceed the bounds of the normal and that, moreover, Germany could count on some certain partisans in the army's upper reaches, such as Labhardt and Bandi. (He mentioned neither Wille nor Däniker.) Pilet also confirmed to Köcher that the Swiss army was impartial and assured the German minister that the army would defend itself with the same determination against the French as against the Germans. But if he voluntarily surrendered to criticisms of the West by way of currying favor, he put German criticisms of the Swiss press in their proper context. And he firmly rebutted the reproaches of the Swiss airmen for supposedly lacking a neutral spirit in their attacks on German aircraft overflying Swiss territory.

As we have seen, the German government interpreted the speech of June 25, 1940 as the announcement of a policy change.[4] Köcher, who did not report on it directly, appears to have interpreted it that way. However, he stated in a conversation with Pilet on July 1 that it was difficult to change Swiss public opinion quickly. A victorious Germany should understand this and find ways to earn Swiss confidence while taking into account their attachment to their special identity. While expressing reservations about the suitability of what General Guisan had said at the Rutli, Pilet supported maintaining mobilization, without stating the essential and obvious reason for it.[5] Köcher was striving in his courteous, naive way to ask which adversary they had in mind.

Was Pilet attempting a diversion with the abundant and critical eloquence he brought to bear on the international situation, the mistakes made by the democracies, and the unhappiness he felt toward the Soviet Union, though it was then an ally of the Reich? The plans for changes that the Germans had thought they discerned in the June 25 speech and random suggestions by the head of Swiss diplomacy allowed time to take action. Köcher found excuses for Pilet in the passivity of public opinion, the frequent hostility to him personally, and opposition to him within the Federal Council, where, as Köcher saw it, only Phillip Etter and Ernst Wetter supported him. His other colleagues avoided the issue and Stampfli, who was not hostile in principle to the Germans, had great reservations about them.[6] These were interpretations peculiar to Köcher, who was not sufficiently aware of the Federal Council's constant need to act as one during these crisis years.

The unfortunate meeting with the Swiss National Movement gave the Germans the premature illusion of a political rapprochement, an illusion that soon evaporated with the strong reaction of Swiss public opinion and by the ban of the frontists in November 1940, which Pilet justified strongly to the German minister, even going so far as to claim, as he willingly played with this ironic paradox, that these bans would improve German-Swiss relations.[7]

From then on, Köcher often encountered the firm attitude of the head of the Political Department. Pilet complained on December 13, 1940 about the obstacles the German blockade placed in the way of overseas trade, which was indispensable for Swiss acquisition of provisions and raw materials and for Swiss exports. That the German minister invited the leaders of the recently banned Swiss National Movement in January 1941 to a reception in honor of Hitler's accession to power was something of a provocation.[8] Pilet warned Köcher and asked him to encourage Counselor of Legation Hans Sigismund von Bibra to be more prudent. Pilet had heard of the ideas that von Bibra, a zealous Nazi, had expressed to the "Swiss reformers."

Was this conditioning—or seduction? On March 8, 1941, before a group of foreign journalists including three Swiss, Propaganda Minister Goebbels described, in a sort of fireside chat, the possibilities for collaboration with the new Europe after the victory of the Axis powers.[9] This collaboration was to extend to currency, the economy, the army, and diplomacy. It did not exclude respect for the cultural and institutional independence of the associated countries, so long as the country became part of the continental system and recognized Axis military supremacy, economic needs, and diplomatic preponderance. Germany's attitude to other countries, according to Goebbels, referred to strategic needs and not at all to any desires for annexation. Thus there was no plan to attack Switzerland because of the behavior of the Swiss press. That, after all, would not be necessary: it would be enough to cut off their coal. After its victory, Germany had no intention of imposing Nazi ideology on other peoples. A country could perfectly well sell its products to the Reich without having an authoritarian structure, and Germany would not convert to democracy as it exported its machines to other countries.

Despite the open door to what one would call today something like the principle of subsidiarity and the respect for relative independence, these ideas of Goebbels were geared less to seducing than to conditioning, to making satellites of the associated nations. In spite of the promise of impunity, the Swiss press rejected these viewpoints unanimously. "It is impossible for a Swiss mind to conceive of collaboration other than in a framework of political freedom and national sovereignty. To agree to give these up, even if it were the smallest thing in the world, would mean to disappear," said a French-language Swiss newspaper. "In reading the first notices in our press," said the *Journal de Genève* for March 13, "one can see the unanimity with which it puts out of the question any military or diplomatic collaboration abroad that could—we do mean *could*—be expected of us some day."

The Federal Council did not have to reply to this unofficial press conference. However, it did not diminish its struggle against the activism of the extreme right and stressed the principles of independence and neutrality. The ideas Pilet presented before the Council of States on June 4, 1941 caused frankly hostile reactions in Germany. The head of the Political Department clearly defended neutrality as one of the pillars of Swiss policy, implying friendly relations with all countries. Certain German newspapers, such as the *Berliner Börsenzeitung,* were hard on "the ideas of one Mr. 'Pilet-Golaz' from Bern," denouncing their hostile tone to Germany, their aggressive stance against the German press, their failure to open up to the new European order, and their servility to England. A summary by the *DNB*, the official German press agency, further stressed the aggressiveness of the replies in the German press. At the same time, German officials expressed themselves to their citizens residing in Switzerland in terms which did not escape the Swiss authorities, in spite of the private nature of the meetings concerned. Thus *Gauleiter* Sauckel gave speeches in Basel, Zurich, and Bern where he stated that Switzerland belonged to greater Germany, referring to the Swiss Confederation as "a putrid appendix" in the heart of Europe. And Weyrauch, German consul at St. Gallen, said that there was nothing more to justify the existence of Switzerland.[10]

Pilet was therefore correct in asking Minister Köcher if the German government supported these ideas. He noted that Switzerland fulfilled its trade obligations to Germany completely. Undoubtedly the climate of relations between the two countries could be improved if an end were made to the attacks against Switzerland and its independence could be assured.

Certainly Köcher was still trying to paint a picture for his foreign minister of a compliant Pilet-Golaz who believed in a German victory, at least in 1940. It would not be well received for the foreign minister of a small, completely surrounded country to tell a representative of the conqueror that its victory would be transitory. For him to say what he really thought would only be a provocation, with serious consequences. But in reading Köcher's letters, we see the head of the Political Department pretending to be disturbed at the Italian defeats in the Balkans and North Africa toward the end of 1940. Peace, he said, would be delayed because of that. However, we should also see in these statements doubts arising about an eventual Axis victory and Pilet's mentioning the tenacity of the English and the refusal of the British government and British public opinion to engage in peace moves, in spite of the destruction on land and sea.

According to Köcher, the German attack on the USSR in 1941 seemed to Pilet to be "in conformity with the interests of Europe as a whole," a formulation, as Bourgeois notes, that was analogous to the Delphic oracle. The federal councilor himself did not believe in the viability of the German-Soviet pact and had opposed a resumption of diplomatic relations between Switzerland and the USSR. That did not prevent him from politely formulating his wishes for the success of the project,[11] without proposing Swiss participation.

On August 1, 1941, the Swiss Confederation celebrated the 650th anniversary of its founding. The Axis countries and their satellites united in declining to send a message of congratulations. Pilet noted his disappointment to Köcher. The state of German-Swiss relations did not allow it, said the diplomat. To keep the peace, the federal chancellery prudently kept silent about the congratulatory telegram from King George VI of England.[12]

After the entry of the United States into the war and the German difficulties in Russia during the winter of 1941–42, Pilet sketched out the possibilities of prisoner exchanges between the belligerents. But Germany would not let anything develop that could appear as a sign of weakness. Köcher warned Pilet that "[w]e would not want to cast doubt on Germany's final victory." However, the fact that the question could arise meant that a certain balance of forces had developed and that from then on, Switzerland dared to express itself. Pilet returned to the problem at a meeting in April 1942. England's generous overture toward prisoner exchanges with the Italians implied other possibilities. An atmosphere of confidence had developed which could lead to peace talks. Köcher interrupted him: it would be impossible to expand the prisoner exchange negotiations to other subjects. Because the English had impudently rejected the führer's offer, the time for peace talks had passed. There must be no more dreaming of compromise. The Reich and its allies were irretrievably set on pursuing the war until the total defeat of the enemy. There could be no doubt of German victory.

Pilet persisted. Köcher told him that if he obstinately linked the problem of prisoner exchanges to some vocation as a mediator, he did not understand. The federal councilor then noted the serious losses England had suffered. It "is still nothing but an island." Canada and Australia will turn to the United States and what England will have lost will not come to Germany. Continuing the war would cause immense suffering. If the belligerents were totally opposed to peace talks, the situation would be made so tense that the end would be all the more bitter. Pilet's insistence was such that Köcher wondered if England had not chosen Switzerland as a good place to begin these approaches. A conversation with former Federal Councilor Edmund Schulthess confirmed it.[13]

Köcher sent these prophetic statements of Pilet to the Foreign Ministry in a memorandum on April 16, 1942. It cannot be excluded that the diplomat, given the detailed and exact nature of his report, took them to some extent for his own; at least he did not appear to be indignant about them. Pilet showed obvious courage, if not imprudence. Germany was making progress in the Soviet Union; the Americans were withdrawing in the Pacific and the British had not yet reversed the course of the war in North Africa at El Alamein. To doubt the incontrovertible nature of the German victory at that time was to run risks for the small neutral country, the planned invasion of which was in the files of the German armed forces. At least the ideas Pilet expressed in those circumstances exonerated him from charges of complacency with respect to Germany, levied by so many ill-wishers, who persist to this day in these accusations.

Even after the defeats at El Alamein and Stalingrad in October 1942, the head of the Political Department confided to Köcher that Germany had "lost the peace."[14] Perhaps it would win the war and regain the peace by force? However, the peace that could have been envisaged after the defeat of France was now made impossible by all the hatred the Germans aroused in the countries they were occupying, as a memorandum from the legation noted.[15]

At that same time, Berlin was making its usual complaints about the lack of sympathy of the Swiss for the new Europe. Pilet stated to Köcher on October 20, 1942 that "[w]e do not know the new Europe. We do not know what it will be. The war is not over. As long as the war is going on, Switzerland, in accordance with its traditional policy, its international obligations, and its solemn declarations, can and will only remain neutral. It cannot take part either in the new Europe or in the Atlantic Charter [signed in August 1941 by Roosevelt and Churchill]. It is only at the end of the war that circumstances will allow Switzerland to decide. Before that, not only in its own interest, but also in everyone's interests, it must stay out."[16] These statements that Bonjour modestly cites in a note led him to declare: "Only such strong language could still make an impression on the German leaders."

The reversal of the situation over the winter of 1942–43, the American landing in North Africa, and the threat hovering over Italy would give greater importance to transit through Switzerland at a time when all troop transport, as well as the passage of war materiel, had been prohibited since 1941.[17] Germany might have been tempted to seize Switzerland in order to control the passes and exert better control over a militarily and politically disrupted Italy. Germany might also have feared that the Allies might launch a coup to seize the tunnels and airports or to destroy them. It doubted the good faith of General Guisan, whom it suspected of connivance with the Anglo-Americans. This may be an explanation of the meeting between Guisan and General Walter Schellenberg, chief of SS Foreign Intelligence, at Biglen in March 1943, where Guisan confirmed the will to resist any aggressor. The declaration was praiseworthy in itself, but it belonged more to the federal council than the army commander to make it. Guisan was appropriately reprimanded.[18]

Pilet's replies to the oft-repeated German discontent conveyed by Köcher could not be regarded as complacent. The tunnels and railroads were carefully guarded against sabotage, but the federal councilor recalled the prohibition against war materiel passing through them. In September 1943, Pilet even suggested refusing the transit of 100,000 Italian workers to Germany. The Federal Council accepted his recommendation unanimously. As for the risk of bombardment of factories working for Germany, there was no question of their receiving antiaircraft protection. Oerlikon, after all, which was delivering antiaircraft guns to the Reich that it had been selling to the Allies up to 1940, was well guarded. As to the precision mechanical industry in the Jura, it was too near the border not to be protected effectively (but Pilet did not add that half its production in the middle of the war was for the Anglo-Americans). He regretted that Germany refused to deliver antiaircraft searchlights. According to Köcher and the German military attachés, an Allied air attack encountered Swiss resistance.[19] But this would have been unlikely in 1942, given the distances involved.

At the beginning of 1943, Pilet contemplated the prospect of an Allied attack through Italy or through the Rhône Valley. Colonel-Brigadier Roger Masson, head of the Swiss intelligence service, reportedly had exchanges with the Italian military attaché with a view to the collaboration of Axis troops in case of Swiss difficulties. Pilet tried to set matters straight. He affirmed Switzerland's capacity to defend the alpine passes. He warned the Germans against a preemptive strike on Swiss territory. They should not come to the aid of the Swiss unless appropriately requested.[20]

Ribbentrop reacted very unfavorably to the information Köcher gave him. Because Pilet did not believe an Allied attack would come from the south and, furthermore, did not envisage German assistance, the ideas he had on defending Switzerland were directed against Germany. As rumors were circulating about possible conversations between General Guisan and the Anglo-Americans, Pilet renewed his protestations of neutrality. Perhaps the Germans had concluded from Guisan's meetings with SS General Schellenberg—which Pilet disavowed because the commander in chief had exceeded his authority—that countervailing conversations had taken place with the Allies. Köcher gave assurances for Pilet-Golaz's statements. There is no example in history where the Swiss did not keep their word.[21]

But Ribbentrop was not convinced. He brought up the contacts revealed by the papers found at La Charité-sur-Loire and doubted that Guisan could have acted without the consent of the Federal Council. He asked Köcher to get to the bottom of the affair: were the Swiss more credible today than they were in 1940 and would they defend themselves against an Anglo-American attack? He doubted the validity of Pilet's statements. The German foreign minister and his diplomat were clearly not on the same wavelength.

In April 1943 Pilet, who had been opposing Nazi threats in Switzerland since 1940, intervened against German espionage.[22] He requested the recall within fifteen days of a consul involved in spying. Shortly after, he severely denounced the activities of spies and their interest in military installations, which supported the notion of Germany's aggressive intentions. Admiral Canaris, however, as the German Foreign Office claimed, had suspended espionage in Switzerland, given its lack of military interest and appropriate political targets. However, the *Abwehr* was not the only intelligence organization in the Third Reich.

Köcher's reports for the years 1942–44 pictured Pilet as undoubtedly impressed by the strength of the German army's combat capacity, for which he had a certain esteem, but he often doubted a German victory. He was disturbed at Soviet progress, expressing the reasonable fear of a communist takeover of Europe and the vain hope of a compromise between England and the Reich to safeguard Europe.

This was the source of the suggestion, which cropped up here and there, of a détente and possible arrangements in the west that could avoid the total collapse of Germany. But the head of the German mission in Bern, following Ribbentrop's strong reaction in 1942 and irritated that anyone could doubt a German victory, did not again risk making this reasonable suggestion on his own.

Köcher certainly encouraged Pilet to follow a policy of concessions, to which the latter appeared open in 1940. The diplomat defended the Nazi organizations in Switzerland, but he also attested to and defended the Swiss neutrality policy on several occasions. Certainly, Pilet gave Köcher the impression that he was seeking an accommodation. Köcher transmitted this impression to Berlin and undoubtedly amplified it, as well as stating that he benefitted from Pilet's confidence, in order to give a good impression of his mission. But action was slow to follow the ideas. Pilet discussed without ever giving anything essential away, as he firmly defended the rights of a neutral state and, beginning in 1942 expressed his doubts about a German victory. The confidence he had inspired to Köcher was seriously reduced.

NOTES

1. Daniel Bourgeois, *L'Image Allemande de Pilet-Golaz*, 69–128; and Edgar Bonjour, *Neutralité*, vol. IV, 79–106.

2. Daniel Bourgeois, *L'Image*, 122–25.

3. Daniel Bourgeois, *L'Image*, 72–75.

4. Daniel Bourgeois, *L'Image*, 77–80.

5. Daniel Bourgeois, *L'Image*, 80–82.

6. Daniel Bourgeois, *L'Image*, 86.

7. Daniel Bourgeois, *L'Image*, 83–91.

8. Daniel Bourgeois, *Le IIIe Reich*, 266–68.

9. Edgar Bonjour, *Neutralité*, vol. IV, 237–41.

10. Daniel Bourgeois, *L'Image*, 96–98.

11. Daniel Bourgeois, *L'Image*, 99.

12. Daniel Bourgeois, *L'Image*, 99–100.

13. Daniel Bourgeois, *Le IIIe Reich*, 415, note 39; and Edgar Bonjour, *Neutralité*, vol. V, 146–47.

14. Edgar Bonjour, *Neutralité*, vol. VII, 243–44.

15. Daniel Bourgeois, *L'Image*, 103.

16. Edgar Bonjour, *Neutralité*, vol. V, 254, note 40.

17. Richard Ochsner, "Transit von Truppen . . . Zugunsten einer Kriegspartei Durch das Neutrale Land," in *Schwedische und Schweizerische Neutralität*, 220ff; Edgar Bonjour, *Neutralité*, vol. V, 259.

18. Willi Gautschi, *Le Général Guisan*, 513–29.

19. Daniel Bourgeois, *L'Image*, 103–109.

20. Daniel Bourgeois, *L'Image*, 107–13.

21. Daniel Bourgeois, *L'Image*, 110–11.

22. Daniel Bourgeois, *L'Image*, 113–14.

Chapter Fifteen

An Attempt at a Separate Peace, or the Hausamann Affair?

The change in the course of the war in 1942–43 undoubtedly suggested to many men of good will that an end should be put to the expenses of a war in which German victory appeared less and less assured, but which still presaged its quota of massacre and destruction. Pilet-Golaz was tempted to offer the good offices of neutral Switzerland in favor of peace talks and in fact suggested the idea repeatedly in his diplomatic contacts. But he was surely led to caution by the imprudence of one of his predecessors, Federal Councilor Hoffman, who had allowed himself in 1917 to become involved in negotiations for a separate peace between the Central Powers and revolutionary Russia and was brutally compelled to resign. In this war, was Pilet-Golaz requested to lend a hand in a similar attempt at a separate peace?

On February 5, 1943 Major Hans Hausamann, who operated a small private information service that was in close touch with army intelligence, sent an "important political report" to General Guisan and Federal Councilor Karl Kobelt, head of the Military Department. According to Hausamann, this report contained a telegram that the head of the American Legation in Bern, Minister Harrison, had sent to Washington, in which Pilet had reportedly encouraged the Allies to conclude a separate peace with the Third Reich at the urgent request of the German minister in Bern.

Who was Hausamann? The information provided by Pierre T. Braunschweig in *Geheimer Draht nach Berlin* [*Secret Line to Berlin*] and the detailed investigation which Erwin Bucher instigated on this person who had grown up in intelligence activities and who was later broken by parliamentary intrigues, show how problematical he was.[1] What was his past?

After a few false starts in business, Hausamann held positions as press chief for the Association of Swiss Officers under the sponsorship of Colonel

133

Bircher and for the Military Department, notably concerning military films. In 1938 he set up a military research and information center which he tried in vain to propose to the department.

He was certainly a man of initiative. In 1938 he offered his services to the German Nazi Party, developing a plan for its propaganda abroad. He later claimed that he had tried to infiltrate the organization in order to spy on it. He was successively seen being reproached for his excessively mild reaction to the leftist Swiss press, then being reproached by the Socialist Party, then giving it technical advice, then haranguing gatherings of workers, and finally participating as a patriot in the "officers' plot" of June 1940. He cultivated relationships with members of Parliament from all parties and voluntarily used these to garner publicity. He expanded his private information service, personally gathering information from officers, diplomats, and Swiss residing abroad and filing newspaper clippings. Active and imaginative, he brought information to the Swiss Army Intelligence Service—led since 1936 by Colonel Roger Masson—which supplemented the meager loot which some paltry resources and an embryonic organization were able to gather. The pacifist illusions of the interwar period and the illusory hope of collective security had led to the dismemberment of the intelligence service. When Masson took over command in 1936, it was composed in its entirety of a section head and a secretary. It was expanded to ten persons on mobilization and to sixty-six by 1945. Recourse to Hausamann's service was an empirical, if unfortunate, necessity.[2] In fact, he received some 150,000 francs a year for these services from 1941 to 1944 and supplemented his resources by selling information to western intelligence services on a basis of reciprocity, because a good part of this information came in particular from the English. However, this did not exclude his having sources in Germany.

The reliability of this information has often been put in doubt, even if Edgar Bonjour refers to it as if it were reliable. We recall the criticism by Division Commander Hans Frick, who discussed false news fabricated both by the English and the Germans. Waibel, an intelligent specialist in the information field, wrote to an excessively credulous Masson that a quantity of unreliable, inaccurate, and alarmist information should have required a critical examination of Hausamann's support. He was reproached with confusing his personal opinion with objective fact. He "fabricated" part of the news himself. This was the case of the message of June 30, 1940 which we have already mentioned, the theatrical evocation of the meeting in the Reich chancellery at which Hitler, Goering, Keitel, Ribbentrop, Hess, and Goebbels supposedly participated at which Switzerland's fate was debated. Most of these celebrities, who were at that time scattered in the four corners of Europe, could not have met together either on that day or in Berlin.[3] Bucher cites other examples.

It is astonishing that Masson, who had to construct his intelligence service from start to finish, placed such trust in Hausamann and defended him so often, notably in the matter of the so-called separate peace.[4] This is even stranger since Hausamann did not hesitate, with some of his colleagues, to plot against Masson, especially with the Americans. An investigation by General Guisan's personal staff described the infighting in the intelligence service in April 1943 with respect to Masson, who was generally esteemed by his superiors, the chief of the General Staff, General Guisan, and his subordinates.[5] The investigation was especially harsh on Masson's auxiliary, Müller, an officer of average intelligence who was influenced by his subordinates, especially Hausamann. The latter was severely criticized for "[e]xploiting, above all, information he obtains in Anglo-American circles, active, fanatical, detesting anything around him that smacks of quiet and calm, then hunting it down, he sometimes shows signs of nervous and mental unbalance. The new facets in Hausamann's activities have been his frequent and conspicuous appearances in the corridors of Parliament after the last session."

Hausamann was feverishly active against Pilet in parliamentary circles. The ambiguity of this person who oscillated between political intrigue and military intelligence and the obvious inaccuracy of his information and its fabrication often called for serious reservations about his activities and integrity.

Consider a report Hausamann submitted on February 5, 1943 to the head of the Military Department, Karl Kobelt.[6] Late in January, according to this report, German Minister Köcher, accompanied by Military Attaché von Ilsemann, called on the head of the Political Department. These two men confided to Pilet that their government no longer believed in total victory, or even victory at all. They reportedly stressed the gigantic efforts the Soviets were making in weapons manufacture and in mobilizing new armies. Their objective was invasion and communist takeover of all Europe. Thus the neutral countries must try to demonstrate to and convince the Allies of the importance of Germany and its army in erecting a barrier against Soviet invasion.

According to the report, Pilet was greatly impressed by the arguments of these men, especially the description of the communist danger. Immediately after the meeting (again according to the report), he called in American Minister Harrison to pass on this information and convey the Germans' concern and the exhaustion of German reserves. He voiced the opinion that the Soviets should be left to fight alone, warning the Anglo-Americans against a communist takeover of Europe.

Next, the report claimed that Harrison immediately cabled these arguments to Washington. Roosevelt limited himself to replying as he already had, that the Allies would fight without compromise for the unconditional surrender of the Reich.

German diplomats at the Vatican and in Lisbon presented a similar demarche. Hausamann's report concluded: "This information comes from a reliable source, although we cannot state its terms exactly. But we do know that the American government has been informed of this matter."

Through loyalty to his fellow federal councilor, Kobelt, aware of the explosive nature of the report, immediately informed Pilet, who completely denied its truthfulness. Then Kobelt informed General Guisan, the other addressee, requesting him to see that the matter not be spread about. He wrote the same message to Hausamann, asking him to specify the source of this information. Although guaranteeing the accuracy of his information, Hausamann refused to specify its origin, as he had committed himself to silence to the person who had given it to him.

Guisan transmitted Hausamann's report to Enrico Celio, president of the Confederation, on February 8. Guisan insisted on the seriousness of the matter, guaranteeing that the information was from a good source, even if there had not been an opportunity to verify it. He added that he had met with several persons who were "alarmed at the attitude of Mr. Pilet-Golaz."[7]

It seems clear that there had been leaks and that the rumor of a "separate peace" was part of a plot against Pilet. Kobelt and Celio, the first to be informed, were aware of this. "We cannot allow these repeated attacks on the foreign minister to go so far," Kobelt wrote in his diary.[8] Pilet, for his part, fully intended to counter the accusations brought against him. On February 13, the central committee of the Swiss Radical Party became agitated about the problem without being familiar with its substance and asked whether it were appropriate for Pilet to resign so as not to bring discredit to the party. Pilet confirmed to the Federal Council on February 16 that the report "did not contain a word of truth." His last meeting with Minister Köcher was on January 16; the German diplomat had not been accompanied by his military attaché, and he did not make the request claimed in Hausamann's report. Pilet had not received the American minister since January 11, on which occasion they had discussed the transfer of diplomats. "The contents of the report themselves are absurd. They show a total unfamiliarity with the most elementary possibilities, customs, and precautions. A moment of thought would be enough to make the report's ineptitude clear. An ounce of practical sense is enough to judge its value."[9]

Immediately after the Federal Council session where the problem had been taken up, Celio received the American minister, informing Harrison of the report and the démarche which Pilet had supposedly transmitted to him and to which President Roosevelt was said to have given a negative response. Harrison expressed his astonishment. He had not met with Pilet since the end of December or the beginning of January and had never heard him bring up that issue. The American archives containing the messages from the legation in Bern also do not mention any peace negotiations during this period.

The falsification was obvious. The Federal Council asked General Guisan to institute an inquiry. Hausamann, the prime target in all likelihood, defended himself with evasive lies, asserting certitudes without giving proof, alleging his commitment to secrecy and refusing to give the names of the diplomats or officials who were supposed to have informed him, unless which he did not state—he had set the affair in motion with the obvious intention of overthrowing Pilet-Golaz,[10] which he had expressed in his correspondence with General Guisan. The criminal court martial concluded with a stalemate because of Hausamann's refusal to reveal his mysterious informers in the name of secrecy and diplomatic confidentiality and also thanks to the support of the intelligence service.

It was this support—which was seriously reprehensible—that allowed Hausamann to pursue his agency's activities as a civilian after he had been demobilized. These activities were regarded as indispensable to the Army Intelligence Service. Later, he was fully restored to his status in the army, in spite of the justifiable reservations of Pilet and Celio.[11]

Did Pilet really try to influence the American minister in order to become the inspiration for a separate peace between the Allies and Germany? Certainly the head of the Political Department often expressed his wish for an agreement on a general peace and his concern at Soviet expansion. He proposed his good offices for these moves, as was his duty. On the other hand, to lend support to a separate peace by some of the belligerents would have detracted from neutrality, as Federal Councilor Hoffman had shown in 1917, paying for his mistake with his resignation. Willi Gautschi, in 1989, quoted Bonjour that "Considering how freely Pilet expressed his fear of Soviet penetration in Europe, Bonjour leaned toward accepting the possibility of such a démarche, coming from Pilet. In his capacity as foreign minister of a small neutral state, Pilet played a dangerous game."[12] But as Gautschi, without following Bonjour exactly, concluded: "From documents currently available to researchers, it seems impossible to me that Federal Councilor Pilet-Golaz did not tell the truth during the litigation in question."

The documents published by Erwin Bucher confirm this. If it is true that Pilet did have fears—how justified and partially realized they were, alas!—of Soviet expansion throughout Europe, he would not have been so imprudent as to provoke what Hoffmann did in 1917. Ministers Harrison and Köcher attest to this, as do the American archives. The "informer," whose name Hausamann refused to give out and who might have been the Czech diplomat Kopecky with whom he was in touch, stated to the Basel reporter Oeri (whom no one would suspect of too much sympathy for Pilet) that he knew nothing of this affair. As for the opinion of American governmental circles, Elmer Davis, director of the Office of War Information, put the *Saturday Evening Post* in its place at a press conference on January 20, 1943. The weekly had attacked Switzerland, calling it a "German province governed by von Bibra." Davis praised the Confederation, "whose government successfully tried to maintain strict neutrality." Walter Lippman expressed himself in the same positive manner some days later in the *New York Herald Tribune*.[13]

It thus appears that the report of an alleged attempt at a separate peace fomented by Pilet was a fabrication, taking its place among the shady deals that often characterize the corridors of parliaments and for which Pilet was the predestined target because of his style and some unfortunate moves. But the fabrication clearly exceeded the limits of the imagination of an intelligence maniac who had gone out of control and was badly supervised by his superiors and went beyond the gossip at the Federal Palace. One must note with Erwin Bucher that there was a deliberate plot with Hausamann at the center, even if he intended to stay in the wings. He was the principal instigator and manipulator, and his goal was to unseat Pilet or at least force him to move to another ministry. Additionally, Hausamann clearly intended to drag General Guisan into it and compromise him as well.

In a letter of February 25, 1943 to Guisan, Hausamann referred to the inquiry of which he was the subject, evoked the mysterious informant, a diplomat whose name he would never reveal, and told enough to force the Federal Council to act, despite denials from Pilet, on the basis of his dubious report, on the grounds that a member of Parliament had taken an interest in the matter.[14]

However, he primarily justified the operation by explaining to Guisan the reasons why he believed Pilet should resign from the Ministry of Foreign Affairs. "We are nearing the end of the war. The Allies will win the victory. Switzerland," Hausamann imagined, "will have access to the negotiations where the new world organization will be deliberated. The Swiss delegation will be led by a foreign minister who must enjoy the confidence and sympathy of his colleagues. This is not the case with Pilet-Golaz, who does not enjoy confidence or sympathy even in his own country. The members of the government are aware of this. If our relations with the Allies are more or less cordial, it is not because of Mr. Pilet, but in spite of him. Conversations with the federal councilors give the impression that they are awaiting an opportunity to force him to resign."

"The opportunity has now been given us. I know that the federal councilors consider this a serious matter, but the denials from Pilet prevent them from acting as long as I have not brought out proof that my report is true, which can never happen. The first step has been taken; conditions are at hand. It was a disagreeable duty to submit the report, in the certainty that I was right, and to defend it until it is concluded, in the awareness of serving the country. I have a habit of taking on unpleasant tasks, as I did with the Däniker affair" [to whom he only gave a relative endorsement].

"Do not believe I am the instrument of third parties in the campaign against Mr. Pilet. Up to now, I have revealed this matter to no one. With your permission, I will keep you informed on what the military inquiry will reveal about Pilet's policies. I apologize for pressing you, but I believe I can read in your letters your approval of the actions I am undertaking."

In two letters Guisan had previously sent to Hausamann on February 18 and 22, he had not taken a position on the basis of the report or on the attacks against Pilet, but he had approved of Hausamann's transmitting this information without fully understanding the reasons for it and without revealing the name of the informant. The inquiry that was opened to supplement the evidence regarded this source more than Hausamann as the one who had done his duty.

Hausamann's devotion to Guisan's position and to Guisan personally is praiseworthy in itself. The commander in chief of the army was not influenced by the plot or by criticism, notably in his choice of senior commanders. Thus Hausamann, in a seven-page memorandum of October 1940, defined the respective authority of the government and the high command. He advanced the proposition, which is debatable at the least, that the general was subordinate not to the Federal Council, but to the Federal Assembly that had elected him. There is no doubt that there was a constitutional problem, but the assembly, a deliberative body, was not in a practical position to give orders to the general or follow up on their implementation. The law at that time provided that the general was subordinate to the instructions the Federal Council would draw up. It was in this context that the authority of the commander in chief would be exercised, all the more so in time of peace. General Guisan would not be able to "play a predominant role with respect to the Federal Council," as Hausamann tried to persuade him. Even more, the general could not be allowed to participate in or to influence the election of a member of the government, or in forcing him to resign, whatever his opinions or personal feelings were.

Hausamann committed a serious error by seeking to involve Guisan without previous contact or agreement in the plot against Pilet, especially because the operation was constructed on an obvious fabrication, a piece of deliberate disinformation. That the mysterious source that Hausamann ceaselessly alleged was never revealed, and which he refused to reveal for the obvious reason that it did not exist, only aggravated the error and indicated the extent of the indulgence that kept him in the intelligence service.

Federal Councilor Stampfli more or less put an end to the Hausamann affair on May 16, 1943 in a speech given before a political meeting at Wattwil, by paying homage to the head of the Political Department and stressing the support given him by the Federal Council.[15]

"In time of war, our historic policy of neutrality between the belligerent powers may appear easy to pursue. This is not the case. On the contrary, it is a difficult and unappreciated task requiring tact, intelligence, and firmness for a small country that is obliged to maintain equilibrium between the powers in conflict. . . . The conduct of this policy is in the hands of the head of the Political Department, Federal Councilor Pilet. Throughout all its related problems this policy has enjoyed the support of the entire Federal Council. Especially in a period of international crisis, Pilet is in a singularly unfavorable situation: a strong duty to maintain confidentiality prevents him from informing public opinion on all negotiations and decisions. This sometimes leads to unfounded errors of interpretation and prejudice. The head of the Political Department has been able up to now to clear up misunderstandings and refute criticism before the Foreign Affairs Committee, where he can give explanations without being constrained by the need to maintain confidentiality. History will show that Federal Councilor Pilet has conducted his foreign policy better than is believed by those whose opinions vary with the fortunes of war, rather than those wedded to a firm vocation for neutrality."

Was this solidarity borne of the moment? Stampfli's sincerity appears genuine, and the Hausamann affair supports it. With the exception of von Steiger, who willingly transferred to Foreign Affairs with the benediction of the ambassador of the Vichy government,[16] it appears that Pilet could count on collegial support both in this case and more generally. Etter in particular gave Pilet especially strong support. Celio, like Kobelt, acted loyally and rapidly as he evaluated the potential gravity of the incident. If there is one area where coherence and cohesion are vital to the conduct of a collegial government, it is foreign policy, especially in a time of crisis. Contrary to the practice of presenting important projects only at the last moment in order to save them from risks, Pilet took pains to consult his colleagues in advance and to take their views into account. This, with the decisive clarity of his mind, contributed to increasing his authority in the Federal Council's deliberations.[17]

Because the Hausamann affair was quickly settled, and given the evidence of fraud, it did not lead to interminable repercussions. Pilet's inveterate adversaries, however, did not give up. The reelection of the Federal Council in December 1943 gave them the opportunity to make themselves heard by multiplying corridor gossip and spreading malicious rumors. An opposition coalition grew up, advancing the name of von Steiger for minister of foreign affairs. It had its press in the progressive newspaper *Die Nation* and its supporters in Guisan's entourage. Minger was said to have stated that he left the Federal Council in 1940 because of Pilet. Hausamann discreetly lent his support to the cause.[18]

The Socialists, who had just gained thirteen seats in the Federal Assembly in the October elections, were offered the post of successor to the Radical Wetter and presented Zurich Mayor Ernst Nobs as their candidate. They refused to reelect Pilet, supporting the Neuchâtel Socialist Perret instead. The Independents and Democrats proposed Paul Rossy, director general of the National Bank, a Radical from Vaud, whom they did not consult. On the other hand, the Radicals, the Agrarians, the Conservatives (now known as the Christian Democrats), and the Liberals all nominated Pilet for reelection. Although Hausamann continued to support the struggle against Pilet clandestinely, especially among the Socialists, the fiery Agrarian National Councilor Feldmann, a future Federal Councilor who had often crossed swords with the head of the Political Department, actively supported his reelection.[19]

In the end, Pilet was reelected to the Federal Council by 154 votes to 72 for his opponents and elected vice president by 145 votes to 37. These results were entirely satisfactory. The other results in Federal Council elections were 122 for the newly elected Nobs and 194 for Stampfli. In previous elections Pilet had obtained successively 151, 144, 119, and 145 votes, figures that are within a reasonable average.

But in every election there are votes one is happy to have received and those one is proud to have been denied.

NOTES

1. Erwin Bucher, *Zwischen Bundesrat und General*, 21–261, presents an exhaustive inquiry into this matter and offers harsh conclusions; Willi Gautschi, *Le Général Guisan*, 423–32; Edgar Bonjour, *Neutralité*, vol. VI, 110–15; and Pierre T. Braunschweig, *Geheimer Draht nach Berlin*, 101–4, 447.

2. Pierre T. Braunschweig, *Geheimer Draht*, 65.

3. Erwin Bucher, *Zwischen*, 233–34; and Klaus Urner, *Die Schweiz muss noch Geschluckt Werden*, 62–63.

4. Erwin Bucher, *Zwischen*, 262–94.

5. Erwin Bucher, *Zwischen*, 272–75.

6. Erwin Bucher, *Zwischen*, 21–23 (text of the report).

7. Erwin Bucher, *Zwischen*, 53–57.

8. Willi Gautschi, *Le Général Guisan*, 425, quotes Kobelt's diary.

9. Erwin Bucher, *Zwischen*, 66–67, letter of Pilet to Celio of February 16, 1943.

10. Willi Gautschi, *Le Général Guisan*, 425–27.

11. Erwin Bucher, *Zwischen*, 139–40, 150–51.

12. Willi Gautschi, *Le Générale Guisan*, 430–31.

13. Edgar Bonjour, *Neutralité*, vol. IV, 354–55.
14. Erwin Bucher, *Zwischen*, 100–104.
15. Erwin Bucher, *Zwischen*, 127–28.
16. Erwin Bucher, *Zwischen*, 198.
17. Erwin Bucher, *Zwischen*, 526–27.
18. Erwin Bucher, *Zwischen*, 198–205.
19. Erwin Bucher, *Zwischen*, 200–203.

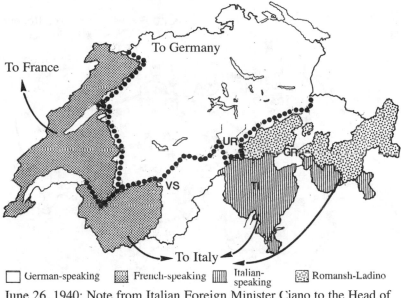

To France

To Germany

UR

GR

VS

TI

To Italy

| ☐ German-speaking | ▦ French-speaking | ▥ Italian-speaking | ▨ Romansh-Ladino |

June 26, 1940: Note from Italian Foreign Minister Ciano to the Head of the Armistice Bureau Pietromarchi

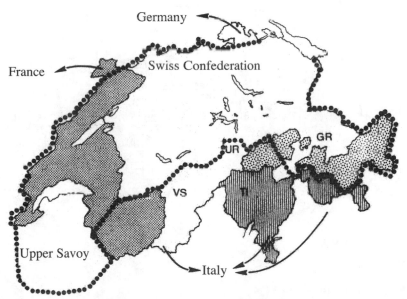

Germany

France

Swiss Confederation

UR

GR

VS

TI

Upper Savoy

Italy

Note from the Operations Bureau of the Italian General Staff of July 15, 1940

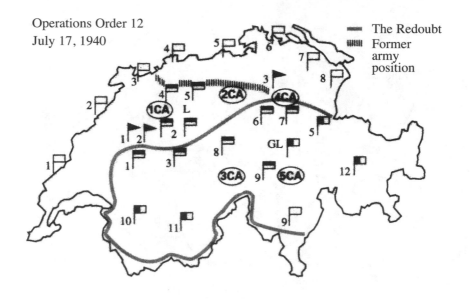

Operations Order 12
July 17, 1940

The Redoubt

Former
army
position

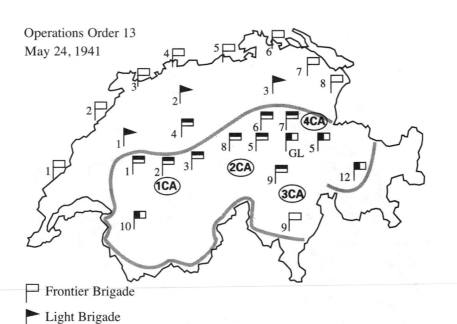

Operations Order 13
May 24, 1941

🏳 Frontier Brigade

▶ Light Brigade

🏴 Mountain Brigade

🏴 Division

Youth welcome Hitler at a Nazi manifestation (1938).

Hitler at the Polish front during the 1939 invasion.

Discussion of operational plans. Hitler at an army general staff.

At the Swiss frontier in June 1940. Reishsführer Himmler on a visit to
Schörner's mountain division.

The Federal Council and the General immediately after his appointment. From left to right: Etter, president of the Confederation; Pilet-Golaz, the General, Motta and Baumann.

The General and Pilet-Golaz.

The General reviewing a detachment of interned Spahis at Porrentray.

Frontier guards: a German soldier and a Swiss soldier.

Mountain artillery in the redoubt.

Chapter Sixteen

Economic Survival and Neutrality

MAINTAINING THE UNIVERSALITY
AND PLURALITY OF TRADE RELATIONSHIPS

Maintaining Switzerland's guarantee of neutrality—by asserting its political independence and democratic liberties and assuring and reinforcing its military defense—was a formidable challenge. Switzerland was at the center of a Western Europe that for five years had been almost totally subservient to the military might and prestige of the two totalitarian powers and to infiltration and ideological pressure from them. Maintaining its political independence in a situation of extreme economic dependence on the Axis for trade and food supplies approached in difficulty the squaring of the circle, all the more because this dependence concerned both warring camps. Yet this was the task of the heads of the Political and Economic Departments, Marcel Pilet-Golaz and Walter Stampfli, who worked closely together.

In the prewar period, no country depended as much as Switzerland on its foreign trade. Out of a national income of 9 billion francs in 1938, foreign trade represented nearly 3 billion francs (1.6 billion francs in imports and 1.3 billion francs in exports). Lacking in natural resources except for hydroelectric production then being developed and some trace deposits of coal and iron ore, the country had to import nearly all its coal, minerals, fuels, chemical products, and textiles. These were indispensable, both for Switzerland's own needs and for its export industries, which with its financial operations conferred its relative prosperity. As to provision of food, though the painful experience of 1914–18 had stimulated productivity and reinforced the protection of agriculture, Switzerland, far from autarchy, still had to import nearly half the calories it consumed.[1]

In 1938, the sources of imports were not equally divided between what would become the Axis in 1940 and the Anglo-American Allies. Overseas countries (which would largely be part of or under the influence of the Anglo-American powers) provided Switzerland with vital imports of grain and other food products, while the Axis area furnished mainly iron, steel, coal, and most manufactured products. Fifty-six percent of the tonnage and 66% of the value of imports came from countries that would be under German or Italian control between 1940 and 1943. Concerning Swiss exports in 1938, 54% went to parts of Europe that would be controlled by the Axis and 26% to countries under Anglo-American influence. This quantitative disequilibrium was worsened by the extreme difficulties in rail communication, the restricted tonnage that could go by road, the insecurity of shipment by sea (Switzerland had to construct its own fleet), harassment from aircraft and submarines, and the conditions placed on the use of Italian and French ports. Finally, the blockade decreed by the combatants against each other forced Switzerland into difficult negotiations to maintain the universality of its commercial and financial relations in conformity with its neutral status. In other periods, perhaps there would have been resignation to alignment and integration into the "New Order."

World War I had caught all governments off guard. In the delusion that modern conflicts would be short because of the destructive effects of firepower and the speed of movement by rail or motor vehicle, governments had foreseen neither the duration nor the extent of the war or its economic implications for weapons and munitions factories, effects on food supplies, and social and political upheavals.

Before 1914, Switzerland had shown the same lack of foresightedness that made it severely dependent on the belligerents and put its economy at the mercy of their interventions and controls.[2] As the war continued it had to improvise a crisis economy, confiding to the military authority, the Central War Commissariat, tasks for which it was not prepared and which went beyond the traditional responsibilities of battlefields to extend over all the country's activities. If "war is too serious a matter to be entrusted to generals," as Böschenstein, biographer of Hermann Obrecht states, quoting Clemenceau, it was all the more true with respect to the wartime economy.[3]

The situation was different in 1939. Hermann Obrecht, who had received modest training as a primary school teacher, had benefitted from military experience in our militia system as an officer of the General Staff and had commanded a brigade before being elected to the Federal Council in 1935. A politician and administrator, he was at twenty-seven the youngest state councilor in Switzerland, heading the finance department in Canton Solothurn. Then he helped manage the city of Solothurn, at the same time sitting on the

National Council. His leadership qualities and spirit of initiative had taken him to the board or the chairmanship of firms ranging from banking to watch-making, passing also through public works and metallurgy. His experience and temperament predestined him to lead the economy during an interna-tional crisis when Hitler tore up the clauses of the Versailles Treaty one by one, dismantling the frail structure of the League of Nations and pursuing a formidable rearmament effort.

The experience of 1914–1918 called for advance planning. As the picture became darker, Obrecht set up an extensive war economy apparatus based less on government intervention than on competition, with the cantons and cities ready to operate as soon as the conflict began. With the cooperation of private firms, the government established reserves of raw materials, fuels, and foodstuffs in advance. Planting was expanded, under what was later called the Wahlen Plan. Strict rationing was adopted, which achieved equi-table distribution combined with controlled prices.[4]

In addition to feeding the population, the government had to assure jobs in an economy which still had an unemployment rate in 1937 of 10% among those with unemployment insurance. Unlike during World War I, minimum social security was now assured, financed by compulsory contributions on work income. This granted indemnities for loss of wages and salaries to the soldiers who had been mobilized. In this way, Switzerland avoided social un-rest and a general strike as in 1918.

BITTER NEGOTIATIONS

However, the establishment of this war economy, its provisioning, and the largely successful attempt at autarchy would not have sufficed to supply Switzerland and provide work for its industries. Switzerland required tena-cious discussions with both groups of belligerents to maintain its foreign trade at a vital minimum and to preserve as much as possible the number and variety of its trade relations. All this did not occur automatically. Hein-rich Homberger, director of the Industry and Commerce Board, delegated by the Federal Council to make trade agreements, worked with Jean Hotz, head of the trade division in the Economics Department, on these dealings throughout the war. Homberger noted, "The neutral country was a thorn in the side of the belligerents, especially in a generalized conflict such as World War II, where each belligerent regarded anyone not taking his side as a powerful enemy."[5]

Paradoxically, it was Swiss relations with the Anglo-Americans and their allies that led at first to the greatest difficulties. On the one hand, there were the problems of distance and long sea voyages made dangerous by the submarine threat; on land there were bombardments, destruction, and lack of rolling stock. On the other hand, the Allies intended to hit the Axis powers and their partners with as strict a blockade as possible. In this context they wanted to prevent the neutral countries from opening a breach in this wall with their imports and production. Yet the totalitarian states surrounding Switzerland and Sweden, which were holding a pistol to their heads, were not prepared to provision the neutrals without something in return. From the Axis perspective, the neutrals observed the conflict from the balcony of the Alps and the banks of the Baltic, enjoying their democratic liberties in peace and operating their factories without a care for air raids. This embittered the discussions, as the neutrals were under the constant threat of a break in food supplies or of military aggression. This troubled outlook, which was conveyed in the Federal Council speech of June 25, 1940, concerned economic stagnation, unemployment, and shortages, with their social and political consequences.

Heinrich Homberger, who took part in these difficult negotiations, distinguishes several stages in the course of wartime economic relationships.[6] In the first period, up to June 1940, the rigor of the western democracies' blockade against the Third Reich led to the principal disagreements. Rejecting all contractual obligations, the Allies intended to allow into Switzerland only what served internal consumption, excluding not only all direct reexports, which was logical, but all exports of products essential to the war economy. The system would be controlled by British officials resident in Switzerland.

Negotiations in Paris between Switzerland, Great Britain, and France had been taking place since the end of 1939. They were conducted, as usual, by a delegation in permanent contact with the Federal Council's committee for economic and financial affairs consisting of Federal Councilors Marcel Pilet, Walter Stampfli, and Ernst Wetter. In addition, there were representatives from the Economic and Political Departments, the Customs Service, members of industrial and agricultural organizations, and diplomats assigned to the Swiss Legation in Paris. After five months of bargaining, the negotiations concluded with the War Trade Agreement of April 24, 1940, which considerably toned down the initial Allied demands. Although imported goods could not be reexported "as is," a list of Swiss or foreign products that could not be sold abroad was drawn up by mutual agreement, as well as a list of products that could be exported from Switzerland only in reduced quantities, according to normal peacetime trade flows. Trade in products not appearing on either list was free. The last-named category was extensive and included notably textiles, perfumes, and pharmaceutical products, but also machinery and apparatus, watches, aluminum and, paradoxically, war materiel which the western Allies, in their lack of preparedness, needed urgently at the time.

THE GERMAN POSITION

In this first phase of the war, Germany was apparently respectful of international law and neutrality. At the beginning of the conflict it addressed a reassuring declaration to the neutrals:

"The German government is of the view that economic neutrality implies the continuation of normal merchandise and transit trade. . . . It is prepared in principle to maintain normal exports and trade with neutral states. It expects that they, in principle, will act the same way with Germany. It follows that Germany will make no objection if these states continue their normal trade, even with countries at war with the Reich. The German government assures the neutral states that it does not consider this activity to be incompatible with neutrality. On the other hand, it considers neutral states allowing other countries to impose restrictions and controls that prevent the normal course of trade and transit with Germany to be contrary to neutrality. Germany's position with respect to the neutrals in the economic sphere has thus been clearly defined, in accordance with international law."[7]

This was the situation during the first months of the war, but Homberger later recalled the fable of the fox and the grapes. When it had the opportunity, the Third Reich unilaterally tried to reduce Switzerland's trade with the West, however, Germany did not actually suppress that trade as it could have. With the continuation of trade, it guaranteed, at least in principle, the universal applicability of neutrality, but it counted on a certain amount of Swiss reciprocity.

The fortunes of war turned the second period of trade relations to Germany's advantage. The reversal of relative strength seriously affected Swiss-German relations. On June 20, 1940, the Reich cut off Swiss coal supplies. Including the countries it occupied, it had nearly a monopoly on coal, thus forcing Switzerland to negotiate under the double threat of economic strangulation and military invasion. Tensions mounted on both sides.[8]

EXPORT OF WAR MATERIEL

The first German demand was to turn the export of Swiss weapons to the benefit of the Axis. Up to that time these exports had benefitted only the Allies. Was this an infringement of neutrality? What were the precedents? In the conflicts of 1859, 1866, and 1870, as with the Swiss Diet in the seventeenth century, the Federal Council had forbidden the sale of weapons to belligerents. Because the Hague Convention on neutrality of 1907 did not have this prohibition, however, the sale of arms had been tolerated in World

War I. The experience had not been convincing, so the Federal Council reestablished the ban on April 14, 1939 in anticipation of a new conflict. Why then did the same government reverse course and free up the sale of weapons to Germany, France, and England only a few months later, on September 8, 1939, at the start of World War II? In fact, this second measure was adopted at the request of the Allies, who were severely behind in equipment and had placed significant orders and called for exclusivity with certain manufacturers. The Federal Council also acted in the interest of the firms, which were barely emerging from unemployment. Finally, the weapons orders were balanced, especially with German aircraft, which Switzerland had to transfer abroad for its own needs. Up to March 1940 France placed orders for equipment worth 121 million Swiss francs. The Reich contented itself provisionally with an order valued at 149,504 francs, even though it was already Switzerland's most important supplier of iron and coal. "To the Germans, Switzerland then appeared as an enormous arms factory working nearly exclusively for the Allies," Bourgeois noted.[9]

Homberger considered the export of war materiel by a neutral country as a "problematic matter." One may well regret, as he did, that the Federal Council did not stick with its earlier decision to ban the trade in arms. But the Allies could not reproach Switzerland for reversing the flow of deliveries, as they themselves had contributed to setting the precedent that would, however, benefit Germany from then on, without Swiss neutrality being questioned.

Weapons trade was only one aspect of a wider and more difficult debate. The inequality of forces in Europe, with Italy joining the Axis in the meantime, and all our borders subject to blockade, placed our negotiators in a position of inferiority, if not of strangulation.

THE AUGUST 1940 AGREEMENT WITH THE REICH

The negotiations with the Reich before the French surrender, taking place in an atmosphere of German military victories, were also tense, with German demands growing in direct proportion to their announced successes.[10] "Since the Swiss delegation did not fail to react, the tension mounted in the meeting room at the German Foreign Ministry," Homberger notes. He attributed the arrogance of the German delegation's leader to the fact that he was careful to appear zealous, as he was not a member of the Nazi Party. Germany was irritated to note that it had made its deliveries of iron and coal in the first months of the war, but that Swiss exports had been modest, slowing down in favor of weapons deliveries to the democracies. Germany desired that Switzerland would be released from agreements it had reached with England and that it would participate in the Axis counterblockade against the Allies. But Switzerland would not hear of departing from the universality of trade that would assure its neutrality, which the Third Reich had duly recognized at the beginning of the conflict. Swiss exports to western countries assured, in exchange, provisions of food and certain essential raw materials which the Axis was not in a position to provide.

Circumstances being as they were, could the trade agreement of August 9, 1940 be considered a humiliating surrender that would lead to Switzerland's integration into the Axis economic system?[11] Certainly Germany attributed to itself a near monopoly of imports of merchandise designated as strategic, with freedom of choice in quantities limited only by available credits. On the other hand, it made certain that Swiss exports of strategic materials did not contribute to the war economy of its enemies. Germany was issued a new clearing credit, covering the trade balance, of 150 million francs. In 1944, this deficit greatly exceeded one billion francs and required payment in convertible foreign exchange for its exports to Switzerland, so that it could make purchases in third countries. Italy, for its part, would benefit from a clearing advance of 150 million, later 215 million, francs, though this amount was never reached.

However, Switzerland received 170,000 tons of coal, iron, and industrial mineral oils annually, which were essential for its economic survival. These deliveries allowed its factories to operate and permitted Switzerland to develop its own weaponry and fortify its defenses more than it contributed to arming the Axis. In spite of German pressure, Switzerland refused to join a counterblockade against England. A list was drawn up of products of no military importance that were freed for export to western or neutral countries to the extent allowed by transport conditions. Further, certain militarily important products were exported to the Anglo-American powers through the Savoy Gap across the battle lines, in complicity with the Vichy customs officials. They went by air, by mail in small lots, by rail, by foreign fleets or the Swiss fleet (there was such a thing), even by smuggling, and the diplomatic pouch.

This was especially the case with certain manufactures of precision lightweight machinery and watchmaking, which could be used in sophisticated weaponry. It was discovered with surprise that at the height of the war (1942–44) exports of Swiss watches passed from 241 million francs in 1938 to an average of 308 million. The Axis, which took 6% of these exports in 1938, continued to import the same proportion, while North American imports passed from 44 million francs in 1938 (18%) to 110 million on average in 1942–44 (36%). At the same time the Spanish and Portuguese tripled their purchases of Swiss timepieces, not necessarily from a concern for punctuality or gifts for their spouses. President Bachman of the National Bank stated before the Full Powers Committee of the National Council on October 14, 1943 that: "[w]e get around the export quotas by sending our deliveries to South America, where drafts in dollars are taken over without limit by the National Bank, while the final destinations are in North America." This statement was the source for the observation of Philippe Marguerat, who noted, "Most of the exports to Central and South America assisted the American war effort."[12]

THE AGREEMENT OF JULY 13, 1941

With the agreement of July 13, 1941, Germany, strong from its first successes in the USSR but troubled by British resistance and their growing aid from the United States, increased its demands and reinforced its control over Swiss strategic exports but allowed some expansion in the sale of nonmilitary products. The clearing credit was raised to 850 million francs, but Germany assured the delivery of 20,000 tons of coal per month. However, in that year, Switzerland prohibited all weapons transport across the Alps. We note in passing that unlike Sweden, which admitted the transit of German soldiers on leave and even allowed the transit of a division and its weapons on its way to Finland in 1941, Switzerland consistently banned the transit of soldiers either in units or alone.

The tension became more intense in subsequent years, to the extent that Germany desperately tried to demand more from Switzerland but was obliged in exchange to expand Switzerland's opportunities to export to the Anglo-Americans. The tension was so strong that there were fears of economic war, or war itself, with the former leading to the latter. Switzerland kept its advantages, consisting of its strategic position—the risk of Allied bombardment, sabotage, or airborne operation—transit through the tunnels, even if military transport was already excluded, its financial position, and its foreign currency, which was useful but not indispensable for the conduct of the war.

As Germany, forced to defend itself on three fronts— the East, Italy, and then in France— became less and less able to satisfy its commitments, especially coal and iron, the Allies stepped up their pressure on Switzerland. Thus, in the spring of 1944, American Secretary of State Cordell Hull presented the neutrals with a new situation.[13] The United States certainly understood their difficulties and the compromises they had been forced into because the Americans were not in a position to help them. At that point there was no further doubt of an Allied victory. From then on the neutrals, if they were to have the benefit of imports from the West, should no longer sell Germany the steel or goods that the Germans could no longer produce for themselves in their ruined factories. "From now on, the neutrals have to cut off their aid to the enemy."

That meant joining an Allied blockade and infringing the rules of neutrality, but Switzerland refused to take undue advantage of Germany. Now it could give a principled reason, the credibility of its neutrality. It also stressed that during the first five months of 1944 it had exported only 126 million francs' worth to Germany as compared to 198 million to the countries of the Allied bloc. A cutoff of economic relations with the Reich would deprive it of German iron and coal while stopping imports from the Allies through territories still under German control. Nevertheless, with the help of circumstances, and because the Reich could not make the promised deliveries, Switzerland severely cut back its deliveries of goods and energy to Germany.

ECONOMIC INTEGRATION?

During the war, a joke circulated to the effect that "The Swiss work six days for Germany and on the seventh they pray for England." It is true that the great majority of the Swiss did pray for England publicly or in the privacy of their homes, but it is obviously false that Switzerland was just a factory with all its machinery humming in the service of the Third Reich.

The period from 1940 to 1945 was one of economic depression for Switzerland.[14] In tonnage, average annual imports fell from 8,358,000 during 1931–1935 to 3,972,000 during the period 1940–1945. Exports fell respectively from 512,000 to 383,000 tons. Sales of metals, machinery, and instruments declined from 121,000 tons in 1938 to 64,000 tons on an annual average for 1941 to 1944. Marguerat notes that the number of employees at the Oerlikon arms factory, where 4,000 were working on orders for the Allies in the spring of 1940, fell to 2,600 at the end of 1943. Swiss real national income fell by 15% between 1939 and 1942. The number of those seeking employment fell from a monthly average of 65,000 in 1938 to 9,000 for the period 1941–44. However, there were between 80,000 and 150,000 soldiers under arms, many of whom were in "surveillance companies" that took in the unemployed. Switzerland hosted only 223,000 foreigners in 1941, whereas there had been 335,000 in 1930. It is true that factory personnel rose from 360,000 in 1937 to 430,000 during the war years, but it exceeded 500,000 salaried employees after 1947. Metallurgy and machinery showed the strongest growth between 1939 and 1945, due as much to the modernization of Swiss weaponry as to weapons exports. With the exception of some factories that earned considerable profit producing weapons, the war period was not a source of prosperity for Switzerland, nor did it stimulate the economy as a whole; however, it is true that the conflict had a profound but momentary effect on the distribution of its foreign trade.

GERMAN PREPONDERANCE

Germany would be the main beneficiary of this redistribution. Had it not long been Switzerland's most important trading partner, as it still is today? In 1930, before the effects of the general crisis of 1929 had made themselves felt on one hand, and the autarchy that the Nazi regime would impose on the other, Germany was first among suppliers of the Swiss Confederation. It provided 28% of Swiss imports, while it was second among customers, taking 16% of Swiss exports, making Germany Switzerland's primary trading partner.

During World War II, German military supremacy, the encirclement of Switzerland by the Axis powers, and the dangers of transport by sea, land, and air conferred a quasi-monopoly of Swiss trade on Germany and brought Switzerland somewhat into the Axis economic block. From 1940 to 1944, Germany provided 2.7 billion francs of Swiss imports, 30% of the total by value, and 11 million tons, or 50% of tonnage There were scarcely any imports from Italy, just 8% (Table 16.4), while the French economy, drained by Germany like those of all the occupied countries, provided only 5% of Switzerland's imports. Axis commerce made up more than half of Switzerland's foreign trade. With no significant increase in tonnage, imports of German coal increased from 54 to 90% of Swiss supplies.

Even though Daniel Bourgeois's dissertation *Le Troisième Reich et la Suisse* [*The Third Reich and Switzerland*] stops at 1942, it already notes that neither the agreement with Germany of August 9, 1940 nor the more restrictive one of July 18, 1941, debatable as they indeed seemed because of their elements of constraint in spite of the extent of the credits advanced by Switzerland, amounted to an economic annexation, such as that of Austria.[15] Switzerland preserved some measure of bargaining power with its firmness and the plurality of its trade, which expanded still further beginning in 1943, despite the restrictions and pressures exercised by the Americans which began at that time. This was a far cry from the idea of German-Swiss trade which Max Leo Keller, with whom Pilet-Golaz had that unfortunate conversation in 1940, referred to in his desires as "close economic ties representing the best way to achieve a cultural rapprochement with the Reich."

The United States alone supplied 10% of Swiss imports in 1940–42, independent of the significant amount of imports that passed through Spain, Portugal, and Latin America. The American contribution fell significantly after 1943 due to the pressure it brought to bear on the neutrals to induce them to break off relations with the Reich. However, for the period as a whole, with more than a billion francs, the United States accounted for 8% of Swiss trade.

THE WEHRMACHT'S ARSENAL?

How much did the Swiss Confederation contribute with its exports to the Third Reich's war effort? Let us attempt to quantify Swiss support for German rearmament. A detailed analysis of arms exports is not easy to make.

Judgments on war materiel exported by Switzerland to Germany (Table 16.3) are subject to certain variations. In the periodical *Der Aufbau*, which appeared on April 8, 1949, Jakob Ragaz arrived at a figure of 242 million francs for arms and munitions exports, which appears modest, coming as it did from the pen of one opposed in principle to arms traffic.[16]

Ragaz characterized 52% of Swiss exports to Germany as military, dividing the remainder among exports to France (66 million francs), England (23 million) for the period 1939–40, Italy (135 million), Sweden (46 million), Romania (40 million), and other occasional and limited customers. However, these data seem insufficient.

Philippe Marguerat, basing his estimates on classified statistics of the Trade Division in 1945, finds that Switzerland delivered 2.5 billion francs of miscellaneous products to Germany between 1940 and 1944. Of this, 600 million consisted of war materiel strictly speaking and 750 million were for strategic products, or 1,350 million francs of products contributing directly to Germany's war effort.[17]

In a seminar paper submitted at Fribourg University in 1982, Marc Hofer concludes with analogous figures: 1.4 billion francs for war materiel in the broader sense of the term, 600 million francs being for weapons in the strict definition. We accept the figures given by the statistics in Table 16.3, which give 605 million francs for weapons in the narrow sense of the term and 1,268 million for military materiel in contributions to the German war effort.[18]

What was the value of this support as a fraction of war production in the Reich? The *Geschichte des Zweiten Weltkrieges* [*History of the Second World War*], published by Ploetz in 1960, evaluates Reich war production as 670 billion Reichsmarks, or 1,172 billion Swiss francs at the exchange rate of 1.75 Swiss francs to the Reichsmark. Reich weapons production was reportedly at an annual rate of 9 billion Reichsmarks, that is, 15.75 billion Swiss francs. Now the annual average of Swiss exports of war materiel to Germany came to about 120 million francs per year in weapons strictly speaking and approximately 260 million in the broader sense. This would give a proportionate contribution to the German war effort on the order of only 0.8% to 1.6% according to the nature of the military materiel.[19]

There are other estimates of the Swiss contribution to German weapons production.

A memorandum of State Secretary Clodius in 1943 estimates this at 0.5% of German production.[20] Philippe Marguerat estimates the total production of German weapons at 120 billion Reichsmarks (210 billion Swiss francs). The 600 million francs supplied by the Swiss in pure weaponry, and the 1,350 million in the broader sense of the term, represent only 0.3 or 0.6 percent of German production. Marc Hofer repeats these figures.[21]

Estimating German war production is problematical. The achievement of exact statistics for historical purposes had a lower priority than rapid production for the front. Subsequently, financing war expenditures by printing money, galloping inflation, and rapid devaluation of the currency made it difficult to evaluate the amounts devoted to weapons. The annual budget of the Third Reich passed from the first to the fifth year of war from 89 to 431 billion Reichsmarks, concluding with a total of 1,470 billion Reichsmarks, of which ordinary receipts covered only 19%. Of this sum, two-thirds was devoted to war expenditures. The Reich's total debt rose from 27 to 388 billion Reichsmarks. The German currency in Switzerland had lost nine-tenths of its value at the end of this period, while the Swiss franc saw its buying power fall by 34%.[22] By way of comparison, expenditures of the Swiss Confederation rose from 965 million francs in 1939 to 2.6 billion in 1944, while its consolidated debt rose from 2.2 billion to 6.7 billion francs. Military expenditures rose from their annual average of 211 million francs from 1934 to 1938 to approximately 1 billion during 1940 to 1944. Armed neutrality has its price, but it costs much less than war.

The Swiss contribution to the German war effort was therefore quantitatively negligible. Was it qualitatively indispensable in terms of certain manufactures, as some would have us believe? Marc Hofer cites the example of a letter from the German high command's Office of War Economy and Weaponry addressed on January 16, 1940 to the minister of foreign affairs.[23] "We do not import war materiel, strictly speaking, from Switzerland, not even detonators made from watch movements." (This was still in the first phase of the conflict, when the democracies were draining weapons deliveries from Switzerland.) "However, Germany is very interested in certain machine tools. Among other things, this concerns machinery for producing detonators essential for antiaircraft guns. If we cannot obtain them, our program will be seriously compromised." A German Foreign Ministry analysis of the situation in June 1943 confirms this concern, deploring the restrictions on deliveries from Switzerland: "However well aware we are of the small quantity of war materiel we import from Switzerland, these are technically specialized items of particular importance." It is doubtful whether even the generally high-performance German technology would ever have been able to fill this gap.

To complete the picture, it should be noted that the Reich obtained its armament purchases from Switzerland almost entirely on credit. The deficit in the clearing account at the end of the war, to the amount of 1.1 billion francs, was nearly the same as the amount of deliveries of military materiel from Switzerland. Was this in some way an infringement of neutrality?[24] Philippe Marguerat makes a limited case for this point of view but also notes that in the context of financial relations between Switzerland and the United States, "Switzerland gave twice as much in advances strictly speaking to the Allies as to Germany." On the other hand, the Washington Agreement of 1946 allowed for at least a partial recovery.

If the clearing credits had been in the form of a sinking fund, it would have meant less of a sacrifice for Switzerland than what the occupied countries went through in the draining, not to say looting, of their economies, in requisition and deportation of "volunteer" workers or prisoners, and financial exactions or drawdowns of material reserves.

Did the trade agreements with and military deliveries to Germany weaken Switzerland's defensive potential? The report submitted by the chief of the Swiss Army General Staff at the end of his active service provides the answer.[25] Credits extended for the replacement and development of weapons and munitions amounted to 1.4 billion francs. Of this, 700 million was devoted to preparations for destruction and to fortifying the country. That would not have been possible without the deliveries of coal and iron provided by Germany in accordance with the trade agreements. Thus, by contributing indirectly to the development of Switzerland's defense, the Third Reich reinforced one of the reasons which, at least as much as the supply of weapons, dissuaded it from attacking Switzerland: the army's capacity to resist.

Regarding Swiss employment involved in manufacturing exports to Germany, which he estimated at 443 million francs annually, Walter Rüdiger, a German historian of the war economy, estimates that between 40,000 and 60,000 persons were engaged in this work, that is, between 10 and 14% of those employed in factories.[26] German war materiel broadly speaking occupied between 2% and 3% of the working population, that is, one day per year, rather than the supposed six days per week.

Ideally, it would undoubtedly have been preferable for the fact and appearance of neutrality if the Federal Council had held to its decision of April 1939 and abstained from trade in weapons in case of war. But it is easy to condemn in the abstract. In hindsight, leaving aside the circumstances and the reactions of the partners in both camps, neither held neutrality in sacred trust. It was under French and British pressure that the Federal Council was forced to review its earlier decision and authorize delivery, beginning in September, to these two countries of the weapons they had already ordered from Swiss firms. The same concession was granted to Germany in the name of equity in neutrality, but Germany made only modest use of it. If Switzerland had not acceded to the request of the democracies, it would have been accused of favoritism to the Third Reich by denying the former the means to fight. Switzerland would have seen its trade with the West paralyzed and would not have been able to maintain its refusal to participate in the blockade declared against Germany. The tension in the negotiations that led to the trade agreement of April 24, 1940 bears this out.

Switzerland found itself under conditions of inverse and symmetrical constraint with the reversal of the military situation in June 1940. It was completely surrounded and under threat of invasion by Army Group C at the Jura border. It could no longer refuse Germany in the name of neutrality what it had conceded to the Allies in September 1939. However, it posed as conditions the delivery of certain quantities of iron and coal which allowed its economic survival, as well as its right, in conformity with neutrality, to trade with the Allied side and the overseas countries and thus assure an essential part of its food provisions and the possibility of continuing the export of its industrial products, with weapons trade being excluded in principle.

On the other hand, as we have seen, weapons deliveries were limited. Switzerland would not be the arsenal of the German armed forces. It would hold firm to receive deliveries of iron and coal and would reduce deliveries to Germany when its side of the bargain began to weaken, beginning in 1943.

To wear a mantle of virtuous neutrality and complete pacifism while refusing all weapons trade would have led to nothing more than economic strangulation, unemployment, stagnation, and in the short term, the invasion of a country unable to defend itself, its absorption by the Axis bloc, and the takeover of its industries.

"NAZI GOLD"

Among the neutrals, certainly Switzerland extended the largest amount of clearing credits, amounting to more than 1 billion francs by 1944. This is explained by the fact that in normal times it was already the most dependent on foreign trade of any country, needing to import all its raw materials to fuel a strongly industrialized economy. It already had financial reserves allowing it to extend these loans. Bourgeois notes that in 1944 Switzerland's debt was much lower than that of countries at war or occupied.[27] According to Bourgeois, debt represented a third of what would have been required for maintaining occupation troops in case of invasion.

Neutrality could not interrupt monetary and financial transactions in case of war without bringing on major disturbances not only for the neutral country, but also for the flow of international monetary exchange, which the war did not interrupt. This applied especially to Switzerland, which since the eighteenth century had played a prominent role in international finance. The bankers in Geneva, St. Gallen, Zurich, and Basel and the government in Bern invested heavily in foreign firms and made loans to neighboring governments.

According to Marc Perrenoud, Swiss capital invested abroad at the start of the war was estimated at between 12 and 17 billion francs at a time when national income was 9 billion francs. This sum included capital placed in Switzerland and reinvested.[28] The geographic distribution of this capital varied widely. The United States was largely in first place, in front of Germany, which, however, was the most important trading partner. This involvement of Switzerland in the multiple channels of the international financial network and its interdependence with the countries of the two warring sides marked the importance of the Swiss banking sector and its prosperity but also its vulnerability. It meant security; to influence the Swiss banking position in one way or another could not have stopped the war, but it would have disturbed the international monetary exchanges affected through its operations in spite of the conflict. Switzerland could not, either for its own economy or for its international monetary role, close its doors and take refuge in a redoubt of monetary autarchy. It had to fulfill its task as a financial transit point as a mission of its neutrality and a condition of its economic survival.

As Philippe Marguerat notes in the well-documented chapter he devotes to this problem in *La Suisse face au IIIe Reich* [*Switzerland Facing the Third Reich*], "The only way to avoid the distortion and total extinction of trade was to maintain the possibility of gold and financial flows to the rest of the world: it was a dangerous but necessary liberty that enabled Switzerland to export to the "dollar area" and the British Empire (advances against Allied gold). This *liberty* assured liquidity on the financial markets by the influx of foreign capital, making it possible to extend the loans needed to sustain sales to Germany (clearing advances). Thanks to this, the country had sufficient reserves in foreign trade to avoid stagnation and massive unemployment."[29]

The management of the National Bank confirmed this to the Political Department on September 5, 1944, stating: "[t]he idea of prohibiting the exchange of gold and foreign currency in order to regulate money creation and encourage foreigners to increase imports has been brought up. The idea was not acted upon because Switzerland did not want to create further needless difficulties in payments abroad; export industries and political considerations were also taken into account."[30]

Although noting that it would have been better to keep the credits extended to both sides equal, which would have avoided friction with the Allies but would have caused tension with the Germans, Philippe Marguerat concludes that "all in all, the National Bank and the Swiss Confederation chose the only course possible."[31] Certain people, such as Werner Rings, who in his pamphlet *L'or des nazis*[32] ["Nazi Gold"] denounces "a dubious association, a criminal companionship with an inhuman dictatorship, a nearly conspiratorial collaboration with a regime hostile to the Swiss Confederation," would doubtless have preferred the Confederation's virtuous abstention from these financial operations in time of war. That would neither have stopped the war nor discouraged aggression, but it would have paralyzed Switzerland's economy and condemned it to political servitude. In its desire for domination, the Third Reich had overcome other monetary difficulties, but here it would have contributed to destabilizing the Swiss economy and presenting the opportunity, in the resulting stagnation, for political agitation, external pressures, and the revival of the frontists on the right; in other words, for totalitarian domination. Thus the Nazi leaders would have achieved the objective of interior disintegration that they pursued when they unwillingly but temporarily gave up their idea of a military operation in 1940. They believed that in time, the Confederation would fall into their hands like a piece of ripe fruit. Thus, in history as in everyday life, the desire to play the angel often gives assistance to the devil.

Further, the Swiss National Bank, like other central banks, has been severely criticized for trading foreign exchange and goods against the gold withdrawn by Germany by right of conquest, especially from the Belgian and Dutch reserves. The conditions under which the Reichsbank acquired this gold, at a time when its reserves were at their lowest, are problematic. Was this a right of conquest, or was it force exercised on the central banks of the occupied countries? The fate of Belgium's gold especially strikes the imagination.[33] At the beginning of the conflict it was transferred to France, then it found refuge in Africa, where the Vichy government repatriated it so that the Bank of France could voluntarily deliver it to the Reichsbank under guarantee of the French state. The Netherlands' gold was handed over under dubious conditions by a governor of the Netherlands Central Bank who was subservient to the occupiers. A part of that gold, extorted or legally handed over, was melted down and reformed into predated ingots carrying the seal of the Reichsbank before being transferred to Switzerland in exchange for foreign currency or in payment for imports.

It is difficult to know exactly the origin of the gold deposited in the Swiss National Bank by the Reichsbank and thus to state that it was illicit. In a postwar investigation, the Allies gave up their request that Switzerland give back "the Belgian gold." They only required a payment of 250 million francs, which could be considered a levy imposed by the belligerents on the Swiss bank's multiple and favorable financial transactions during the war. The Federal Council rejected the juridical basis of the request although it did deposit that sum (see Chapter 23).

Further, the monetary and financial exchanges were largely multilateral and worked to the advantage of both the Allies and the Axis. The gold reserves of the National Bank increased, according to estimates, from 1.2 to 1.6 billion francs from the Axis and more than 3 billion from the Anglo-Americans, in part in deposits in the United States that were frozen until the end of the war. Philippe Marguerat blames the National Bank for having managed the transfers of gold autonomously and in an essentially mechanical fashion.[34] He reproaches the Federal Council for having left the initiative for too long with the bank, because of "lack of intellectual adaptability of the two important superintendents of finance, Wetter and Nobs." Their department did not execute, before or during the war, "an overall study of external economic casuistry and political effects." It is always easy to remake history and to conclude after the fact that things could have been done in a better way. It is not certain that direct political influence from the Federal Council, which was also more subject to pressure from abroad, would have better served the interests of the Swiss economy than the technical empiricism and the words not said by the National Bank. The question that arises is a generic one. What technical autonomy should have been granted to the central bank? Did the political authorities, exposed to fluctuations in public opinion and pressure from economic lobbies, have the independence necessary for the continuity of monetary policy? The solution undoubtedly lies in the National Bank's narrow bounds for action provided by law, which were less obvious at the time.

CONCLUSION

In concluding his report on Switzerland's trade policy during World War II, Heinrich Homberger notes the difficult role the country had to play in order to achieve both economic and political survival.[35] It dealt in very different ways with the constraints, pressures, and threats that varied according to whether they came from the Axis under German domination or the Allied countries led by the Anglo-Americans.

In the economic field, Switzerland had positive services to offer Germany in exchange for raw materials and the opportunity of transit toward the Allies and the rest of the world.[36] These services provided to the Axis were the transit of goods through the Gotthard Pass, which was controlled by Swiss military defense, and delivery of manufactured products, consisting partly of weapons. Switzerland received more in value than it delivered. It assured its supply of raw materials necessary to reinforce its defense. It paid the deficit in its trade balance with the "billion" in the clearing account extended to Germany, a means of economic defense for Switzerland, 650 million of which would be reimbursed in accordance with the Washington Agreement of 1946. The monetary exchanges assured the Reich a certain payment liquidity.

The Allies, on the other hand, issued negative demands, their interest being for Switzerland to cease all deliveries to the Axis powers. This would have threatened employment, caused shortages, and delivered the country to German political and military dominance, all without the cause of European liberty or peace having gained the slightest advantage.

Homberger placed the greatest threat to the economy in 1944 when the Allies, already at the Swiss border, demanded that Switzerland break off economic relations with Germany and close the Gotthard Pass,[37] on pain of cutting off its food supplies. The near certainty of an Allied victory, the promise to speed up provisioning from overseas, and the hostility of public opinion to Nazism all added to the pressure. However easy these concessions might have been and how apparently close they were to our immediate interests, they would have been contrary to neutrality. The Federal Council refused. An alignment with the Allies, by then in a position of strength, like submission to German demands under other circumstances, would have been an easy solution. In refusing to give in, in spite of material inducements, the government gave credibility to Swiss neutrality.

Did it do so in a constant fashion? In his article, "La Suisse et la neutralité dans le domaine économique pendant la Seconde Guerre Mondiale" ["Switzerland and Neutrality in the Economic Field during World War II"] (1985), Philippe Marguerat states that "in the military area, Swiss neutrality was never put in doubt, either by the belligerents between 1939 and 1945 or by subsequent historical writing. That is not the case for the economic area." Concerning some recent historians, "They cast doubt, even accuse Switzerland, which could have assured its economic survival—or its well-being— only at the price of unilateral concessions in favor of the German war effort." Marguerat takes issue with this. He admits a certain amount of improvisation in the conduct of Swiss trade policy during the conflict, but he concludes that "this playing by ear was accompanied by a certain balance of concessions, and there was more of it than has been claimed."[38]

In the *Revue Suisse d'Histoire* (1982, no. 32), Daniel Bourgeois published a memorandum dated 1 April 1944 from German Major Gäfgen, head of the *Deutsche Industriekommission* (German Industry Commission) in Bern, which demonstrates the balance in German and Swiss economic relations.[39] He notes the possibility of a break in relations as a way for Germany to bring pressure to bear during the tense period of negotiations between the two countries, Gäfgen notes the German contribution to Switzerland: the provision of coal and iron, the possibility of goods to be transported toward third countries, and sea transit for merchandise heading to Switzerland, thus assuring freedom of navigation to ships flying the Swiss flag. He then draws up, but without figures, a detailed inventory of weapons and machinery delivered by Switzerland, which were partially financed by the substantial advance extended by Switzerland to cover the significant clearing deficits. The north-south transport permitted the transit to Italy of the iron and coal that was essential to its industry.

Gäfgen continues to say that these negotiations demonstrate that Switzerland was not prepared to make concessions on the issues of the transit and counterblockade. If no understanding were possible, there would have been an economic war with extensive, debilitating consequences.

For Switzerland: the end of coal and iron deliveries, the cessation of transit through countries under German domination, the closure of the port of Marseilles to connections with overseas countries, and the end of guarantees given to the Swiss fleet. It would follow that the Swiss population, the economy, and the press would support their government and that the influence of Germany's enemies would be increased.

For Germany, a break in relations would mean the end of deliveries to the Third Reich, the blocking of German assets in Switzerland, the impossibility of obtaining foreign exchange for purchases in third countries, the withdrawal of credits extended, and the end of north-south transit. Switzerland would be able to withstand a siege for two years under a regime of consumption and labor restrictions.

Daniel Bourgeois deduces from this memorandum that the reciprocal services exchanged between Germany and Switzerland were of a "flagrant inequality." "As to the German orders that allowed Swiss industry to survive, they were very useful to Germany, far more useful than the 150,000 tons per month of coal they delivered to Switzerland. In a word, there was no German service that could be characterized as extraordinary with respect to the situation in peacetime. The services rendered by Switzerland had an entirely different character and derived from a modification of the force relationship caused by the war. A large part of what it offered to Germany would not have been offered in time of peace, which was especially true of the clearing credit." The fair exchange evoked by Heinrich Homberger concerning the main agreements governing German-Swiss economic relations resembles some kind of fiction, according to Bourgeois.

As for the billion franc clearing deficit whose repayment was in doubt, one would have to agree with him. Economic survival, if not survival itself, as well as peace, political independence, neutrality, and the pursuit of trade with the enemies of the Third Reich were paid for dearly. However, did these all have a price?

On the other hand, we need to fine tune Bourgeois's interpretation of the balance of trade and the "flagrant inequality." The German orders were far from "allowing Swiss industry to survive." According to Table 16.3, total Swiss exports had an average annual value of 1,421 million francs from 1940 to 1944, representing 13% of the average national income of 11 billion. Sales to Germany averaged 481 million francs annually and, even though doubling in value, represented only 34% of our exports, or 4.4% of national income. This certainly was significant, but was not enough to "allow Swiss industry to survive." By way of comparison, total exports in 1938, at 1,316 million, amounted to 15% of the national product. The substantial increase in German purchases did not at all result from an overheating of Swiss industry. Swiss sales to the Third Reich, of which 25% on average were weapons strictly speaking, amounted to only marginal support to the German war machine. As we have seen above, Swiss exports represented less than 1% of production of German war materiel in 1943. On the other hand, if they were negligible to Germany, the 150,000 tons of coal and 20,000 tons of iron that Switzerland imported each month at the height of the war, transport assured in the dangerous circumstances of the conflict, amounted to approximately 20% of our trade with Allied countries. For Switzerland they meant the essential conditions for its economic survival and the reinforcement of its defense.

The fact that they were achieved and maintained shows well the firmness, even obstinacy of the Swiss negotiators. In spite of the extreme disproportion in military and economic potential, Switzerland was able to make its significant advantages felt. These advantages led Gäfgen, like Ilsemann, the former military attaché in Bern, to recommend against a break in economic relations. As Bourgeois himself notes, Switzerland did not allow itself to be incorporated into the Axis economic system. If it is true that Switzerland in time of peace never extended the amount of credit to others that it gave to Germany in wartime, the negotiations between the two countries were well carried out, with each of the parties holding solid advantages, on the principle of fair exchange. The German historian Rüdiger Walter states this well in his study published in 1970 on German-Swiss relations during World War II. He ascribes special importance to the economic sphere: "It may be said today that the economic and commercial agreements negotiated by Switzerland showed this country's determination to affirm its identity and its efforts to make its sovereignty and its neutrality respected. The country was able, up to the end of the war, to refuse economic incorporation into either of the two warring blocs."[40]

Table 16.1. Swiss Foreign Trade 1926–1950

	Imports		Exports		Transit
	Swiss Fr (million)	Metric Tons (thousand)	Swiss Fr (million)	Metric Tons (thousand)	Metric Tons (thousand)
	Annual Average				
1926–30	2,598	7,935	1,970	962	3,380
1931–35	1,639	8,358	903	512	2,340
1936–39	1,684	7,541	1,219	488	3,270
1940–45	1,661	3,972	1,430	383	5,147
1946–50	3,629	7,571	3,550	553	1,030
	Annual				
1940	1,853	6,220	1,315	510	5,930
1941	2,024	4,900	1,463	522	8,090
1942	2,049	4,420	1,571	405	7,640
1943	1,727	4,071	1,628	368	5,330
1944	1,185	2,679	1,131	309	3,750
1945	1,125	1,541	1,473	181	140

The tonnage figures reflect the recession of the war years, while the values less so because they were influenced by inflation—the doubling of prices from 1940 to 1945. Transit figures indicate the importance of the Swiss corridor for the Axis powers, even though the passage of troops and war materiel after 1941 was forbidden.

Note the differing ratio of price to weight between exports and imports; exports have a much greater value per ton than imports. This is a constant in Switzerland's economy. During the years 1940–1944, the value of a ton of imports rose from 298 to 442 francs, a 48% increase, while the value of a ton of exports rose from 2,578 to 3,660 francs, a 42% increase. The increases in value were therefore comparable.

Sources: *L'Annuaire Statistique de la Suise 1950*, from *Documents Diplomatiques*, vol. 15, 1078–85 and the documentation provided by the Federal Statistical Office for the years 1930–1950.

Table 16.2. Swiss Imports from Germany

	1930	1938	1939	1940	1941	1942	1943	1944	1945
Value—in millions of Swiss francs									
Coal	62	66	64	121	195	168	145	107	2
Iron	69	51	71	43	120	156	96	70	3
Copper	19	5	5	4	6	5	3	1	*
Other metals	20	16	14	13	33	39	25	14	2
Machinery	69	37	41	36	43	44	38	24	6
Vehicles	12	19	32	15	6	3	4	10	3
Watches	5	4	2	1	2	1	1	1	*
Instruments/Equipment	31	14	13	13	20	21	21	16	4
Pharmacy	7	8	12	8	9	9	8	8	3
Chemicals	39	23	32	24	33	36	38	35	6
Dyes	13	10	15	9	9	10	10	9	1
Other	363	120	139	124	180	168	143	138	24
Total Imports from Germany	709	373	440	411	656	660	532	433	54
Percent of Swiss Imports	28%	23%	23%	22%	32%	32%	31%	37%	5%

Swiss Francs

Volume—in thousands of metric tons

Total Imports from Germany	2,578	2,226	2,402	1,994	2,613	2,499	2,356	1,698	NA
Percent of Swiss Imports	29%	29%	27%	32%	53%	57%	58%	63%	NA

Memo: Coal—in thousands of metric tons

Total Imports of German Coal	NA	1,783	NA	1,565	1,985	1,830	1,632	1,168	NA
Total Swiss Coal Imports	NA	3,336	NA	NA	2,215	1,908	1,945	1,369	NA
Percent of Swiss Coal Imports	NA	53%	NA	NA	90%	96%	84%	85%	NA

NA = Not Available.
* = Less than .5 million.

The preponderance of imports was clearly from Germany, but these imports (in value terms) exceeded one-third of total Swiss imports in only one year. The average tonnage of imports from Germany from 1940 to 1944 at 2,234 thousand tons did not significantly exceed the 2,226 thousand tons in 1938 and remained notably lower than the tonnage for 1930. Coal imports were only 60% of prewar tonnage, but the portion from Germany rose from 53 to 96% with nearly constant tonnage.

Table 16.3. Swiss Exports to Germany

	1938	1940	1941	1942	1943	1944
Value—in millions of Swiss francs						
Finished Weapons	0.9	19.0	58.5	41.7	37.0	*14.0
Weapons Parts	—	0.5	5.0	17.0	19.0	—
Detonators	0.6	0.5	31.0	62.0	67.0	16.0
Ammunition	6.5	14.0	59.0	53.0	77.0	12.0
Other Weapons	—	.7	.5	.3	—	—
Total Weapons Exports**	8.0	34.7	154.0	174.0	200.0	42.0
Strategic Products	58.0	91.0	162.0	201.0	209.0	—
Total War Materiel Exports	66.0	125.7	316.0	375.0	409.0	42.0
Total Exports to Germany	206.0	284.0	577.0	655.0	598.0	293.0
Percent War Materiel	32%	44%	55%	57%	68%	14%
Total Swiss Exports	1,316	1,315	1,463	1,571	1,628	1,131
Percent to Germany	16%	22%	39%	42%	37%	26%
Percent War Materiel to Germany	3%	10%	22%	24%	25%	4%
*Includes Weapons Parts						
**Percent of German Weapons	1%	3%	11%	11%	12%	4%

The 2.4 billion francs of Swiss exports to the Third Reich from 1940 to 1944 represent 34% of total Swiss exports. Germany was far from having a monopoly on Swiss exports, all the more because with an annual average of 1.42 billion francs, total Swiss exports were only 8% above the figure for the crisis year of 1938, and these figures were in nominal values at a time of considerable inflation. This does not point to an economy overheated by weapons exports to Germany. The proportion of deliveries of war materiel to the Third Reich furthermore represents an average of only 18% of total Swiss exports. At the same time, Switzerland was devoting 2.14 billion francs to the material reinforcement of its defense in weapons, aviation, fortifications, and munitions, made possible in large measure to the coal, iron, and aircraft imported from Germany.

Table 16.4. Trade with France, Italy, Spain, and Portugal

	France		Italy		Spain	Portugal
	Metric Tons (thousands)	Swiss Francs (millions)	Metric Tons (thousands)	Swiss Francs (millions)	Swiss Francs (millions)	Swiss Francs (millions)
Imports						
1930	2,380	451 (17%)	268	185 (*7%)	35	2
1938	—	229 (14%)	267	116 (7%)	5	4
1939	1,423	275 (14%)	264	135 (7%)	6	8
1940	404	138 (7%)	245	164 (9%)	17	11
1941	200	75 (4%)	270	244 (12%)	26	103
1942	153	77 (4%)	187	154 (8%)	62	113
1943	120	78 (5%)	103	131 (8%)	106	57
1944	70	58 (4%)	12	28 (2%)	94	13
1945	275	130 (11%)	21	47 (4%)	93	31
Exports						
1930	295	183 (11%)	122	120 (*7%)	28	4
1938	—	121 (10%)	88	91 (7%)	5	8
1939	52	140 (11%)	62	81 (6%)	6	9
1940	37	112 (9%)	5	142 (11%)	15	10
1941	—	92 (6%)	60	185 (13%)	25	11
1942	14	66 (4%)	24	158 (10%)	38	19
1943	27	51 (3%)	15	93 (6%)	70	35
1944	17	24 (2%)	2	5 (-)	61	39
1945	81	165 (11%)	6	11 (1%)	100	60

*These figures for Italy are for the year 1931.
Trade with France, which was Switzerland's second or third largest trading partner in ordinary times, collapsed beginning in 1940, when France was exploited and plundered by the Third Reich, up to 1944. Trade with Italy grew modestly in value, but scarcely at all in tonnage, beginning in 1940. Trade with Spain, and more so with Portugal, grew beginning in 1940, favored by their neutrality, trade agreements with Great Britain and the United States, and the rapid expansion of transit trade more than from their economic expansion.

Table 16.5. Trade with Countries under Anglo-American Influence

	1938	1939	1940	1941	1942	1943	1944	1945
	Swiss Imports—in millions of Swiss francs							
United States	125	133	199	151	235	56	21	137
England	95	109	88	16	20	4	1	21
Canada	24	31	19	22	13	80	14	103
Mexico	3	3	2	4	1	1	—	2
Brazil	12	17	14	1	1	14	2	48
Argentina	58	78	115	109	112	52	41	120
Other America	27	41	61	14	24	43	49	81
Australia/Oceania	11	112	3	—	—	—	—	3
East Indies	28	31	26	11	4	5	2	10
South Africa	3	3	7	3	3	—	—	9
Turkey	6	7	12	53	53	39	30	53
Total	392	565	546	384	466	294	160	587
Percent of Total Imports	24%	24%	30%	19%	23%	17%	14%	49%
	Swiss Exports—in millions of Swiss francs							
United States	90	130	140	108	102	153	141	385
England	148	164	95	23	21	36	31	32
Canada	15	15	15	12	14	19	17	35
Mexico	7	9	10	9	9	10	11	27
Brazil	17	18	21	19	23	29	24	65
Argentina	36	33	28	26	40	40	40	87
Other America	26	29	27	20	30	45	37	93
Australia/Oceania	21	19	12	4	5	16	7	13
East Indies	28	31	30	22	19	18	26	49
South Africa	16	14	11	10	10	12	8	14
Turkey	4	3	7	7	13	25	25	53
Total	408	465	396	260	286	403	367	853
Percent of Total Exports	34%	27%	30%	18%	18%	25%	33%	57%

Conclusions to be drawn from these figures:

During the five years (1940-1944) that Switzerland was surrounded by the Axis powers, it had to deal with Germany to obtain the coal and steel it needed for economic and social survival, but also to have its rights as a neutral state recognized and to pursue its economic relations with the Allies and the overseas countries. It resisted Allied pressure to join the bloc against the Axis powers, which would have had the inevitable practical consequence of forcing it to join the economy of the Third Reich.

The figures provided support our previous findings. Switzerland was not some pulsating arsenal with all its factories in the service of German rearmament. If these factories, beginning in 1940, produced for Germany the weapons that, up to then, had been ordered by France and England, then equally it must be said that German iron and coal also enabled the reinforcement of Swiss weaponry and the construction of the redoubt network of fortifications. The period 1940 to 1945 was one of little trade, in both tonnage and value. The Third Reich was far from holding a monopoly; tonnage of exports to Germany was only 15% greater than the normal year 1930 and 30% over 1938, a year when Germany systematically reduced its trade relations. From 1940 to 1944, Germany took 50% by value of Swiss exports, while the Allies, in spite of the extreme difficulty of transport along Axis lines and the dangers of ocean navigation, took 25%. Under the most unfavorable conditions Switzerland maintained the plurality of its trade in conformity with neutrality, to the greatest extent possible under wartime conditions, and while surrounded militarily. It was a remarkable achievement.

NOTES

1. Klaus Urner, "Une Mobilisation pour les Besoins de l'Économie de Guerre," in *Revue d'Histoire de la Deuxième Guerre Mondiale* (Paris, 1981), 121, 63–69; and *Annuaire Statistique de la Suisse, 1950* (Basel, 1951).

2. Jakob Ruchti, *Geschichte der Schweiz während des Weltkrieges 1914–1918* (Bern, 1930), 2 vol., vol. II, Kriegswirtschaft.

3. Hermann Böchenstein, *Bundesrat Obrecht* (Soleure, 1981), esp. 241–61, 232.

4. In general: Hans Schaffner, "Centrale Fédérale de l'Économie de Guerre," in *L'Economie de Guerre Suisse 1939–1948*; Report of the Federal Department of Public Economy, Bern, 1951, 2–48; Heinrich Homberger, *La Politique Commerciale de la Suisse durant la Deuxième Guerre Mondiale* (Neuchâtel, 1972), 14–15; and in general: Klaus Urner, "Neutralité et Politique Commerciale," in *Revue d'Histoire de la Deuxième Guerre Mondiale* (Paris, 1981), 121, 35–39, and the articles there by Heinz K. Meier and Daniel Bourgeois, 41–61; Daniel Bourgeois, *Le IIIe Reich*, 158–82; and *Annuaire Statistique de la Suisse, 1950* (Basel, 1951).

5. Heinrich Homberger, *La Politique Commerciale*, 15–21.

6. Heinrich Homberger, *La Politique Commerciale*, 22–26.

7. Heinrich Homberger, *La Politique Commerciale*, 27.

8. Heinrich Homberger, *La Politique Commerciale*, 38–42.

9. Daniel Bourgeois, *Le IIIe Reich*, 163–82.

10. Heinrich Homberger, *La Politique Commerciale*, 42–47.

11. Heinrich Homberger, *La Politique Commerciale*, 23; and Daniel Bourgeois, *Le IIIe Reich*, 173–76.

12. *Annuaire Statistique de la Suisse, 1950* (Basel, 1951); and Philippe Marguerat, *La Suisse Face au IIIe Reich* (Lausanne, 1991), 155–56.

13. Heinrich Homberger, *La Politique Commerciale*, 97–101.

14. *Annuaire Statistique de la Suisse, 1950* (Basel, 1951) and Tables 16.1 through 16.5 of this chapter.

15. Daniel Bourgeois, *Le IIIe Reich*, 178–82.

16. Jakob Ragaz, "Die Ausfuhr von Kriegsmaterial aus der Schweiz Während des Zweiten Weltkrieges," *Der Aufbau* (Zurich, April 8, 1949).

17. Philippe Marguerat, *La Suisse Face au IIIe Reich*, 94–97.

18. Marc Hofer, *Die Schweizerische Kriegsmaterialexporte nach Deutschland Während des Zweiten Weltkrieges,* Seminar paper at the University of Fribourg, Economic History, Professor Tanner, 1992, 11–16.

19. A.G. Ploetz (ed.), *Geschichte des Zweiten Weltkieges* (Würtzburg, 1960), part 2, 3–30.

20. Daniel Bourgeois, *Le IIIe Reich*, 417.

21. Willi A. Bœlke, *Die Kosten von Hitlerskrieg* (Paderborn, 1985), 98–102.

22. Philippe Marguerat, *La Suisse Face au IIIe Reich*, 110; and Marc Hofer, *Die Schweizerische Kriegsmaterialexporte nach Deutschland während des Zweiten Weltkrieges*, 17.

23. Marc Hofer, *Die Schweizerische Kriegsmaterialexporte nach Deutschland Während des Zweiten Weltkrieges*, 17–18.

24. Philippe Marguerat, *La Suisse Face au IIIe Reich*, 98–99.

25. Report of the Chief of the General Staff on His Active Service, 1939–45, 50.

26. Walter Rüdiger, *Die Beziehungen der Schweiz zu Deutschland Während des Zweiten Weltkieges, Studien der Herresoffizierschule* (Munich, 1969), 321.

27. Daniel Bourgeois, *Le IIIe Reich*, 180.

28. Marc Perrenoud, "Banques et Diplomatie Suisses à la Fin de la 2e Guerre Mondiale. Politique de Neutralité et Relations Financières Internationales," in *Etudes et Sources,* 1314, (1988), 7–27.

29. Philippe Marguerat, *La Suisse Face au IIIe Reich*, 162; and *Documents Diplomatiques,* vol. 15, 1108–41.

30. *Documents Diplomatiques*, vol. 15, 587–89.

31. Philippe Marguerat, *La Suisse Face au IIIe Reich*, 161–63.

32. Werner Rings, *L'Or des Nazis* (Lausanne, 1985), 150.

33. Werner Rings, *L'Or des Nazis*, 17–24.

34. Philippe Marguerat, *La Suisse Face au IIIe Reich*, 172–74.

35. Heinrich Homberger, *La Politique Commerciale*, 115–17.

36. Klaus Urner, "Neutralität und Wirtschaftskrieg. Zur Schweizerischen Aussenhandelpolitik, 1939–1945," in *Schwedische und Schweizerische Neutralität* (Basel, 1985), 255–84.

37. Heinrich Homberger, *La Politique Commerciale*, 92–105.

38. Philippe Marguerat, *La Suisse et la Neutralité dans le Domaine Économique Pendant la Seconde Guerre Mondiale* (Neuchâtel University, Faculté des Lettres, 1985), 84–85.

39. Daniel Bourgeois, "Les Relations Économiques Germano-Suisses Pendant la Seconde Guerre Mondiale. Un Bilan Allemand de 1944," *Revue Suisse d'Histoire*, vol. 32 (1982), 563–73.

40. Walter Rüdiger, *Die Beziehungen der Schweiz zu Deutschland Während des Zweiten Weltkieges*, 132.

Chapter Seventeen

Neutrality and Openness

The third paragraph of the declaration of neutrality published by the Federal Council on August 31, 1939 stated that "The Confederation will be honor-bound to facilitate the impartial humanitarian activity it performed during the last few wars that can contribute to mitigate the sufferings a conflict can cause." [1]

This declaration, which essentially repeated that of 1914, confirmed the essential element of human solidarity which neutrality implied, as it had been practiced, especially in 1870–71 and 1914–18 and as it had been announced in 1863 on a private initiative by some citizens of Geneva, among whom were Dunant and General Guillaume Henri Dufour, for the establishment of the International Committee of the Red Cross, and then by the several conventions of Geneva and the Hague (1899 and 1907) for "humanizing war" and defining the rights and duties of neutrality.

On September 18, 1939, the Federal Council approved instructions to Swiss representatives abroad stressing the role not of propaganda but of explanation and information that they were expected to play. This action should remain prudent and discreet in order to be effective and not resort to methods that would be counterproductive. The themes to be developed were that: [2]

1. Neutrality is an organic necessity for Switzerland. It derives from historical developments.
2. It is in Europe's interest.
3. Switzerland is resolved to defend its neutrality against anyone and is capable of doing so.
4. This neutrality is not selfish, but generous, because it enables the mitigation of the evils of war for the belligerents.

Justified by law and reason, neutrality could not remain passive. With some effort, it could maintain the openness and universality of diplomatic relations and exchanges. It especially needed to demonstrate its solidarity with refugees by helping them materially and taking them—in however limited a fashion was necessary—by the activity of the International Committee of the Red Cross, adhering as much as possible to the guarantees provided in the successive Geneva and Hague Conventions that sought as much as possible to humanize (if one may use that term) warfare and its results. It also fell to Switzerland to be the site of meetings and contacts of every variety and to offer its good offices to the governments and peoples of the world to mitigate the evils of war and to contribute if possible to ending the conflict, without detracting from its commitment to neutrality.

Pilet defined the openness policy, the vocation of neutrality, on November 5, 1941 at a press conference, of which he has left the manuscript outline:[3] "The policy to be pursued for accomplishing our international tasks. To make ourselves useful to everyone under the rubric of neutrality; that goes without saying. Liaison between peoples. Foreign interests. Humanitarian aid. Wherever there is suffering, to intervene according to the limit of our resources. Even at the cost of sacrifices. With no political ideology, like the International Red Cross. We will take advantage of every opportunity. We will seek these opportunities."

Switzerland believed in maintaining diplomatic relations with all. Thus the Federal Council refused to break all relations with an invaded Poland, in spite of German pressure. Certainly it could not regard the government in exile in France and later in England as a government with full rights. However it maintained a compromise solution that was unofficially tolerated by the Reich: the recognition in Bern of a Polish chargé d'affaires with the title of minister plenipotentiary, who could remain in constant touch with the Polish division interned in Switzerland throughout the war. In the same spirit, and in spite of opposition from the Axis powers that wanted Switzerland to recognize the de facto situation arising from the military occupation, the Swiss Confederation insisted on the de jure situation of the end of August 1939 and retained the diplomatic representation in Bern of Norway, Denmark, Belgium, the Netherlands, Greece, and Yugoslavia as governments in exile, like that of Poland throughout the war.[4]

To what extent did Switzerland propose to become involved to end the war? In his study of the "good offices," the former secretary of state for foreign affairs, Raymond Probst, recalls the caution to which its total encirclement and its unfortunate experience in 1917 guided Switzerland during the Second World War.[5] He notes the incident of November 1941 when Pilet is said to have informed the ambassador from the Vichy government of a German diplomatic initiative for calling a conference for the consideration of a new European order. Berlin, which was beginning to feel the severity of the Russian winter following its invasion of the Soviet Union, hoped to have France, Spain, Portugal, Sweden, and Switzerland join. This, the Germans hoped, would have led Britain to a compromise. Pilet, according to the French ambassador's report to the authorities in Vichy, said the move would be inappropriate. Faced with England's reaction to the project, the Political Department took an unequivocal position: this problem had nothing to do with the neutrals but concerned the belligerents. As it happened, he recommended a high level of caution. Pilet also thereby freed himself of the suspicion of encouraging an undertaking which too many would have seen in the perspective of integration into the European order. Churchill's speech of November 10 made short shrift of German soundings by excluding all negotiations with the National Socialist regime. In 1942, Pilet took advantage of a certain détente on the occasion of some exchanges of wounded and ill soldiers between Britain and Italy to proffer good offices proceeding in the direction of peace feelers. As it happened, Pilet had made it clearly understood to German Minister Köcher that "if the British losses had been heavy, they did not do Germany much good . . . if the belligerents persisted in rejecting all offers of peace talks, the rope would be stretched to the breaking point and the issue would be all the more bitter."[6]

We need not repeat the story of the Hausamann affair and the alleged offer of a separate peace that had been used in an attempt to trap Pilet. If Hausamann's plot—pending more complete purely personal information—had failed because of its improbable construction it is none the less true that Germany had showed some signs of disquiet. The Swiss Councilor of Legation Feldscher wrote from Berlin on February 23, 1943 in a private letter to Pilet that hope was growing in certain German leadership circles of convincing the western powers of the increasing danger from Soviet power and that appropriate action should be taken. It is in this context that the Vatican's intervention is to be seen. On February 11, 1943, Monsignor Bernardini, the apostolic nuncio in Bern, reported to Secretary of State Cardinal Maglione on an interview he had had the previous day with Pilet-Golaz, who shared his concern for the communization of Europe by the advancing Soviet troops.[7] He noted Stalin's plans for Germany and the favorable treatment of the German generals and soldiers at Stalingrad. However, one must not harbor too many illusions about the interests the Americans and British would bring to bear on Europe after the war.

Pilet reported these concerns, shared by many diplomats, to the Foreign Affairs Committee of Parliament. Had the time come to undertake peace moves by associating the Holy See with the four neutrals, Switzerland, Portugal,

Spain, and Sweden? The latter country had already provided positive assurances. The Vatican's answer came on March 3.[8] The undertaking was praiseworthy, but premature. The German foreign minister, furthermore, had declined a papal intervention in favor of peace. One should not hold against Pilet an interpretation of the situation which the end of the war and the subsequent events tragically confirmed or a proposal to put an end to the massive massacres and destruction two years earlier than would in fact be the case. This was very much in keeping with Switzerland's vocation of neutrality. However, the Vatican's prudence is understandable. It is easier to start a war than to brake its infernal machinery once it is started.

It is appropriate to recall once more Switzerland's refusal in 1943 to participate in a peace initiative of Franco's Spain and sponsored by Portugal and the Vatican. In August 1943, the Political Department could not accept providing the services the Royal Italian Government was requesting from Switzerland. In that delicate phase this government, whose territory was partially held by the army of Germany with which it was officially allied, was seeking to disengage itself from the alliance with Hitler to join the Allied side. Switzerland clearly could not enter into and participate in an imbroglio of this kind, which would be counter to neutrality.[9]

As it happened, the Political Department's position was reasonable, but Edgar Bonjour poses the dilemma between the extreme caution prudently observed and a more active contribution that could have advanced the cause of peace. This is undoubtedly an illusion: history showed that belligerents at daggers drawn do not accept these moves until they feel their forces weakening. It is at that point that they have recourse to the neutrals for establishing the necessary technical contacts. However, previously, with the war machine at full steam on both sides, proposals to mediate, whether from Roosevelt or the Vatican, much more from a small neutral whose very neutrality was under suspicion, had little chance of being heard. More often than not, they served to shed suspicion on their authors of favoritism to the adverse side, from a constant mistrustful reaction against neutral countries.[10] Certainly some private individuals may have been led by their generosity or their concern for playing some role to work for peace. In this connection, General Staff Major Max Waibel of the Swiss Intelligence Service, one of the "conspirators" of 1940, was involved, in his private capacity, and unbeknownst to his superiors, in the conclusion of an armistice in northern Italy in March and April 1945.

Waibel would put an end to the confusion where the occupation forces of the German army, exhausted and eroded by the slow climb up the Italian boot, were scattered in disorder, dealing inefficiently with opposition from remnants of the Italian regular army under the contested authority of the royal government and the indecisive command of the Italian leaders in northern Italy. The bands of republican antifascists in conflict with the fascists loyal to Mussolini and the eruption of regional autonomous entities such as the Republic of Ossola had the sporadic and unofficial support of certain Swiss politicians. It was in this situation, dangerous for his country, that Major Waibel, acting independently, initiated contacts with both the scattered Italian forces and the Germans and, without having received any such assignment, obtained a general agreement for peace and disarmament for northern Italy.

These negotiations, which departed from official procedures and took place without the participation of the Swiss government or the army's high command, were a clear violation of neutrality. They therefore provoked the irritation of the Soviet government;[11] however, the agreement, achieved without official Swiss participation but through the initiative of a Swiss officer, opened a decisive breach in the confrontations of the war and was the prelude to the general armistice. Neither the army's high command nor the government of Switzerland had a role in the matter, and they did not approve these actions until after the war.

A leader's initiative is sometimes the result of successful disobedience. Even though the credit of blame could morally be ascribed to the army, these negotiations risked setting a dangerous precedent.

THE UTILITY OF CONTACTS WITH ALL BELLIGERENTS

The protection of a belligerent country's legitimate interests with the countries it is fighting is a permanent duty and justification of a neutral country. The presence of Swiss representatives in nearly every country at war in the world made it possible in the heat of the conflict to maintain contacts, to conclude lesser agreements, to prepare the way for negotiations on larger topics, to offer a place for meetings, and to some extent to prepare the postwar world. It also enabled the safeguarding of national or private interests and especially protecting human rights and to free or transfer a number of innocent victims, within the severe limits where this was possible.

During World War II, Switzerland represented forty-three countries which had four-fifths of the world's population in countries with which they were at war. That represented more than 1,200 Swiss and foreign diplomats and officials, in Bern and in the wartime capitals, and some 70,000 diplomatic dossiers. In this way, Switzerland assumed the defense of the interests of the principal countries at war, from Germany in the United States, passing through Italy, Japan, Britain, and Vichy France[12] This discreet but important role maintained a trace of solidarity in a world in discord.

NOTES

1. *Documents Diplomatiques*, vol. 13, 323.

2. *Documents Diplomatiques*, vol. 13, 413–18.

3. Erwin Bucher, *Zwischen Bundesrat und General*, 558.

4. Edgar Bonjour, *Neutralité*, vol. IV, 99–110.

5. Raymond Probst, "Good Offices in the Light of Swiss International Practice and Experience," *Dordrecht*, (1989), 293–306.

6. Edgar Bonjour, *Neutralité*, vol. VI, 99–110; and Daniel Bourgeois, *L'Image Allemande de Pilet-Golaz*, 102.

7. Edgar Bonjour, *Neutralität*, vol. IX, 374.

8. Edgar Bonjour, *Neutralität*, vol. IX, 374–76; Letter from Monsignor Bernardini to Cardinal Maglione of 11 February 1943 and the latter's response; and Raymond Probst and Paul Stauffer, "Mediationstätigkeit der Schweiz im Zweiten Weltkriege," in *Schwedische und Schweizerische Neutralität* (Basel, 1985), 295–96.

9. Edgar Bonjour, *Neutralität*, vol. IX, 121–23.

10. Raymond Probst and Paul Stauffer,"Mediationstätigkeit der Schweiz im Zweiten Weltkrieges" in *Schwedische und Schweizeriwche Neutralität* (Basel, 1985), 293–306.

11. Edgar Bonjour, *Neutralité*, VI, 119–27.

12. Martin Schärer, "La Suisse Puissance Protectrice," in *Revue d'histoire de la Deuxième Guerre Mondiale* (Paris 1981), 121–29; and Konrad Stamm "Die Vertretung fremder Interessen durch die Schweiz im Zweiten Weltkriege," in *Schwedische und Schweizerische Neutralität* (Basel, 1985), 307–20.

Chapter Eighteen

Solidarity Actions

The movement later to be known as the International Committee of the Red Cross (ICRC) was established in 1863 by a group of Geneva citizens including the philanthropist Henri Dunant and General Guillaume Henri Dufour. A private foundation, the ICRC assigned itself the mission of humanizing war by protecting the wounded, prisoners of war, and the civilian population through international conventions that defined and limited the rights of belligerents. The ICRC, with its headquarters in Geneva and composed essentially of Genevans and other Swiss, monitors respect for these conventions and assumes something of a management role through its delegates, who enjoy official recognition in most countries and carry out their mission of humanitarian assistance in case of war or natural catastrophe. Financing is provided by private donations and contributions from governments, primarily Switzerland.

The activities of the ICRC are an essential witness to the good offices rendered by Swiss neutrality throughout World War II. Professor Jean-Claude Favez, in *Une Mission Impossible?*, has written an analysis that is both positive (in spite of the title) and critical.[1] Switzerland saw its moral obligation as a neutral but did not make a show of it, and the results of Red Cross activities during World War II emerge from the statistics. The Committee, its 173 delegates, and some 3,700 members worked on behalf of 7,000,000 prisoners of war, their primary mission, and of 175,000 civilian internees. They visited the camps bringing provisions and medical supplies, establishing contacts, seeking out identities, informing and reassuring family members if possible, and promoting the application of the Geneva Convention. They made 600,000 investigations, filled out 50 million forms, and delivered 100 million letters and 33 million packages weighing 400,000 tons and worth 3 billion

Swiss francs. Added to this figure were 750,000 packages distributed to persons deported to concentration camps.[2]

Aside from the Red Cross's extensive and permanent activities, carried out impartially in various areas in conflict in collaboration with national Red Cross groups, other activities arose sporadically that were more sectoral and targeted, sometimes debatable[3] yet often positive. This was the case on the Russian front and on the German side. The Third Reich had not officially requested Swiss participation in the "antibolshevik crusade" set in motion in June 1941, which would gather all European forces against communism. However, there were some persons, survivors of the rightist fronts or nostalgic for a greater Germany, who demanded that Switzerland join the struggle "for freedom from Jewish-Asiatic bolshevism" and recruit a "legion of volunteers," following the example of other countries such as France, Belgium, and Spain, for the campaign in the USSR. Of course there was no reply to this request, and joining a foreign army remained subject to punishment by Swiss military courts.

In July 1941, a proposal from some prominent Zurich citizens close to the extreme right demanded that Switzerland, after twenty years of opposing the communist regime, show its complete solidarity with the peoples and armies who were caught up in the struggle against bolshevism and assist them with all their means. In their view, Red Cross member nations in particular should do their duty by assisting war victims in this sector, especially the oppressed and tortured Russian people who had been freed by the Axis armies. Pilet replied unequivocally. The principle of neutrality governed Swiss policy in the current conflict. He would not tolerate placing the emphasis on this front more than the others, all the more so because that would bring more assistance, humanitarian as it was, to one side only.

The dispatch to the eastern front of a military-medical mission, proposed by Eugen Bircher, a Swiss division commander, and some other doctors and citizens close to the German cause, gave rise to some reservations, aggravated by Bircher's uncommon personality. He was a remarkable surgeon and a competent commentator on military affairs, an admirer of the German army, but a difficult subordinate often in conflict with his superiors. Had he not referred to the Rütli report as "an anti-German provocation"? His project, this unilateral mission, clashed with General Guisan's strong opposition and Pilet's reservations. However, the Federal Council finally gave in, because the matter had been pushed so hard by its inspirer. Nevertheless, the mission was to be neither official nor military, and its personnel would be clad in uniforms with no rank insignia and sufficiently inelegant so as not to attract attention, to the great disgust of Bircher. The mission would not originate with the Swiss Red Cross, much less with its International Committee, and would be subject to German military law.

The "medical mission," which consisted of some eighty doctors and assistants, brought only a little relief to the wounded, due to its short duration and difficult working conditions. But it was received in Germany with a certain amount of publicity and served to prejudice Swiss neutrality policy because of Bircher's impetuous pronouncements. Despite warnings, he stressed the example provided to the young Swiss of the "new German man," and on the analogy between the construction of the new Europe and that of the old Swiss Confederation. He thanked the führer for allowing its members to participate in this "great struggle." It is true that the enthusiastic and disorderly division commander was later to distance himself from the evils of National Socialism, and when he painfully left his military command he deplored its exuberance and combativeness from the sheltered atmosphere of the Federal Parliament. Meanwhile, the mission had reinforced German defiance of the Soviet Union and its allies, without gaining for Switzerland useful recognition from the Germans. Some doctors on the mission expressed their frank opinions on the severity in the conduct of the war when they returned home.

Other similar missions organized on several fronts were more effective and garnered less publicity. As part of their active vocation of neutrality, these missions could have been on a larger scale, as is the case today in several theaters of war.

Added to the geographic extent of the conflict, the millions of men involved, and the destruction from the blind, massive bombing which struck the civilian populations was an element which, if not unheard of, was at least new in its dimension: deliberate genocide. This included massive deportations, concentration camps, and mass murders. The ICRC, like the Vatican and other neutral states, has been reproached for not having officially denounced these crimes to the world, as the "final solution" and the extermination of the Jews had been known since 1942. Yet neither the International Committee, which had the mission of overseeing the application of the international conventions, nor the governments, especially the Swiss Federal Council, had any coercive power available that could enforce respect for elementary human rights.

In 1942 the ICRC extensively debated a public declaration that would denounce the violations of basic human rights and genocide then underway in the totalitarian states, whose names it intended to publish. The organization feared that in unleashing fanaticism, a solemn protest on a worldwide scale such as the later one tardily issued by the Allies on December 17, 1943 would only make the persecutions worse, aggravate the fate of the victims, and prevent the pursuit of humanitarian assistance by the committee, other neutral states, and the churches. This move would have closed more doors to humanitarian assistance than it would have saved victims. Consciences would have been morally appeased to the detriment of the concrete fate of the prisoners. Humanitarian aid occasionally needs to take place on the margin of principles.[4]

The ICRC is a private Swiss organization, essentially and qualitatively elitist and Genevan in its leaders, which is not to depreciate either its quality or its vocation. It is not answerable to political institutions, even though they contribute substantially to its financing. However, instances of interference are multiple, constant, and inevitable, because Switzerland's services as a protecting power make use of agents of the Red Cross. This interference sometimes provokes controversies, when the activities of "the protecting power" take precedence over other Red Cross activities, either its mission of maintaining respect for international conventions or in specific activities such as exchanges of the wounded or prisoners.

On the whole, however, the collaboration has been positive. For instance, Pilet supported the committee in June 1940 in a project to assist refugees in France. He also encouraged the ICRC to "carry out a new project by enlarging the field of its activities more and more and in all areas, being bound neither by tradition nor convention." In 1942, the head of the Political Department and his colleagues advised against putting out a worldwide appeal for human rights, which the dictators would not even consider, but in that year the Federal Council established the position of delegate for international assistance.[5] In 1944, Pilet renewed his encouragement to the ICRC and promised Red Cross President Carl Burckhardt all necessary assistance. For Bern, in principle, "What is good for the Red Cross is good for Switzerland."

The refugee problem certainly brought out the saddest of considerations in Switzerland. The tradition of welcoming refugees—though in actual practice, this welcome was constantly selective for practical reasons—is morally tied to the neutral country's humanitarian vocation. This is so strongly the case that the right to receive refugees is a prerogative of the state that exercises it and not at all the right of the refugee to claim. "We do not grant the right of asylum, we exercise it," Pilet was to say. This brief formula summed up the definition that his predecessors at the Political Department had given to the right of asylum. Thus Jonas Furrer, first president of the Confederation in 1848, had stated, "The right of asylum is totally false. We do not recognize in any way the right of a foreign refugee to asylum. The right of asylum is a right belonging to the state, with respect to other states, to receive refugees as a moral obligation, to the extent that the duty of humanity requires it and to the degree that the state's interests permit it."[6] This declaration was issued at a time when the Holy Alliance had revived a reactionary spirit and Austrians, Prussians, and French were considering an ultimatum demanding that the Confederation expel the libertarians who had found asylum there.

In a similar situation in 1889, Federal Councilor Numa Droz used the same language to the Austrian minister: "Our right of asylum is not the result of our neutrality, but an attribute of sovereignty that every state possesses. In this connection, we have never accepted the erroneous conception that Switzerland, by reason of its neutrality, would be a Temple of Delphi where criminals are safe." He continued, "Although neutral, Switzerland has the same right as any other state to rid itself of people who are not convenient and to admit those it wants to admit, even if it does not exercise that right. It only has to conduct itself in this matter, like every other state, in accordance with its sovereign rights and in agreement with its obligations to other countries. . . . The fact that a country is neutral does not detract from its sovereignty. Neutrality without sovereignty would be only an illusion if one were not independent."[7]

The recent and massive flow of refugees to Western Europe from the Middle East, Africa, and Eastern Europe demonstrates to us today the limits of the capacity to receive them. These limits are material, economic, and psychological. The western countries, even the European Community, at a time when it is contemplating the abolition of its internal borders, is obliged to limit strictly the number of refugees and resort to painful and often arbitrary rejections of them.

The situation was especially tragic in 1939–45. It was not, as it frequently is today, a case of lack of resources or the search for a job which would lead to repaying the right of entry, but often the last hope of surviving the concentration camps and the "final solution." This situation applied both to Jews and political opponents of Nazism, as it does now to peoples facing massive deportation or deliberate massacre who do not share the same ethnicity, the same god, or the same ideology, despite the ineffective efforts of pacification by the United Nations and the European Union.

Samuel Werenfels carefully studied the stages of Swiss refugee policy from 1939–45.[8] During the first wave of Nazi persecution beginning in 1933, refugees were almost never admitted unless they were on their way to another country. This provision was to be strengthened after 1938 by the ignominious J stamped by German and Swiss officials on all passports whose bearers were of Jewish origin. In addition, an entry visa was obligatory. The initiation of hostilities increased the pressure at the border, but reinforced the restriction on authorizations, leading to the removal of all clandestine refugees. The distinction between soldiers who had not been interned in units such as the French army corps and the Polish division in 1940, deserters, escapees from prison camps, civilians driven out by the fighting, or inhabitants of Alsace-Lorraine who refused annexation and mobilization was not easy to make. Restrictions were particularly severe in 1942, and the border was to remain closed to Jews up to the middle of 1943, yet that measure was not universally applied in all its rigor everywhere or by everyone, for a strong minority of public opinion opposed it. The year 1943 marked a relative softening in refugee policy, especially in view of events in Italy and the flow of deserters and prisoners fleeing from all the camps and every country. Werenfels concludes from this that it is not fair to criticize those who had to take restrictive steps against the refugees, even if they may be reproached for excessive prudence. We must bear in mind the force, threats, and uncertainties of the war, during which decisions had to be made in an effort to save those who could be saved.

"To grant asylum is certainly the best fruit of neutrality," Edgar Bonjour wrote in 1943. "To accord a safe retreat to one persecuted for political reasons is a right possessed by every state. . . . Such a tradition has its responsibilities. By giving up the idea of asylum, we stain our sense of national honor and we will recover from that only with difficulty. . . . Our total neutrality obliges us to be totally humane."[9]

This generous idea of universality was replied to in advance by Federal Councilor Edouard von Steiger in 1942. "When one is in command of a rescue boat that is already fully loaded with no extra space and is provided with a limited quantity of food, and when thousands of victims of a maritime catastrophe are calling for help, one can appear heartless if one does not take everyone on board. However, one would be even more humane by warning people in time against deceptive hopes and by trying to save the ones already taken aboard."[10]

Was the boat fully loaded? The answer, then and now, is difficult to discern. The future then was uncertain and taking people in freely, though desirable in itself, could have led to an uncontrollable flood. Switzerland took in nearly 400,000 refugees and internees in successive stages, provisionally or on a long-term basis. To this must be added a number, naturally impossible to define, of clandestine refugees who were unknown or tolerated, disguised or enjoying a private welcome, where disobedience had occasionally mitigated official rigor. In 1943, 26,000 refugees were recorded entering; there were 46,000 in 1944, a year at whose end 103,000 refugees were recorded. Of these, 16,000 were interned soldiers, escaped prisoners of war, or Italians refusing to serve in the German army or the neofascist commands. The rigor of the quota policy became a little more flexible after 1943, showing that there was still room in the Swiss boat after it had been shaken a bit. But would it have been possible to receive in neutral Switzerland or Sweden the millions of Germans, Poles, French, and Hungarians scheduled for the "final solution" or the millions deported or held in concentration camps? At that time the outcome and duration of the war were uncertain, the precarious supply of food was constantly put at risk, and there was a permanent threat of invasion or military reprisals.

It has been asked whether Switzerland could not have provisionally sheltered larger contingents which could have been sent overseas thereafter, excluding all European countries in advance, to the extent that transport could be organized. Yet, to take perhaps the most important example, "Washington was granting entry visas to Jewish refugees in Switzerland from an eye dropper. A more generous passage downstream, even under deferred conditions, could not have failed to encourage the Federal Council to be even more open upstream," stated Mysyrowicz and Favez in the *Revue d'histoire de la Deuxième Guerre mondiale.* Thus, from 1940 to the summer of 1942, that is, a period during most of which the United States was not at war, only 1,563 refugees could be evacuated from Switzerland through Geneva and Marseilles, of whom 638 proceeded to the United States.[11]

The opening or closing of the refugee gates, based on the Federal Council's joint decisions, was not controlled by the Political Department, but rather by those of Justice and the Police. Following his colleagues' example, Pilet contracted it only when necessary, and then unwillingly. "It is extremely painful not to be able to open our doors wide to the refugees," Pilet stated in 1942 before the parliamentary National Committee for Foreign Affairs. His interest in good offices and refugee policy brought on criticism from the impulsive Feldmann, who reproached Pilet with being dazzled in his vanity by the august surroundings. After having supported Pilet's reelection in 1943, Feldmann deplored the fact that he had fallen back into his charitable conception of Swiss foreign policy.[12]

Pilet could not distance himself much from the generally restrictive attitude of the Federal Council. However, we see him replying in 1944 to an initiative of the president of the United States to establish an interministerial committee to handle the refugee problem. Pilet described the efforts Switzerland had already put forth and explained why an unlimited reception of refugees would be impossible: "The security of Switzerland is also that of those who have found refuge there." Switzerland's neutrality precluded its associating itself with a committee made up of belligerents, but it very much desired to "reinforce the position thanks to which it was still possible to continue its contributions to render practical assistance to victims of war." Pilet made these statements before the parliamentary Committee for Foreign Affairs in September, adding that we Swiss "cannot uselessly risk our external security to exercise the right of asylum," nor could we compromise our internal security. It was not a question of receiving those who would act in a manner detrimental to Switzerland. However, Pierre Laval would not be admitted either, "nor those who had committed acts against the laws of war," Pilet added before Parliament.[13]

Pilet never let pass an opportunity to humanize the harsh refugee policy. This may be seen in what he did for Jews in Hungary in 1944. Great Britain, which held a League of Nations mandate over Palestine, had planned to transfer about 40,000 Hungarian Jews there. In spite of all the efforts in which Pilet participated personally, the establishment of a Jewish quarter in Hungary under Swiss protection and the emigration of a certain number of Jews were all that could be accomplished.

The activities of Consul Karl Lutz, an attaché at the Swiss Legation in Budapest, although not officially sanctioned, nevertheless prevented the annihilation of more than 50,000 Hungarian Jews. Of these, 2,000 found asylum in Switzerland in 1944, and the initiative of former Federal Councilor Jean-Marie Musy in 1945 enabled the reception of more than a thousand detainees from the Theresienstadt concentration camp.[14]

In December 1943, the Federal Council authorized the Political Department to prepare the reception of children from the bombed areas of Germany, "without distinction of nationality or race," adding to the activities that had been underway since 1940 on behalf of French and Belgian children.[15] Nevertheless, it was only in November 1944 that Chief Rothmund of the Swiss Division of Police informed Berlin through Minister Hans Frölicher of a Swiss protest against the deportation of Jews accompanying an offer to take them in. Also, it was only on February 6, 1945 that the Federal Council decided to make a protest against genocide; there was nothing more to fear, as there had been in the past, that such a protest would unleash retaliation against Switzerland and make it worse for the powerless victims. This at least is the explanation that can be imagined at this late date.

However, in this critical period, with Switzerland surrounded economically and militarily and under threat of invasion, we cannot reduce the country's image to a redoubt closed in on itself, its borders bristling with barbed wire, and its customs officials and policemen driving back the refugees and the persecuted. In line with this official rigor, which was both selective and forced by necessity, a largely unwritten history has developed on the margin of the law, regulations, statistics, and the Gestapo. It concerns transit traffic and clandestine shelter, cross-border cooperation in merchandise, printed matter, and doubtless weapons as well in aid of the resistors. A Swiss citizen of Italian-speaking Ticino, Renata Broggini, leaves the most vivid if not the most turbulent image of the Swiss Federal Police and the protests by fascist activists on the far side of the border. She evokes this idealistic agitation in her thesis on Italian refugees, *Terra d'asilo*.[16]

The episode of the ephemeral Republic of Ossola illustrates these close relations. In September 1944 the Italian antifascist partisans, who were especially active in the mountainous region bordering Swiss Ticino, took the Italian town of Domodossola away from the German troops occupying it and installed a city council that governed the valley for forty days. They made contact with the legation of the Royal Italian Government in Bern. The reception the partisans gave the Ticino deputies Borella and Canevascini, then to Mayor Rusca of Locarno, amounted to an official recognition. The Red Cross and the Caritas Association took up a general collection of food and money in aid of the valley. Weapons crossed the border, but an unfortunate neofascist counterattack brutally put an end to this ephemeral liberty. Tracked down, many of the partisans were able to cross the border under the protection of Swiss troops, who kept their pursuers at a respectful distance. Along with the resisters, several families and thousands of children, driven out by the last remnants of fascism and the nervousness of the German army, found refuge in Ticino.

Neither statistics nor archival documents contain any data on the clandestine traffic in people, refugees, emigrants, secret agents, merchandise, and weapons that crossed the wooded border of the Jura into Switzerland or took advantage of the Schweizer Loch between Geneva and Chamonix, which greatly disturbed the Germans. They tried to strengthen their control, but totally in vain. Blocked traffic of official transport would move to the "green frontier," with or without the complicity of the Swiss or French border guards. [17] Some recent studies (published in 2000) confirm that the frontier controls were applied only with relative rigor.

The vocation of welcoming refugees, an expression par excellence of humane solidarity to which Switzerland should bear witness, is a noble mission. It was not an easy task to welcome thousands of unexpected guests at the border, distribute them, house and often clothe and feed them at a time of precarious and severe rationing, and live with them and encourage them if necessary for months. This uprooted and demoralized population was housed often in only relative comfort, in crowded, desperate conditions where some quantity of dubious antisocial elements could have slipped in along with political activists spreading division. They could not be left to themselves in depressing idleness. This population had to be encouraged and kept busy, whether through the initiative of the refugees themselves whenever possible, or through the intervention of the civilian and military refugee organizations. This required a combination of both humanity and firmness among the refugees and those assisting them, as well as a degree of cooperation with churches, local authorities, and the population in general, which was not always spontaneous.

The 9,000 soldiers of the Polish division that had taken refuge in Switzerland in 1940 represented a special case, with their four years of internment, even though the 30,000 French soldiers had returned to their country. Divided up into several camps, the Poles, in military formations and under military discipline, continued their physical and intellectual training or worked for pay, while some pursued university studies or professional apprenticeships. Pilet recommended repatriation in stages. However, the circumstances, the Poles themselves and their leaders, as well as the federal commissioner for internment who had regarded the idea "as a forfeiture contrary to the spirit of national honor," prevented the move. Finally, General Guisan undoubtedly contemplated using the rearmed Polish division to resist a German invasion. Pilet accepted this reasoning and gave up the idea of repatriation, which would at the least have been difficult.[18]

Switzerland's neutral status, especially in time of crisis, and its immediate proximity to the scene of operations made it a meeting place very much in demand. There were embassies and legations from nearly all the countries engaged in the conflict. International institutions—the Bank for International Settlements at Basel, the dying League of Nations in Geneva, the Universal Postal Union in Bern, and the ICRC and other charitable organizations—enabled easy contact and could commence or facilitate negotiations.

Switzerland's central location and its neutrality also encouraged the intelligence services of the warring parties. When Swiss citizens became involved it was sometimes useful to their country, but compromising at other times. This does not mean to say that *La guerre a été gagnée en Suisse* (The war was won in Switzerland), as Pierre Accoce and Pierre Quet assure us of that in their 1966 book of that title, which evokes Otto Pünter (Pakbo), Radolfi-Rado, Alexander Foot, and especially Rudolf Roessler-Lucy. This last-named, in the words of Allen W. Dulles, the very active head of the American intelligence service in Switzerland from 1942 to 1945, found out within twenty-four hours all the decisions of the German high command concerning the eastern front, more reliably than the Swiss intelligence services.[19]

It was also in Switzerland, or through Switzerland, that certain resistance organizations arrived at their decisions and executed their deliveries, notably Ticino for the Italian antifascists. It is not well known that in the spring of 1939 in Ouchy, the port of Lausanne, Carl Goerdeler, the former mayor of Leipzig; Dr. Hjalmar Schacht, former president of the Reichsbank and then a cabinet minister; and Hans Gisevius of the German consulate in Zurich laid the basis for resistance at the highest political and military level against Adolf Hitler's fury. This resistance, which enjoyed the support of Admiral Canaris's *Abwehr* counterespionage organization, found its tragic epilogue in the failure of the plot of July 20, 1944 and the bloody reprisals that followed.[20]

Switzerland was a liaison point for German resistance, which was centered around German Consul General Voigt in Zurich. Allen Dulles's office in Herrengasse in Bern was concerned not only with coordinating American intelligence in Europe but also maintained close relations with the liberation movements of our neighbors. Furthermore, Dulles established rapport with German emissaries beginning in 1943. Neutral Switzerland, which favored secret contacts among the belligerents, could, if need be, initiate attempts at peace feelers.[21]

Finally, the role of a free press—despite protests from the Axis powers, recommendations for prudence, and a censorship more inept than effective— must be evaluated for its role in this, alas limited, initiative of openness where newspapers could be read by neighboring countries. Nothing, on the other hand, could rein in the radio, in spite of prohibitions and official recommendations, controls by the German police, and denunciations. Neutrality constrained the radio to prudence but kept propaganda of the occupying powers from crossing the borders. Even though one René Payot of French-speaking Swiss radio displayed relative complacency for a time concerning the Vichy regime in Nazi-occupied France, he made clear and objective information on the international situation shine over the airwaves. Each Friday evening his factual serenity rebutted the triumphant euphoria of the totalitarian news and gave hope to the population in occupied territories. After the British BBC's French language transmissions, the Swiss French radio transmissions earned second place in number of listeners in its range.[22]

In February 1940, Pilet requested the historian Jean Rodolphe de Salis to provide a weekly radio chronicle of international politics, giving him complete freedom. "The Swiss broadcasting company was not a government organization. The government did not take responsibility for its broadcasts and had no intention of giving it instructions." This did not prevent Salis from getting into difficulty and controversies with military censors. Salis, in spite of the glorious regiments where his ancestors had served abroad, had only a moderate affection for the uniform and did not want to irritate the German Legation in Bern. The extensive audience for his broadcasts in German-speaking countries, in spite of incidents with the censors that he prudently bypassed, itself justified neutrality, the need for openness that it implied, and the comfort it could bring to people waiting for liberation, to which they listened at risk of their lives.[23] Pilet was aware of this mission, knowing that the war engaged peoples' hearts and souls. He would have preferred to replace early military censorship with a more flexible political censorship that was less imperative and restrictive and more suggestive to editors in chief. However, when he met with Salis in February 1943 he recognized with his fellow Federal Councilor Edouard von Steiger, who had been in control of the press since 1942 when that function was taken from the army, that it was not yet time to mitigate the regulations, given the tensions of the moment.[24]

Neutrality and the redoubt, the military symbol of neutrality, therefore did not turn the country back onto itself. Pilet did not consider the redoubt as a permanent idea, a sterile and virtuous isolation. He was aware that neutrality proclaims its justification and its value only by a policy of openness. It was in this state of mind that he oversaw the report that his department submitted on February 16, 1944 to the Federal Council.[25]

This report, drawn up in keeping with directives from the head of the department by Daniel Secretan, in charge of the Postwar Section of the Political Department, was entitled *Ebauche d'une politique suisse d'après-guerre. Considérations générales* ("Outline of a Swiss Postwar Policy. General Considerations").

The first need was to be constantly informed of other countries' intentions for the postwar period and the measures they planned to take. Next, there should be balance in the neutrality policy, judging whether and how this neutrality should confront political, military, economic, financial, and humanitarian problems and then set out the praise and criticism received from our partners and prepare our replies.

The policy to be pursued was to be extracted from these two elements, from a study begun in 1942. First, the fundamental points of foreign policy needed to be set out: independence, prosperity, and solidarity. Neutrality must be maintained. "We owe two inestimable benefits to it: peace, which allows employment, and prosperity. Without neutrality there is no peace and without peace there is no employment, and therefore no prosperity." Did we need to have this neutrality recognized again, which the powers had already recognized? It seemed to go without saying, but guarantees were needed from the new great powers, the United States, China, and the Soviet Union.

The integrity of Swiss territory appeared beyond discussion. It should not be allowed to fall prey to temptation, as it was in 1919, by its neighbors who wanted to annex us.

Would the League of Nations survive, or would it be absorbed into a new international organization whose idea had been voiced by the three great powers at the Teheran Conference? The second solution seemed to gain the upper hand. The Swiss Federal Council had already approved this measure. "No country would acclaim more than Switzerland an international organization established for tranquillity, prosperity, and the good of mankind."

The report stressed the close contact between the Federal Council and the ICRC. "Switzerland and the committee are united. What affects one affects the other as well." Swiss participation in the rebuilding of Europe must be on both humanitarian and economic terms. Maintaining armed neutrality makes membership in a general security organization problematical. With concern for the economic future and the ghost of 1930s unemployment, the report finally opened the perspectives for emigration overseas.

NOTES

1. Jean-Claude Favez, *Une Mission Impossible? Le CICR, les Deportations et le Camps de Concentration Nazis* (Lausanne, 1988). Followed by *Point de Vue du CICR, Signé par son Président Cornelio Sommaruga*, 376–79.

2. Jean-Claude Favez, *Une Mission Impossible?*, 365–66.

3. Edgar Bonjour, *Neutralité*, vol. IV, 439–49; Daniel Heller, *Eugen Bircher*, (Zurich, 1988), 192–216, preface by Hans Senn, 7–11; and Felix Steiner, *Die Freiwillige, Idee und Opfergang* (Göttingen, 1958), 373.

4. Jean-Claude Favez, *Une Mission Impossible?*, 155–66, 376–79.

5. Jean-Claude Favez, *Une Mission Impossible?*, 46.

6. Edgar Bonjour, *Neutralität*, vol. I, 326–27. Letter from Jonas Furrer to Alfred Escher.

7. Edgar Bonjour, *Neutralität*, vol. II, 44–45. Messages from Numa Droz to the minister of Austria and the minister of Germany (1889).

8. Samuel Werenfels, "Die Schweizerische Praxis in der Behandlung von Flüchtlingen [...] im Zweiten Weltkrieg," in *Schwedische und Schweizerische Neutralität* (Basel, 1985), 377–404.

9. Edgar Bonjour, *Die Schweizerische Neutralität. Ihre Geschichtliche Wurzel und Gegenwärtige Funktion* (Bern, 1943), 31ff.

10. Edgar Bonjour, *Neutralité*, vol. VI, 20, note.

11. Ladislas Mysyrowicz and Jean-Claude Favez, "Le Refuge," in *Revue d'Histoire de la Deuxième Guerre Mondiale* (Paris, 1981). 121, 112–20.

12. Erwin Bucher, *Zwischen Bundesrat und General*, 590–95.

13. Edgar Bonjour, *Neutralité*, vol. VI, 31, note.

14. Edgar Bonjour, *Neutralité*, vol. VI, 31–33.

15. Edgar Bonjour, *Neutralité*, vol. VI, 143.

16. Augusto Rima, "Appoggio della Resistenza 1944–1945" in *Actes du XVIIe Colloque de la Commission d'Histoire Militaire* (Bern, 1993), 473–88; Renata Broggini, *Terra d'Asilo: I Refugiati Italiani in Svizzera 1943–1945* (Lugano, 1993), especially 325–30; and *Documents Diplomatiques,* vol. 15, 651–53, 657–58.

17. Klaus Urner, *Die Schweiz muss noch Geschlukt Werden*, 117–27.

18. Ladislas Mysyrowicz and Jean-Claude Favez, "Le Refuge," 119.

19. Pierre Accoce and Pierre Quet, *La Guerre a été Gagnée en Suisse. L'Affaire Roessler* (Paris, 1966), 300; and Stephen P. Halbrook, *Target Switzerland,* 172–73.

20. Hans Bernd Gisevius, *Jusqu'à la Lie: de l'Accord de Munich Jusqu'à l'Attentat du 20 Juillet 1944*, vol. II, 76–205.

21. David Kelly, *The Ruling Few* (London, 1952), 272.

22. The Community of the French Language Public Radio, *La Guerre des Ondes Pendant la Deuxième Guerre Mondiale* (Paris-Lausanne, 1985), 251–63.

23. Hans Rudolf von Salis, *Grenzenüberschreitung* (Zurich, 1978), vol. II, 79ff, 251–63; and Alice Meier, *Anpassung oder Widerstand* (Frauenfeld, 1965), 85.

24. Edgar Bonjour, *Neutralité*, vol. VI, 155–91.

25. *Documents Diplomatiques*, vol. 15, 229–34.

Chapter Nineteen

Permanence of the Threat

THE COURSE OF THE WAR

Lacking the accommodation with London that he had desired, Hitler began the Battle of Britain on July 10, 1940. After achieving air superiority, he would start Operation Sea Lion, which would enable a landing on the British coast. But Hitler underestimated the effectiveness of the Royal Air Force and the will to resist of a people who stoically endured the Germans' massive air raids. From July until mid-November the Luftwaffe lost 1,818 aircraft to the RAF's 915. As Churchill said, "Never in the field of human conflict was so much owed by so many to so few." With its solitary resistance, Great Britain was the first to stop the inexorable expansion of the Third Reich. After October 1940, Hitler gave up the task of conquering Britain, all the more because the United States, with its logistical support and with Roosevelt steadily emerging from neutrality, was constantly reinforcing British defenses. Shortly after that, Mussolini's presumptuous activities in North Africa, Greece, and the Balkans presented his German ally with unexpected concerns and delayed by two months the invasion of the Soviet Union, of which the führer had been dreaming since June 1940.

These concerns, on an entirely different scale from the Swiss theater, did not indicate that the Axis powers had lost interest in that country. Switzerland's strategic location, its secure communications, the systematic advantage it took of its industrial apparatus and financial resources, and its political alignment toward the "New Order" made the Swiss "wasps' nest" "one of the last of Great Britain's positions on the continent," as Mussolini wrote to Hitler in October 1940. And so the German and Italian general staffs continued to fine tune their invasion plans.[1]

Both Axis plans assumed the Swiss would surrender on receipt of an ultimatum or during negotiations. However, a vigorous resistance was generally expected, because the German and Italian general staffs were aware of the deterrent effect of the redoubt and were adapting their personnel to it. Their concentrations near Switzerland were still significant in the winter of 1940–41. As in other theaters, the general staffs certainly did not urge an invasion and sought to dissuade Hitler, "the politician," as General Franz Halder, the army chief of staff, wrote in his notes, from a military operation. However, other episodes show that Hitler's political impulsiveness often overthrew reason.

The movement of Axis forces to the east was soon to ease the concerns of the Swiss command. However, on June 2, 1941 the two dictators again met at the Brenner Pass and were prolific in their bitter recriminations against Switzerland. According to the memorandum prepared by Paul Schmidt, the interpreter, "[t]he führer characterized the Swiss as the most repugnant of people and their government as the most lamentable. The Swiss were the mortal enemies of the new Germany and they declared—their way of speaking is significant—that only a miracle could prevent 'the neighboring Swabians' from winning the war. They are obviously opposed to the Reich, because they had hoped to strike out on a better course . . . abandoning the common destiny of the German people. But now they see, in light of most recent events, that their calculations were wrong. It is Swiss hatred of renegades that shapes their attitude, to some extent."[2]

Schmidt's report continues: "To the Duce's question about the future of Switzerland, most likely an anachronism, the Reich's foreign minister replied that it was up to the Duce to discuss that with the führer. The Duce then remarked that in Switzerland only the French Swiss are for France, while the Italian Swiss and the German Swiss are hostile, respectively, to Italy and Germany."

Daniel Bourgeois notes that Hitler's violent diatribe against Switzerland was the only point which General Halder, who was present, noted in his diary.[3]

The threats and hatred were real, especially from one who listened more to his impulses than to reasonable calculations or the advice of his generals. It is appropriate to describe this behavior with respect to a larger theater than the microcosm of Switzerland. After the defeat of France in June 1940, Hitler revived the interpretation of the European geopolitical situation that had led Napoleon I to his ruin one hundred thirty years before. He soon grasped that British insularity was irreducible. General Franco of Spain, when asked, refused to enter the war and open the Gibraltar route. Thus it was to the east that Hitler turned. Victory in Russia, which, however, was then his ally, would assure him the undivided domination of the whole continent and the realization of the great design set out in *Mein Kampf*. Since July 1940 he had been confiding his intentions to the generals closest to him: Jodl, Keitel, and von Brauchitsch. They combined to dissuade him from the undertaking with military arguments, at least for 1940, while Secretary of State von Weizsäcker and the armaments minister warned him against the economic risks it would entail.[4]

In preparation for the move on the USSR, the Germans invaded Yugoslavia on April 6, 1941 on the pretext of the Russo-Yugoslav Pact and then Greece, where they came to the assistance of their helpless Italian allies, took Athens, and parachuted into Crete. On June 22, in spite of the complacency Stalin displayed on the matter, Hitler brutally attacked the Soviet Union, where 200 divisions penetrated rapidly and deeply, reaching the outskirts of Moscow in November and encircling Leningrad jointly with the Finnish army. Since war was also raging in the Middle East, where the Third Reich was obliged in February 1941 to transfer General Rommel's Afrika Korps to save the Italians from a rout in Cyrenaica in northeast Libya, the immediate danger was removed from Switzerland's borders. We were able, in successive stages, to reduce the Swiss army to a minimum of 150,000 men, complete the rearmament, bring the network of fortifications and preparations for destruction to total and detailed completion, perfect the army's training, and inspire it with combative spirit so as not to bury it in the static defensiveness of the redoubt.

The following year, 1942, was made famous by the battles of El Alamein, where Montgomery's British liberated Egypt and drove out Rommel's Afrika Korps; the Coral Sea and Midway, where the American navy took revenge for the attack on Pearl Harbor and halted Japanese expansion; the resistance at the symbolic city of Stalingrad, a prelude to the German army's retreat; and finally the Anglo-American landing in French North Africa. These marked the turning point in the war, the "end of the beginning," in Churchill's phrase.

This reversal of the general situation, though, had consequences for Switzerland and restored the probability of an invasion. The vigor of Soviet resistance made it possible to anticipate a vast counteroffensive; the powerful American war machine was going at full speed; the Allied landing in North Africa and Allied naval supremacy made an attack likely against Italy, whose government was vacillating under its defeats. Clearly the vise was tightening around Germany. Switzerland's position thus again increased in strategic and logistical importance for the two Axis powers. It was perhaps feared that the Reich would include this mountain bastion in its defensive preparations or that the Allies could come in one way or another to disrupt transit, even though this was forbidden to both troops and war materiel. The Germans were disturbed and mistrustful of Allied connivance with Switzerland, "the Anglo-Saxon forward position in Europe." On November 10, 1942, in retaliation for the Allied landing in North Africa, Hitler ordered the occupation of southern

France. A few days later he reportedly met in his headquarters with Heinrich Himmler and General Eduard Dietl, who had led operations in Norway in 1940. They now insisted on the importance of occupying Switzerland and its strategic interest. This surprise attack would call for massive bombing, airport operations, and fifth column operations in the interior.

General Guisan explained the matter to the Federal Council on January 6, 1943. "Past examples show that the German high command does not wait until the last minute to take measures it deems necessary for the conduct of the war. It would try to occupy our country, if the operation did not seem too costly, assuring itself the twofold advantage of strategic surprise and the time needed to reestablish our lines."[5]

Did subsequent events bear him out? Did the warning of March 1943 portend "one of the most immediate dangers we had to face during the war," as Samuel Gonard claims?[6] Gonard's view tends to refute H. B. Gisevius's statement in his 1946 interrogation before a Swiss examining magistrate. This collaborator of Admiral Canaris's *Abwehr*, who was close to Swiss interests, claimed that the warning of 1943 was only a gesture to bring pressure to bear on Switzerland or to enhance the role of SS General Walter Schellenberg as an intermediary in the eyes both of the Swiss and the Nazi leaders. German counterintelligence knew nothing about it. Secretary of State von Weizsäcker also expressed doubts in his memoirs. But one must remember that Hitler was not in the habit of divulging his plans, not even to his own government.

BLUFF OR THREAT?

H. R. Kurz, Samuel Gonard, Willi Gautschi, and Hans Senn, who doubts but largely confirms the various hypotheses, all admit that the threat was real, according to Bonjour. The troop concentrations in southern Germany; the mission given in 1942 to General Dietl, a specialist in mountain warfare, to study Operation Switzerland;[7] the "Viking" source of the intelligence service that provided a direct line between Masson and Schellenberg; and the inevitably appearing Hausamann also confirm this threat.[8] It appears to have taken form early in March 1943. Why then? The Soviet army was catching its breath after the reconquest of Stalingrad on February 2, 1943, which left a few Reich divisions available for an operation in Western Europe. Finally, the defeats in the Soviet Union and Africa and the United States' entry into the war led to a rise of combative zeal among the leaders of the Third Reich which Hitler expressed in his Munich speech of November 11, 1942. "There is no way out for us," Goebbels was to say in the same vein, "and people who burn their bridges behind them will fight to the end without holding back much better than those who still have a possibility of retreat."[9]

The warnings issued since that fall took serious form in the spring of 1943. On March 18–19, 1943 it was announced that an attack was likely before April 6. The problem would be discussed urgently at Hitler's general headquarters. A special commando unit would be given the task of eliminating General Guisan.

The Swiss command took this news very seriously. Leaves were denied; soldiers on leave were called back; there were mobilization exercises and preparations for a general mobilization, which Pilet, through his liaison officer, wished would be gradual so as to prevent disorder.[10]

Then, all of a sudden, the problem vanished as if by miracle. On March 22, the "Viking" intelligence source stated that the view of the generals, and also perhaps the economists, had won out over the führer's fantasies. "The Swiss plan will be abandoned," Bernard Barbey states in his book, *PC du Général.* For Roger Masson, head of intelligence, this confirmed that the source established with SS General Schellenberg had proven a success. "The threat had disappeared: Switzerland was no longer in danger."

THE SCHELLENBERG ENIGMA

At this point the miracle becomes an enigma.[11] What role was played here by the close and paradoxical relationship established in 1942–43 between the modest head of the Swiss army's intelligence service, General Masson, and the high-spirited Nazi officer, already an SS general at age thirty-two? From 1942 on Schellenberg had been in charge of counterintelligence, inevitably encroaching on the intelligence service. Further, he exercised an obvious political influence as a creature of Heydrich and Himmler and through them had contact with Hitler. According to those in contact with him, as relayed by Masson and Dr Francis Lang of Romont, who secretly took him in and treated him at the Billens hospital in 1951–52, which Lang attests in his memoirs, Schellenberg was a cultivated and brilliant personality, appealing in his free spirit, but ambiguous and without scruples in his ambition. Hence it is difficult to understand the report he submitted in 1944 convincing Himmler of the treason of Admiral Canaris, whose reservations concerning the regime and its aggressive policy Schellenberg appeared to share.

It seems certain, in the last years of the war when the wind clearly had shifted, that Schellenberg, with several other senior officers including Canaris and paradoxically even Himmler himself, was among those who sought a way out of the foreseeable disaster. This was behind his approach to the neutrals Sweden and Switzerland, useful intermediaries. His testimony and that of his collaborators at the Nuremberg trial in 1946 confirm it. Schellenberg was counting both on Switzerland's firmness in neutrality and the possibility of finding a contact with the Allies. He was also using his office to verify the will to resist among responsible Swiss military leaders in case of a German invasion and to inform the command and political leaders.

Masson, for his part, had inherited a rudimentary intelligence service on taking command. He was anxious to improve his information by direct contacts with responsible leaders at a senior level. He also set store by mitigating a controversy that was still active. Thus, his service distributed information in 1936 to the Czech general staff on the organization, training, and tactics of the German army. Something similar had happened with the papers found at Charité-sur-Loire which the Third Reich was keeping in reserve or the Nazi press campaign throwing doubt on General Guisan's reliability, raising suspicion of connivance with the Anglo-Americans.

Certainly, direct relationships with foreign counterparts entailed serious problems, notably those of the service's employees who were trying, not without difficulty, to maintain and nourish their own sources only to be short-circuited and passed over by their supervisor's personal contacts. In addition, the political authorities had particularly strong reservations, for they harbored an understandable and logical fear of confusion of jurisdiction and diminution of their authority, as was seen in 1939–40 in the dubious support agreements between the Swiss and French general staffs.

In January 1943, Albert Müller, an editor of the *Neue Zürcher Zeitung*, had published a study of the Third Reich's expansion policy under the title *Erweiterte Strategie* [Global Strategy], of which the Federal Council became aware. In Müller's view, diplomacy and military operations, closely connected, deliberately short-circuited traditional hierarchies and procedures. The division of authority should favor direct contacts with political and military personalities, which were both more responsible, more flexible, more diligent, more able, and less bogged down in hierarchy than diplomatic or administrative personnel. At the instigation of Willy Bretscher, his editor in chief, Müller was disturbed at the risks this direct diplomacy could entail for the Swiss high command and for the country. In December 1942 he called the attention of the Federal Council to the importance and dangers of this new procedure. The connection between Masson and Schellenberg and the meeting at Biglen was evidence of this.[12]

Thus, without the knowledge of the Federal Council but with the consent of General Guisan, Masson met Schellenberg in the German border town of Waldshut on September 8, 1942. Masson put forth great efforts to resolve any doubts on the question of Switzerland's neutrality, complaining of the unfounded accusations of partisanship laid at Guisan's door. Schellenberg, for his part, expressed sympathy for Switzerland. Masson obtained the release of one Mörgeli, an intelligence officer who had been sentenced to death, an easing of press articles, and the repatriation through Switzerland of a niece of General de Gaulle and of the family of General Giraud.

A second meeting between Masson and Schellenberg took place on October 16–18 at the Wolfsberg chateau near Ermatingen. Masson was hard put to reassure the German leaders with regard to Guisan. Schellenberg brought up the removal of Labhard, Wille, Bircher, and Bandi, officers favorable to Germany. Masson contemplated a trip to Germany, but Guisan opposed it. On the other hand, Schellenberg eventually obtained Hitler's authorization to travel to Switzerland, not without objection, to meet Guisan, a meeting that had in fact been in preparation since January 1943.

On March 3, Guisan, with some hesitation and despite Barbey's concern, and also, astonishingly, omitting to inform the head of the Military Department, who doubtless would have objected, met Schellenberg at the Bären Hotel in Biglen. Also present were Masson, two Swiss officers, and one collaborator of Schellenberg, the SS officer Eggen, who was in charge of liaison with Switzerland and who also attended to some personal business matters. What the two generals said when they met face to face was of course not published. Guisan probably thanked Schellenberg for the steps he had taken after the meeting at Waldshut and he also tried hard to play down the various contentious matters between the two countries, notably the papers of Charité-sur-Loire. Nothing has come down to us from either side indicating that the two officers presented a general appreciation of the situation or said anything about their governments' intentions and preparations for the near future. However, in Guisan's eyes the only justification for the meeting, when an Operation Switzerland appeared to be under study, was the unchangeable will of the Swiss people, army, and government to defend their country's independence in neutrality. He confirmed his statements in a written note which he delivered to Schellenberg three days later at Arosa. In it Guisan referred to Switzerland's historic vocation for neutrality, which had been confirmed in its time by Bismarck. He stated the unconditional resolve: "Whoever penetrates our country will thereby become our enemy" and noted "We are especially prepared to defend our alpine border."

Did Hitler become aware of the note and these meetings? Although there is no proof, nothing disproves it either. This information falls among the privileged relations between Schellenberg and Himmler, who was himself close to Hitler. Ribbentrop, whose influence was then on the wane, was aware of the note. However, he gave no credence to Guisan's justifications for his relations with the French general staff in 1939–40 with, as Ribbentrop thought, the tacit connivance of the Federal Council.

What weight did the Biglen meeting and the note delivered at Arosa have on the decision to abandon Operation Switzerland, to the extent that the operation had been planned? Around the same time, on March 22 when concern was at its highest, the "Viking" and Schellenberg sources transmitted the message that "we should be content with the result." Masson, in transmitting this news to Guisan, was sure that "these activities, which have been going on for more than a year, have had significant influence in this matter" and cordially thanked Schellenberg. Guisan was more reserved. He limited himself to stating in 1947 in *l'Illustré* that, "I could not say to what extent Schellenberg's influence was felt by Hitler or his entourage. Some people claim that my meeting did not lead to anything. In any event, it did no harm."[13]

These "some people" were numerous. On Guisan's personal staff, Barbey, had he been consulted, would have advised against meeting Schellenberg. "But I am not sure I was right. This was a typical case where the boss takes the risk."[14] Others in the intelligence service were unhappy and felt frustrated by the competition from this direct source. The high command—where the chief of the general staff, the most loyal Huber, who approved Masson's initiative and his direct line to Schellenberg after the fact—was informed of nothing at the time, and the general officers were hard put to hide the chronic animosity reigning in the upper reaches of the hierarchy against Guisan, his entourage, and his personal initiatives.

However, the Federal Council showed the greatest irritation which, it must be admitted, was most understandable, on grounds of principle. Add to that the fact that the head of the Military Department was not informed, given its unusual character, of the Masson-Schellenberg connection. Yet an intelligence service where, more than elsewhere "the end justifies the means," should not be bound by the rigidity and transparency of administrative procedures. It could compromise the government by certain actions. It needed to enjoy, under the responsibility of its direct supervisors, a certain freedom of action and initiative, as well as strict confidentiality. It should under no circumstances implicate the political authorities. Furthermore, Masson undertook nothing without requesting Guisan's consent. The direct connection with Schellenberg turned out on the whole to be useful.

However, it was a different matter for the commander in chief and the mandate he had from the Federal Assembly and the government, even if by his actions he only reaffirmed the will to independence, neutrality, and resistance that the Federal Council had frequently declared. External relations, the definition of policy, and contacts with foreign leaders were the business of the government, not the army commander. In the days following these meetings, Guisan informed the Swiss president as if they did not matter, and Karl Kobelt, the head of the Military Department, heard of them only by hearsay. Questioned by Kobelt, Guisan was hard put to admit that it had been a private meeting that took place by coincidence, which contradicted the importance he had himself ascribed to the meeting and its results.

On April 5, the Federal Council took up the matter and debated it at length, but, paradoxically, did not hear Guisan. In the terms of a letter drawn up by Kobelt, the government recognized the commander in chief's good intentions and his desire to serve his country. The declaration to Schellenberg was in agreement with the policy the Federal Council had often publicly proclaimed. However, by meeting a high-ranking politico-military official without informing the government and by giving a declaration that inevitably had an official character, the general had gone outside his role and intervened in the area of relations and decisions reserved to the Federal Council. The council strongly stressed that it reserved to itself the presentation of declarations to foreign officials and that it alone decided on the army's involvement in instructions it would issue to the commander. The general was to abstain from such meetings in the future, unless he previously informed the Federal Council and obtained its approval in advance. In his reply, Guisan noted that "his only purpose had been to reestablish confidence and that this purpose had been served." "One should not read 'declarations of a political nature' into this, since it was a matter only of confidence."[15]

According to the minutes of the Federal Council meeting, Pilet did not take part in the discussion. However, given his conception of the separation of powers and the primacy of the political power, he must have agreed on the sanction inflicted. He was questioned on June 1 by Deputy Bringolf of Parliament's Foreign Affairs Committee, who wanted to bring out the harm the Biglen meetings had done to neutrality. Pilet responded tersely that the committee should ask the Military Department, stating: "In any case, the head of the Political Department and" (Pilet thought he could add) "the Federal Council believed that foreign policy belonged exclusively to the government and that the army should concern itself only with preparing the troops for war and studying the military situation." Pilet doubted that danger was imminent and mistrusted the fancy taken to Schellenberg.[16]

The principle of subordination was undeniable and needed to be affirmed. However, it was admitted that Guisan had only repeated what the government had constantly affirmed. It may be that the heavy language of the military man better expressed a partisan conviction than would a démarche with kid gloves by a diplomat. Infinitely regrettable in this affair, more than the obvious lack of liaison, communication, and planning, were the personal differences, the concern for prestige, and the rivalries and antipathies explicable as much by the susceptibilities of the responsible persons as by the reciprocal twists, turns, and animosities of their entourages. The pettiness of personal reactions can weaken the most just of causes.

Guisan, while continuing to defend the soundness of his actions, was very reserved thereafter. This did not prevent the Masson-Schellenberg line from continuing its activities. Masson, in 1948, summed up the services he attributed to Schellenberg, with confirmation from Guisan, in order to defend his partner. To what we have already noted concerning the meetings at Waldshut and Biglen, he added the rescue of numerous deported people, prisoners, and hostages threatened with death and the interest in the Frenchmen Léon Blum, Edouard Herriot, and Paul Reynaud, enemies of Germany. He mentioned the recall of Hans Sigismund von Bibra, first counselor at the German Legation in Bern and a notorious activist for Nazi propaganda. He noted the incident of the German Me-110 Cg aircraft, equipped with secret instruments and compelled to a forced landing at Dübendorf. To preserve its secret construction, the Swiss allowed the destruction of the aircraft in exchange for the sale of twelve Me-109s which the Germans allowed on Schellenberg's intervention. Schellenberg also lent his concurrence to an operation for the liberation of some Jews undertaken by former federal councilor Jean-Marie Musy, which, however, succeeded only in part.

Masson was ill-rewarded for expanding a nearly nonexistent intelligence service and for the services he rendered it with limited resources, empirical methods, and activities that were problematic in quality and sometimes even in honesty. At the time when Switzerland was celebrating the end of the war that it had survived in peace and freedom in the middle of the European furnace, Masson was appearing before an examining magistrate. On the basis of rumors and complaints it appeared "that Colonel-Brigadier Masson had not been faithful to the instructions that had been given him, that his actions not only gave gross offense to the neutrality policy set by the Federal Council but also involved acts contrary to several provisions in the criminal law." Under these conditions, Swiss President von Steiger requested Guisan to open a supplementary investigation.[17] At the conclusion of the inquest, on the recommendation of the chief investigator, Masson's direct superior Major General Jakob Huber, chief of the general staff, putting the rumors in their place, limited himself on August 10, 1945 to issuing a reprimand for violating the border-crossing regulations.

It is true that some time later Masson made the imprudent mistake of confiding to a foreign journalist that he had had a connection with Schellenberg. These revelations caused a furor in the press and Parliament, with Hausamann feeding the fire. A new investigation was assigned to Federal Judge Couchepin. In his report of November 29, 1945 the judge condemned Masson's naiveté and his violation of the requirement to be discreet, but noted that no military or diplomatic secrets had been revealed. "In considering all the facts," Willi Gautschi concluded, "according to this report, and especially in view of Masson's merits, his blameworthy actions seem to be insignificant, and we should only confirm the reprimand from Parliament by the head of the Military Department."[18] However, the busybody Hausamann, with his strong political support, continued to inveigh against the wartime head of intelligence, who furthermore had made the mistake of showing too much indulgent naiveté toward the person involved, his problematic channels, his dubious connections, and his political intrigues.

In the light of history, the Federal Council's obstinate pursuit of Masson, who had certainly made some mistakes in the pursuit of his duties, may have constituted so many indirect blows at General Guisan.

As to the dashing SS General Schellenberg—who was neither hero, martyr, nor savior of Switzerland, but who had certainly rendered it great service and had tried to temper Hitler's rages—Masson drew up a report countersigned by Guisan for Schellenberg's defense at the Nuremberg trials.[19] For his efforts he received another written reprimand from Kobelt. Despite Swiss and Swedish testimony and the support of the British and Americans, Schellenberg was sentenced to four years in prison. Released in 1951 with his health seriously endangered, he found refuge, which had to be temporary and clandestine, at the Billens hospital in the canon of Fribourg, thanks to Masson and Dr. Francis Lang. However, they sought in vain to obtain the right of asylum for him, running into the obstinate wall of the government. He had to go to Italy to die. He did not harbor any rancor against Switzerland. The day after his death in Turin in 1952, the priest who had heard his final confession told Masson: "I bring you the last messages from Schellenberg. After his long confession, I know what Schellenberg has done for Switzerland."

NOTES

1. Klaus Urner, *Die Schweiz muss noch Geschluckt Werden*, 65–84, 161–76; Hans Senn, *Dissuasionsstrategie, Etat-major VII*, 235–72; Alberto Rovighi, *Un Secolo di Relazioni Militari tra Italia e Svizzera 1861–1961*, 521–37; and Georges-André Chevallaz, *Les Plans Italiens Face à la Suisse 1933–1943* (Pully, 1988).

2. Daniel Bourgeois, *Le IIIᵉ Reich . . .* , 297–98.

3. Franz Halder, *Kriegstagebuch 1939–1942*, 3 vols., (Stuttgart, 1962–1964) vol. II, 450.

4. Pierre Renouvin, *Les Crises du XXᵉ siècle*, T. 8, vol. II of *L'Histoire des Relations Internationales* (Paris, 1958), 292–97; and Edgar Bonjour, *Neutralité*, vol. V, 51–53, 58–60.

5. *Rapport du Général Guisan à l'Assemblée Fédérale sur le Service Actif* (Lausanne, 1946), 47–49; and Hans Senn, *Dissuasionsstrategie, Etat-Major VII*, 360–65.

6. Samuel Gonard, *Die Strategische Probleme der Schweiz im Zweiten Weltkrieg*, cited by Willi Gautschi in *Le Général Guisan*, 47.

7. Willi Gautschi, *Le Général Guisan*, 539; Hans Senn, *Dissuasionsstrategie*, 372–75.

8. Edgar Bonjour, *Neutralité*, vol. V, 64–86; Hans Rudolf Kurz, *Histoire de l'Armée Suisse*, 133–34; and Willi Gautschi, *Le Général Guisan*, 530–32.

9. H. A. Jacobsen, *Der zweite Weltkrieg* (Darmstadt, 1961), 380; and Henri Bernard, *Les Dossiers de la Seconde Guerre Mondiale* (Verviers, 1964), 45–46.

10. Bernard Barbey, *PC du Général*, 143, 154, 158; and Marcel Pilet-Golaz, *Aperçu*, 406–7 [French text].

11. On the Biglen Affair and Schellenberg: Edgar Bonjour, *Neutralité*, vol. V, 64–86; Dr. Francis Lang, *Mémoires d'un Médecin de Campagne* (Fribourg, 1991), 70–89, 209–29; Pierre Th. Braunschweig, *Geheimer Draht nach Berlin* (Zurich, 1989), 295–325; Erwin Bucher, *Zwischen Bundesrat und General*, 262–72, 283–89; Walter Schellenberg, *Le Chef du Contre-Espionnage Nazi Parle* (Paris 1957). He concisely describes his relations with Masson and the events of 1943, and brings out his personality and his purposes; and Hans Senn, *Dissausionsstrategie*, 367–72.

12. Edgar Bonjour, *Neutralität*, vol. VII, 232–40. Correspondence concerning the Schellenberg affair.

13. Willi Gautschi, *Le Général Guisan*, 529.

14. Bernard Barbey, *PC du Général*, 156.

15. Edgar Bonjour, *Neutralité*, vol. V, 79–106.

16. Marcel Pilet-Golaz, *Aperçu*, Annex 30–31.

17. Edgar Bonjour, *Neutralité*, vol. VI, 79–106.

18. Willi Gautschi, *Le Général Guisan*, 639ff.

19. Willi Gautschi, *Le Général Guisan*, 644–45; Dr. Francis Lang, *Mémoires d'un Médecin de Campagne*, 73–79, 211–29; and Edgar Bonjour, *Neutralité,* vol. V, 86. Cites Roger Masson.

Chapter Twenty

Beginning of the End

THE MILITARY SITUATION

In 1942, the battles of El Alamein and Coral Sea, the Soviet resistance at Stalingrad, and the Allied landing in North Africa marked "the end of the beginning," to use Churchill's phrase. Allied successes continued on all fronts in 1943; the year 1944 sounded the beginning of the end for the armies of the Third Reich and Japan.

Compared with 1940 and its immediate threats, after the serious alert of 1943 Switzerland underwent a quieter period from a military point of view. The army, while keeping guard at the borders, had settled in the redoubt. With its fortifications, armaments, troop training, and its very concept, the redoubt served for a generation as the symbol of fidelity and independence for some and, for others, Switzerland's turning in on itself. The army was to come out of the redoubt in the summer of 1944 after the Allied landings in Normandy and Provence, the methodical conquest of the Italian peninsula, and the massive unleashing of the Soviet armies in the east all brought the war closer to Switzerland's borders.

In Italy, Mussolini was placed in a minority position in government on July 25, 1943 by the Grand Council of Fascism. King Victor Emmanuel III had him arrested and entrusted the government to Marshal Pietro Badoglio. Badoglio affirmed his desire to continue the struggle on the side of the Reich and then negotiated an armistice with the Allies, who occupied the south of Italy, where the royal government had taken refuge. In the north, the Germans disarmed the Italian troops and extended their support to the Italian Social Republic, which Mussolini, whom they had liberated, pretended to govern under their control with the last of the black-shirted fanatics. But the Allied advance northward was slow. The Swiss Federal Council did not recognize the neofascist government and continued its official relations with the Royal Government of Italy.[1] Pilet summed up the Italian situation in a February 10, 1944 letter to Stampfli: "I would be the first to rejoice in the excellent relations we could have with our neighbor to the south. But we obviously cannot forget Italy's political situation at this time: it is not to be confused either with the Badoglio government—if it really is a government—or with the Mussolini government, which is more apparent than real. Hence, we must confine ourselves to generalities without expressing our views and avoid stirring up publicity."[2]

This did not preclude de facto relations, especially economic relations, with the neighboring areas in northern Italy occupied by the German army with the dispatch of a plenipotentiary delegate to see to the protection of Swiss citizens and interests. The Swiss consul in Milan urged prudence in the more than unofficial assistance rendered by the Italian-speaking canton of Ticino to the partisans at Ossola, which was the subject of vehement protests by the neofascists, who also denounced the partiality of the Swiss press.

As we have seen, Renata Broggini recalled these idealistic uprisings, especially the ephemeral Republic of Ossola.[3] A fascist counterattack cut off its brief independence. When the partisans were tracked down, many crossed the Swiss border under the protection of Swiss troops, who kept their pursuers at bay. The influx of all types of fugitives—fascists, antifascists, and military internees—forced Switzerland to guard its borders more closely and caused numerous problems in the reception and lodging of refugees. However, no threat of invasion was now conceivable on this southern front.

It was a different story in the west, where the fighting was coming dangerously close to the Swiss border. It could be breached either by accident or by troops seeking refuge, as with the Bourbaki army in 1871 or General Daille's army corps in 1940, or by operational calculations, infringing Swiss neutrality to take the enemy in the rear. Thus, in November 1944 Stalin, calling the Swiss "pigs," proposed to Roosevelt and Churchill an invasion of Switzerland in order to continue fighting at the rear of the German Siegfried line. The idea does not appear to have been the subject of any special study. In December, the day before a Moscow meeting, Churchill gave Foreign Minister Anthony Eden a mandate to defend Switzerland's honor and to attest that "Of all the neutrals, Switzerland has the greatest right to distinction."[4]

But it is clear that blocking the Rhine line would have given either of the belligerents the idea of a more or less wide detour through Swiss territory. In spite of obvious logistical problems, the Allies could have tried it both to save their forces and to penetrate more quickly into southern Germany and arrive there before the Soviet armies. Would the Swiss have put up a savage resistance when such an attack would have placed Switzerland in the camp of the Third Reich, then in desperate straits? Hans Senn brings out the dilemma. Some soldiers in Aargau, a canton bordering on Germany, wondered what they would do if the Allies crossed the border, and concluded that "there would be no question of firing; we should rather hoist the white flag." But Hitler, acting impulsively and desperately, as at the Battle of the Bulge, could have imagined a reverse operation.[5]

A JURISDICTIONAL CONFLICT BETWEEN THE GENERAL AND THE FEDERAL COUNCIL

In addition to the risk of a deliberate invasion, Switzerland also had to be prepared for some local incursions, whether by ignorance of the map or from the sudden influx of troops that had been surrounded and were requesting internment. Foreseeing these possibilities, General Guisan had been soliciting the Federal Council since the Allied landing in Normandy in June 1944 for a remobilization of the border guard, the air force, and the antiaircraft service. Kobelt, the head of the Military Department, supported the idea. However, the government contented itself with a partial reinforcement of troops, as no obvious threat had materialized. The struggle against the Allied landing and the aggressiveness of the Soviet troops were taking up all the German forces. Further, it was necessary to avoid dramatizing the situation in the eyes of public opinion, as well as causing economic problems which would follow an excessive call-up.

A heated controversy followed on the interpretation of Article 210 of the Military Law: "When the general requests the call-up of supplementary troops, the Federal Council orders it and carries it out." Did this article confer an obligation on the government? Was the government to be subordinated to a decision of the commander in chief? It might be granted that the right of mobilization be delegated to him under given circumstances. However, to maintain that a proposal from the general had the force of an order to the government would have detracted from the fundamental subordination of the military. A compromise was achieved: a partial mobilization that would suffice for the moment. Was not Guisan in the same situation as General Herzog in 1871 when he had only 20,000 troops, and the Federal Council's refusal to mobilize enough troops to intern 87,000 French forced him to resort to mobilizing the cantonal contingents?[6]

After the landings in Normandy, the rapid progress of General Eisenhower's armies across France and the Franco-American landing of August 15 in Provence, the First French Army of General de Lattre de Tassigny proceeded up the valley of the Rhône River and was soon skirting the Jura. General Guisan then obtained from the Federal Council a more substantial remobilization. The army order for the redoubt had been withdrawn, and five divisions went to reinforce the border guards or join the three light brigades to form a mobile reserve in French Switzerland. Actually, this was only a relative mobilization because, although antitank weapons were reinforced, the tanks themselves were nonexistent and the army's mobility scarcely exceeded the level of 1939. The scenario and pace of maneuvers in bygone years was restored: there were long columns of infantry and teams of horses on the roads; the cavalry patrolled in the forests and the general staff officers rode over the harvested fields like a "ride into glory," as in a painting by Detaille. "The general is aware of this," noted Barbey, "and he accepts it."[7]

Although Guisan did not receive authorization from Kobelt to accept an invitation from General de Lattre to a "military lunch" at the border by Neuchâtel, there was nevertheless permanent contact between the two generals, which made it possible to avoid all border incidents of any importance. In the final phase of the war, Guisan even obtained from General de Lattre a modification of an operational plan on Ulm in order to adhere to a request of the Swiss commander who, for Switzerland's security, wanted to see the remaining pockets of German resistance north of the Rhine eliminated. De Lattre granted the request most unofficially at the insistence of Colonel Guisan, the general's son, who had been assigned to the French general as a liaison officer.[8]

Disturbed by the advance of the Soviet troops in the east and the difficulties of the Allies in the west, Guisan wrote on January 22, 1945 to the chief of the general staff that, "The extent and initial successes of the Russian offensive on the eastern front compel us to contemplate the situation that would arise if the Soviet forces were to conquer still more areas toward the center of Europe, and where their penetration as far as Bavaria and the Tyrol, for example—that is, beyond the demarcation line set by the Allies for the occupation of Germany—would constitute a direct threat to our territory." The measures to be taken needed to be studied. An operational exercise was to be set for the beginning of April.[9]

The Allied advance resumed, meeting the Soviet troops at Torgau on the Elbe on April 25, 1945. Reaching Bavaria and the Vorarlberg, the Allies ensured respect by the Soviet armies for the demarcation line and eliminated the disturbing possibility of Soviet troops approaching the Swiss borders. However, without the presence and determination of the western armies, especially the Americans, there would have been considerable danger that the Soviet steamroller, with obvious numerical superiority and aided by resistance organizations in the liberated countries, would go all the way to the Atlantic coast, liquidating the reactionary Swiss redoubt on the way.

DIPLOMATIC TENSION WITH FRANCE

Although with the exception of some minute, nearly domestic incidents, the relations between the Swiss command and the First French Army were positive, the same cannot be said for the situation between the two governments. Certainly, at the beginning, the Vichy regime benefitted in Switzerland (as in France, whatever may have been said later) from a favorable image in the catastrophe that had stricken the neighboring country. "Our relations with France are those of assistance and pity," Pilet stated in May 1942 to the Foreign Affairs Committee of the National Council. The venerable Marshal Pétain, who "had given France the gift of his person," wore the halo of his military prestige. He had been the victor at Verdun, who in 1917, with an authority both firm and humane, had reestablished confidence in the French army. At least as much as the impetuous Marshal Foch, Pétain had gained the victory with the aid of the Americans. He had expressed his esteem for Switzerland on many occasions, notably while visiting the maneuvers of the Swiss First Division in 1937. The French National Assembly, under circumstances that were certainly exceptional but after all legitimate, had conferred full powers on him, by a strong majority, to govern France in the most dramatic of conditions. The regime of the Third Republic, already strongly criticized from the top of the Alps, was looked down upon in Switzerland as it was in France, because of the defeat for which it was blamed. The authoritarian regime that took power in Vichy did not appear to inspire demagogic fantasies in our neighbor. It was rather a return to the traditional patriotic order. "Family, fatherland, work," conservative and corporatist, initially struck a more paternalistic than dictatorial tone. Pétain surrounded himself with mediocre politicians of varying allegiances but also with competent senior officials and technicians, academics, generals, and admirals. Certainly, a minority of Frenchmen, after the manner of Doriot or Déat, writers and politicians, desired an ideological, political, and military alignment with Germany. But a majority saw the Marshal's regime as the only way to get through a dangerous period in relative freedom, while awaiting in enforced neutrality the return to independence with the defeat of the Third Reich. Finally others, who grew in numbers as the pressure from the occupying power grew, fought in the resistance while the Vichy police were busy persecuting the Jews and the opponents of the regime. Pétain himself was divided: "I have no particular reason to like the Germans," he stated to Walter Stucki, the Swiss minister, in

January 1942. "They are and will remain our hereditary enemies. But I must frankly admit that by fighting Russia Hitler has protected all Europe, therefore including France, from an immense danger." The collaboration Pétain was hoping for did not bear fruit, as he recognized. "Germany is imposing insupportable burdens." "With collaboration, an unfortunate and dangerous stagnation is prolonged and I see no possibility of changing anything."[10]

This did not prevent Switzerland, thanks to the exceptional effectiveness of Minister Stucki, from maintaining positive relations with the Vichy regime as long as the latter was free to govern unoccupied France. He intervened for the continuance of trade relations, the free circulation of persons, the exchange of refugees and internees, the protection of Swiss residents in France, and especially for the Jews, victims since 1941 of a rigorous segregation law. In this connection, we need to recall the "window" which the Germans, to Hitler's great annoyance, had left open between Geneva and Chamonix, through which so much authorized or prohibited merchandise passed—weapons, money, refugees, intelligence agents, and resistance fighters—with the complicity of the customs officials and the police. The German inspector general of customs resigned himself to the "Swiss hole." No matter how many French customs officials there were, there was no way of preventing the passage through the "green border." Hans Thalberg, later Austria's ambassador in Bern, who took advantage of this passage, expressed his gratitude: "I cannot keep silent about the importance of that fissure in the encirclement of Switzerland. The 'hole' at Geneva played its role in the course of the war. Hitler's irritation that he did not think of plugging it in time is perfectly justified."[11]

But the return of Laval to power in 1942, after the interlude of Flandin and then Darlan, and especially the occupation of all French territory in November 1942 following the Anglo-American landing in North Africa, led the situation to deteriorate seriously. The Vichy government's sovereignty became pure fiction, and Marshal Pétain was reduced to the role of a hostage, stripped of the last bit of authority, even the right to protest. The Third Reich imposed its law on the government, administration, and police, which were too often complaisant, forcing more than 600,000 French into forced labor in Germany, deporting tens of thousands of Jews toward the death camps, and cooperating with the SS and the collaborationist French "Milice" in repressing an increasingly combative resistance. The Swiss Legation in Vichy was reduced to giving information, to timely humanitarian and problematic interventions, and to maintaining a minimum of economic relations, transit trade, and their financial regulation.[12]

Stucki informed the Political Department objectively of the dramatic events the Vichy government was living through. He benefitted from the old marshal's confidence without sharing his politics unconditionally, and he conveyed his solicitude in the tragic circumstances marking the end of the Vichy regime in 1944: German pressure to send a congratulatory telegram to Hitler after the unsuccessful attempt on his life on July 20, 1944, the order to leave Vichy under threat of bombardment, and finally, on August 20, the marshal's arrest and his deportation in stages to Germany. It was to Stucki and the apostolic nuncio, direct witnesses of the event, that Pétain stated that he was no longer capable of exercising his functions as chief of state and that he was a prisoner. This was the tragic end of the fiction of a French state that had exercised only the semblance of sovereignty and that had pursued a massive persecution of the Jews, when it was not taking the initiative for it.

At the instigation of his colleagues in the diplomatic corps, Stucki stayed on in Vichy until September 1944, trying to avoid the depredations of the Germans exasperated by their defeat and bloody settling of scores among the resistance, in which the communists tended to take the upper hand before the arrival of the American troops. Then, with his mission at an end, he returned to Bern with the gratitude of the Vichy population, to assume the position of chief of the foreign affairs division of the Political Department to which he was naturally suited by his expertise, service, and abilities as a statesman.[13]

For some time, Pilet had harbored no illusions about the representative character or the sovereignty of the Vichy government. In September 1942 he remarked at a meeting of the Foreign Affairs Committee that, "France represents the past and probably the future, but not the present. It is not an independent element in international politics." His views were still more critical at the end of 1942, after its total occupation: "France is nothing more than a facade." However, following the example of other neutral states, Portugal, Spain, Turkey, and the Vatican, diplomatic relations were maintained up to the last minute, that is, up to the marshal's abduction. There were two reasons for this: a continuation of the historic tradition and loyalty. One does not abandon one's neighbor in his misfortune. In the same spirit, Switzerland, in spite of the desperate situation of the Third Reich, did not give in to pressure from the Allies, who wanted it to break both de jure and de facto relations with the Reich. It was only on May 8, 1945 that Frölicher was recalled and Köcher had to leave Switzerland.[14]

Also, and this applies just as much to Vichy France as to the dying Third Reich, Switzerland had to ensure vital trade on both sides as long and as much as possible, especially the provisioning and the protection of Swiss expatriates; the defense of foreign interests that had been entrusted to Switzerland; and, of course, the humanitarian vocation of a neutral and neighboring country.

With the disappearance of the fiction of the Vichy government, the full recognition of France under General Charles de Gaulle and the establishment of official relations posed certain problems. It was through the mediation of the British government that Switzerland was able to have occasional and un-official relations with the liberation committee that de Gaulle established in London in June 1940.[15]

The French Committee of National Liberation was established in Algiers on June 3, 1943 under the provisional coleadership of Generals de Gaulle and Giraud as a unique French organization fighting from then on at the side of the Allies. It claimed "to exercise French sovereignty over all territory taken from its power by the enemy and to assure the management and defense of all French interests in the world." This committee, through the mediation of the Swiss consul in Algiers, did not formally request that Switzerland recognize its sovereignty, but it hoped that the Swiss government would relinquish in its favor the representation of French interests in all those countries where the committee was in a position to have its own diplomatic and consular agents accredited. But in fact this request amounted to an indirect recognition of its sovereignty.[16]

Accordingly, the Federal Council declined to promise this. Certainly it was ready to find favorable solutions to concrete problems, but a recognition of sovereignty seemed premature under the circumstances. Neutrality implied the recognition of states according to the status quo immediately preceding the conflict. Thus, Switzerland had maintained diplomatic relations with the governments in exile of Poland, Belgium, the Netherlands, and the govern-ment of Vichy, which, whatever one might think of its policy and the extent of its real sovereignty, derived its powers from a strong majority of the French National Assembly that had been elected in 1936. The United States and Great Britain, like other of the United Nations countries, recognized these de facto jurisdictions, and not the state sovereignty of the committee that their armies had installed. This could appear as legal formalism; however, neutral-ity, to remain credible, must be adhered to, without vacillating in the wind. Pilet expressed this firmly on March 30, 1944 before the Council of States, the upper house of Switzerland's Parliament: the maintenance of strict neu-trality is "a necessary, salutary, and saving inflexibility, an absolute necessity. We must carry it out coolly, reasonably, realistically, and with foresight, con-sideration, and prudence. There should be no impetuous moves in the short run, no sentimental distractions, no balancing of unequal extremes, but the will to follow the right course up to the end."

To these justifications based on law was added an understandable Swiss mistrust, a sentiment that many Frenchmen shared. Pétain had lost a good part of his credibility by the progressive loss of his authority to the occupying power and to collaborationist activists. However, if only because of his con-tinuing good fortune, he still retained some of his reputation in both Switzerland and France. If General de Gaulle benefitted from undoubted prestige for defying fate and believing in France's future, there was an obvious distrust of him by certain elements in the resistance. To a majority of authentic patriots were added a few dubious characters, motivated more by opportunism than conviction or docile and obedient to communist instructions, causing some concern for the future of France. The British and Americans shared this concern. Their relations with de Gaulle—"a disturbing undesirable element," reportedly said by Roosevelt according to Churchill—were not perfectly peaceful. The Soviet Union, on the other hand, granted a status to the committee which was nearly the equivalent of de jure recognition. The obvious reservations of the western Allies only reinforced Pilet's legal prudence, shared also by a portion of the French living in Switzerland. "The shadow of the extreme left hiding behind Gaullism is harmful to the basic options."[17]

It was no less thanks to Britain, which showed its understanding of Switzerland's special conditions, that unofficial relations were established between Switzerland and the Committee of Liberation. The designation of a committee delegate in Bern was laborious: Pilet's obstinate insistence on sustaining the legitimacy of the Vichy regime, beyond any evidence, when it was increasingly being stripped of its sovereignty; the reception, even in July 1944, of a new ambassador from Pétain (the writer Paul Morand), which served as a provocation to the Committee of Liberation and showed excessive legalism that was not adapted to the real situation or the interests of the two countries. But there was also an important financial controversy arising from the clearing account (then in deficit), the mutual freezing of funds and the wrongs done to Swiss citizens residing in France, especially the Jews, as much under the Vichy regime as under the ill-managed excesses of the Liberation.[18]

"Absurd moves," concluded Gérard Lévêque, in strange opposition to the lucidity of Pilet-Golaz and his close collaborators. "Perhaps they were due to the fatigue of extreme tension built up over the years."[19] Pilet can certainly be reproached for his legalistic rigidity, hesitation, and delays in recognizing an inescapable fact, perhaps even his weariness. But can we deny the hostility to Swiss neutrality of certain French leaders, the shock of reciprocal intransigence, and even an element of emotional disturbance creeping into both sides of these diplomatic relations? The diplomacy of a small country garners more respect for its firmness—even though it is rigid—than by accommodating attitudes or haste to move with the fad of the day and celebrate the victor of the moment.

By October 24, 1944 General de Gaulle's provisional government controlled the greater part of French territory. It saw the de jure recognition of its sovereignty by the Allies, but real authority, even in diplomatic affairs, was reserved to the Allied high command. Sweden and Spain followed. The Federal Council recognized the French provisional government on October 31 but was in no hurry to appoint a minister.[20] Paris and Bern, however, continued to exchange legal reticence, protocol sensitivities, ill-humored controversies, halfway measures, and successive refusals to accept the other's appointed representatives, to which was added the Allied pressure on Switzerland to break off all trade relations with the Reich, contrary to the rules of neutrality.[21]

It was only in February 1945 that Professor Carl Burckhardt, former high commissioner of the League of Nations in Danzig and president of the International Committee of the Red Cross, received the French government's agrément as minister in Paris and the Federal Council agreed on the candidacy of Henri Hoppenot, "a faithful follower of de Gaulle from the first and one motivated by sympathy for Switzerland," as ambassador in Bern. "A crisis that had become very difficult was finally solved. Unfortunately for Max Petitpierre, Pilet's successor as head of the Political Department, the troubles were not over," wrote Gérard Lévêque[22]; the controversy in relations with France was not tied exclusively to the rigor of Pilet's policy.

THE ECONOMIC AND SOCIAL SITUATION

In that year of 1944 when the course of the war was precipitated and approached its borders, Switzerland pursued its normal economic activities and the usual course of its political life, alone in the heart of Europe in its armed peace. The net national income increased from 9 billion francs in 1938 to 12.8 billion in 1944. However, in real terms, the cost of living index rose by 50%; it recorded a decline of 11% when direct taxes are taken into account. In real terms, Swiss expenditures passed from 604 million to 1.33 billion francs, a growth from single to double figures, rising from 7% to 15% of the national product. Multiplied by six in nominal terms, military expenditures took up 46% of the federal budget in 1944 and 9% of the national product. The deficit in Switzerland's balance sheet rose from 1.5 to 6.7 billion francs.[23]

Foreign trade, affected by the wartime environment, fell dramatically, to the lowest figures of the war. In nominal terms, imports fell from 1,600 million (18% of GNP) in 1938 to 1,185 million in 1944 (9% of GNP), while exports fell from 1,316 million (15% of GNP) to 1,131 million (7% of GDP). Of imports, 64% came from Axis-controlled countries and 39% of exports were directed there. In 1942, the Axis absorbed 68% of Switzerland's exports and provided 81% of its imports.

The 4.4 million Swiss population remained stationary. Residents of foreign origin fell: they formed 15% of the population in 1910 and 9% in 1930 but only 5% in 1941. Work permits fell from 19,000 to 2,200 between 1938 and 1944. In 1941, Italians, at 95,000, were in the lead, followed by the Germans with 78,000. Unemployment was marginal—statistics gave the figure as 13,000 in all. However, we need to take into account the steep fall in foreign workers, the thousands of unemployed soldiers in the companies designated "surveillance," and an average of 150,000 men under arms. Considering the 50% rise in consumer prices, salaries lost between 6% and 15% of their real value since 1939. Over the same period the tax burden rose from 255 to 403 francs per inhabitant, or 382 francs in real terms, rising from 12% to 14% of national income. However, these difficulties and the full powers of the Federal Council enabled the country to have an equilibrated and stable tax system.

The Wahlen Plan extended grain planting in order to increase the harvest from 200,000 to 300,000 tons and caused the production of indigenous sugar to increase from 8,000 to 20,000 tons. This was not enough, however, to keep consumption at its prewar level, given the sharp drop in food imports. Estimated in nutritive calories, domestic consumption fell 30% from its prewar value. While domestic production and imports were approximately equal before the war, domestic production provided 80% and imports 20% during the conflict. Daily calories per inhabitant fell from 3200 to 2167. Today, a normal ration is considered to be 2500 calories, and the current estimate is 3400 for Switzerland. Based on these estimates, 1944 was far and away the most critical year for Swiss food supplies, yet its neighbors were not any better supplied. There was strict rationing and more progressive taxation. Direct federal taxes on income and wealth increased from 50 million to 431 million francs in four years. The partial compensations for salaries and profits of drafted men, which did not exist in 1914–18 and whose financing served as the basis for old age insurance and price controls, were efforts to provide an equitable division of charges and sacrifices.

These conditions, and the fact that the Swiss had known neither war, bombing, ruin, deportation, concentration camps, nor massive and arbitrary genocide allowed them to count themselves privileged among Europeans. Were they well aware of this? Of course it was not decent to take pride in this, because besides an undoubted will for independence and incontestable resistance, and a diplomacy at once supple and firm even though it had certain partisan intrigues, providence had played an important role. But in this period when the war gave its last gasp among ruins and blood, the awareness of privilege and the expression of recognition were scarcely to be seen, nor that of generous solidarity with a world in disarray. This was especially true because the hegemony of the Soviet army over Central Europe justified the concern many felt and gave encouragement to the extreme left, which was to achieve some electoral successes as soon as the ban was lifted.

It was certainly due to the immediate and durable threat and nearly unanimous cohesion that the Switzerland of 1939–40 did not experience the political and social differences or the divisions and errors that it had gone through between 1914 and 1918, in the face of a less serious external danger. There had not been that committed and passionate antagonism between a French-speaking Switzerland and a German-speaking, Wilhelmine Switzerland that said to Clemenceau: "Paris can forgive, but Lausanne never will!" German-speaking Switzerland—the reports from the Axis intelligence services confirm it—showed, in the vast majority of public opinion and in its press, a more passionate opposition to Nazism than the rational and ironic allergy of the French- and Italian-speaking Swiss.

The war of 1914–18 had aggravated the latent conflict between the working class and the bourgeois social and political "establishment." Wages did not keep up with inflation. Mobilized soldiers did not receive compensation for their lost wages and had to dip into savings or seek public assistance. In his Swiss refuge, Lenin pondered and distributed his program of "war against war," universal revolution, and dictatorship of the proletariat. Without being unconditional partisans, some Swiss socialist leaders participated in the meetings in Zimmerwald and Kiental where the foundations were laid for the communist international and the Soviet revolution was prepared. In addition, some, even among the Allied general staffs, feared that the general strike unleashed in Switzerland on November 11, 1918 was the beginning, in the disorders of Central Europe, of a Bolshevik revolution and contemplated military intervention. Willi Gautschi minimizes this intention in his work on the strike of 1918, but Edgar Bonjour, on the basis of diplomatic reports, points up the concern of the Allied governments and the possibility of such an action.[24]

The situation was different from 1939 to 1945. Faced with the consequences of the economic crisis and the rise of Hitlerism, labor and management substituted a "labor peace" for the class struggle by the introduction of collective bargaining agreements. Beginning in 1935, the Socialist Party had ceased its anti-militarism on principle and rallied to the country's defense. During mobilization, the institution *Armée et Foyer* (Army and Home), founded in 1939 by General Guisan and under the supervision of the adjutant general, worked to help maintain troop morale, to fortify patriotic feelings, and to bring the army closer to the population. It organized lectures on national problems where union leaders and management joined together with officers and politicians.[25] In this way, a spirit of concord developed that contributed to the country's cohesion during the war and allowed the important economic, technical, and social changes of the postwar period to take place without too many partisan controversies.

André Lasserre takes the temperature of Swiss morale in *La Suisse des années sombres* [Switzerland in the Somber Years] and notes in particular that people learned from experience that the army was not the instrument of one class, but the concern of all the people, and that a more humane atmosphere had grown up between officers and men.[26] Rigid formalism, more particularly Germanic, generally gave way to pragmatic, effective, and more flexible instruction. Certainly, morale could vary from one company to another according to the personality of the commanders. Without defeatism and depression taking over, one could understand that at the end of five years of border guarding, lassitude and the monotonous problem of lying fallow could result. As in the novel by Dino Buzzati, many Swiss lived through their own *Tartar Desert*, the unsettling and vain waiting for the announced enemy. The triumphant advance of the Soviet legions under the Zhukovs and the Malinovskis could give certain frustrated idealists the tragic illusion that soon "our tomorrows will sing," but many others became justifiably disturbed.

However, Lasserre notes that most of the atmosphere in public opinion remains gray in the absence of motivation "for something great," to happen, and in the passivity born of someone else's war, which drowns the breath of great ideas in administrative necessities. In short, it was the congenital sluggishness of the Swiss, little concerned as they were with the international scene, caring little for the fate of others, cultivating their comfortable boredom and their nostalgia for impossible hopes in the austere existential colloquia with heads bent over our malaise.

But this sluggishness was far from being unanimous. Freed from this anxious waiting and the military service that interrupted the continuity of their work or studies, many young people in particular were now able to devote themselves full time to their work, career, and family. This was all the more true that, overthrowing pessimistic predictions and the elaboration of the Zipfel Plan that opened up job opportunities, an unprecedented period of expansion and technical revolution of growth and full employment for western countries and Switzerland in particular now began. The trials of the mobilization period, with its constraints, reinforced the country's cohesion, developed its sense of social interdependence, and inculcated a spirit of service.

NOTES

1. Marcel Pilet-Golaz, *Aperçu*, 419 [French text].
2. *Documents Diplomatiques*, vol. 15, 28–29, 32–33, 48–49, 219–20, 238–39, 478–80, 651–53, 657– 61.

3. Renata Broggini, *Terra d'Asilo. I Refugiati Italiani in Svizzera 1943–1945* (Lugano, 1993), 325–30.

4. Churchill to Eden, 3 December 1944, quoted in Winston Churchill, *The Second World War*, vol. VI *Triumph and Tragedy*, 712.

5. Hans Senn, "Die Armee von Versailles Vertrag bis Beute," in *Revue d'Histoire Militaire* (1988), 65, 254, 360–65; and Willi Gautschi, *Le Général Guisan*, 610.

6. Louis Edouard Roulet, "Un certain 6 Juin 1944 en Suisse," in *Festschrift Walther Hofer* (Bern and Stuttgart), 1980, 483–94; Bernard Barbey, *PC du Général*, 211–27; Edgar Bonjour, *Neutralité*, vol. V, 132–38; Hans Rudolf Kurz, *Histoire de l'Armée Suisse*, 33–34; Hans Senn, *Dissuasionsstrategie, Etat-Major VII*, 427–33, 438–39; and Marcel Pilet-Golaz, *Aperçu*, Annex, 422–24 [French text].

7. Bernard Barbey, *PC du Général*, 232.

8. Willi Gautschi, *Le Général Guisan*, 610–17; and Hans Senn, *Dissuasionsstrategie*, 420–23.

9. Hans Senn, *Dissuasionsstrategie*, 435–38.

10. Edgar Bonjour, *Neutralité*, vol. V, 295.

11. Klaus Urner, *Die Schweiz muss noch Geschluckt Werden*, 127–30.

12. Oscar Gauye, "La Crise Politique de Novembre-Décembre 1943 à Vichy," in *Cinq Siècles de Relations Franco–Suisses* (Neuchâtel: 1984, Hommage à Ls. Ed. Roulet) 281–92.

13. *Documents Diplomatiques*, vol. 15, 236–37, 240–41; and Edgar Bonjour, *Neutralité*, vol. V, 295–330.

14. *Documents Diplomatiques*, vol. 15, 419, 610–11.

15. Gérard Lévêque, *La Suisse et la France Gaulliste 1943–1945* (Geneva, 1979), 2–4.

16. Gérard Lévêque, *La Suisse*, 5.

17. *Documents Diplomatiques*, vol. 15, 778–81.

18. *Documents Diplomatiques*, vol. 15, 672–73; and Gérard Lévêque, *La Suisse*, 124–29.

19. Gérard Lévêque, *La Suisse*, 227–30.

20. Gérard Lévêque, *La Suisse*, 135–43.

21. Gérard Lévêque, *La Suisse*, 144–54.

22. Gérard Lévêque, *La Suisse*, 186–92.

23. These and the following figures were taken from the *Annuaire Statistique de la Suisse 1950* and from Jakob Tanner, *Bundeshalt, Währung und Kriegswirtschaft, Eine Finanzsoziologische Analyse der Schweiz Zwischen 1938 und 1953* (Zurich, 1986).

24. Willi Gautschi, *Der Landesstreik 1918* (Zurich, 1968), 339–40; and Edgar Bonjour, *Neutralität*, vol. II, 281–92.

25. Willi Gautschi, *Le Général Guisan*, 318–30.

26. André Lasserre, *La Suisse des Années Sombres*, 287–342, especially 328.

Chapter Twenty-One

Relations with the USSR

On June 2, 1944, Pilet gave an extensive report on the overall situation to Parliament's Foreign Affairs Committee, discussing first the military state of affairs.[1] Germany was resisting tenaciously, and its air force was far from being annihilated. The British and Americans had finally understood that their bombing raids were not going to win the war and they would have to fight on the ground, "otherwise the war would last a very long time, while ruins and misery piled up in Europe." This explained the hardening of the conflict. Where and when would the Allies land? "Let us leave that to the clairvoyants and the ignorant, which are sometimes one and the same; even some professors have not succeeded."

Allied pressure on the neutrals increased and sometimes took the form of a strong hand, as in the case of chrome exports to Germany from Turkey which were completely blocked, as well as tungsten from Spain and ball bearings from Sweden. In Portugal, the Azores were occupied with no prior notice.

"A general nervousness holds sway in every country. Dangerous reactions could come out of it at any moment. A wave of pessimism is sweeping through Europe. There is a feeling that the happiness and prosperity of this continent are at an end and that prosperity is passing elsewhere."

"Russia will make its influence felt in Europe and Asia, but its goals are still a mystery. The Anglo-Saxons are just as unaware of these goals, as they say they are convinced that the alliance with the USSR will stay together until the Germans are defeated."

"And Switzerland's situation? From the diplomatic viewpoint, it is certainly not good. The country is exposed to changing and threatening situations, all the more because it is no longer possible to talk reasonably with others, who have become susceptible and nervous."

Then Pilet brought up the difficulties with commercial exchanges. "We are stuck between the blockade and the counterblockade, in which the Allies are being as hard as the Germans, the Foreign Office always being more understanding than the State Department."

"Above all," Pilet cautioned, "stay away from illusions about economic obstacles, military dangers, or the difficulties of our position; we dare not allow ourselves a state of euphoria."

"Let us not forget that there is no common thought among the belligerents for the postwar world. We must not attach ourselves to either of them, and we should do the work of neither one nor the other. The general peace will allow us to reconstruct, but we must be reserved without, however, exposing ourselves to reproach for being too negative or not understanding what is happening. . . . Our neutrality must be whole and sincere."

The report of this session did not allude to relations with the Soviet Union, which were not in the front rank of issues faced by the head of the Political Department at that time. Pilet explained why at the September 12, 1944 meeting of the same parliamentary committee. If he spoke but little about relations with the USSR, "it was because some tasks have to be carried out in the silence of the chanceries."[2]

At that time, despite the seriousness of the situation, the walls of the Federal Palace already had ears.

Pilet did not discuss his state of mind, and if he had, he would rarely have entrusted it to paper. This is frustrating for historians who must make do with official texts or reports of conversations that often became distorted and reinterpreted. However, the following general reflection of July 16, 1943 is found among his papers:[3]

"My God, what a cataclysm! What misery we have to look forward to, without counting the epidemics that will probably come. Our poor Europe is being ruined. Every day and night there are air raids on France, Belgium, the Netherlands, the Ruhr, and especially Italy, after the conquest of North Africa by the United Nations. Sicily is being hammered mercilessly, and so is Sardinia. Naples and the southern part of the boot are not much better off. All that beauty and those treasures destroyed. . . . A whole civilization is collapsing— that's the word—and it's going to disappear. What madness! Why? They claim it's to make people happier and assure their future! What irony! The Germans would be happy to make peace, but on conditions that would be unacceptable. However, they are hated everywhere. The British have some old scores to settle with them and the Americans—who seemed to have been afraid—are showing themselves merciless. However, our neighbors to the north have some great qualities: they work hard; they are systematic, disciplined, and courageous. It is their desire to *dominate* that is bringing them down: 'the master race.' They do not understand that real collaboration is based on consent. If they could have been more moderate and done without fighting, they would have become the first among European peoples. The Anglo-Saxons have been more adroit: their dominions are attached to them. As for the Russians, this is the great mystery: are they communists or slaves? Clearly they are both. What will they do to us if they achieve a definitive victory? Distress at first and them collectivism."

Pilet's concern was genuine and his pessimism justified. But in spite of that, for its survival Switzerland had to consider the increasing force of Soviet power, which for half a century was to divide with the United States the leadership of the world in the tragic polarization of the Cold War.

The question of resuming diplomatic relations between the Soviet Union and Switzerland was difficult for both sides to negotiate, without there being cause for criticism as to the course of the negotiations themselves. Edgar Bonjour claims to see a failure to foresee events, ill will, and deliberate delaying tactics by Pilet.[4] Yet between Switzerland and the Soviet government there was a serious historical controversy to overcome: a series of disagreements, starting with the basic hostility of the majority of the Swiss people both to communist ideology and especially to its brutal, repressive, and totalitarian application, just as a mistrust of this small, "reactionary" country held sway in the Kremlin, diligently supported by the direct contact of a handful of Swiss communists.

Certainly the Soviet Union could have been grateful to Switzerland, which in its time had given asylum in its mountains to so many Russian rebels and revolutionaries, from Bakunin to Trotsky, Zinoviev, Radek, and especially to Lenin himself. From 1915 to 1916 he set up the foundations of International Communism and the Russian Revolution of 1917 in the rustic atmosphere of Zimmerwald and Kiental.

Over time, however, various events eroded relations on both sides. In May 1918 the Soviet government established an unofficial delegation led by Jan Berzin who obviously, and in spite of warnings from the Federal Council, added propaganda activities to his diplomatic mission, which made Switzerland a center of communist agitation in Western Europe. When the involvement of the Soviet delegation with some leaders of the general strike of November 11 was established, Berzin and his accomplices had to be conducted to the border. The Swiss mission in St. Petersburg, robbed of its archives, followed the same road in the opposite direction.[5]

An attempt to resume unofficial relations was cut off by the murder in Lausanne in 1923 of Worowski, the Soviet observer to the Straits Conference. The assassin, Conradi, a Swiss who had returned from Russia after his wanderings for the revolution, was acquitted by a minority at the criminal court in Lausanne. Any resumption of relations was thus excluded for a long time. The Federal Council obstinately refused de jure recognition of the USSR despite the resumption of commercial relations.

In September 1934 the Federal Council opposed the admission of the USSR to the League of Nations, resisting pressure from France, England, and Italy. In the Federal Council's delegation for foreign affairs, contrary to William Rappard who, reasonably, recommended abstention, Pilet intervened for rejection, noting that the League of Nations had failed in everything it had undertaken. It was no more than the instrument of the great powers, whose démarche to the Federal Council on the subject was most unpleasant.[6]

In an address to the General Assembly of the League of Nations on September 17, 1934, which had wide international repercussions, Swiss Foreign Minister Giuseppe Motta denounced communism in the Soviet Union as "contrary to all our ideas about religion, morality, the social structure, politics, and economics." Had not Lenin called the League an "association of bandits?" However, the die was cast, but Switzerland had the duty to warn against "Geneva becoming the seat of destructive propaganda." Motta added: "Soviet ideology and practices have offended the most respectable of opinions. This ideology is an agent of public disorder and social disintegration. It has trampled underfoot the highest aspirations of Christian consciences and even those of other religious doctrines." Despite this, only Portugal and the Netherlands followed the Swiss example.[7]

In principle, these sentiments certainly merited respect. They were undoubtedly shared by the majority of Swiss and justified by the Soviet regime's bloody brutality, the repressions, deportations, and summary executions. However, it must be granted that the concert of powers had never had the purity of an angelic choir, and the great powers often gave preference to their short-term interests, known as "reasons of state," over due respect for the law. Relations between states being necessary for life in common, it was not possible to have moral, ideological, or religious criteria prevail in the absolute. And was it not the mission of a neutral country, without being silent about its opinions but also without isolating itself in its claim to virtue, to maintain diplomatic relations with all states, which could serve world peace? Motta's speech of 1934 went against the principle of universality of the League of Nations. Although it deserved the respect due to strongly held convictions, the speech could have weakened the credibility of our neutrality giving it a differential character, which would weigh heavily on our relations with the Soviet Union to the extent that Motta took pains to use equally severe language with respect to the dictatorships near Switzerland.

Other events aggravated the controversy. The Ribbentrop-Molotov Pact of 1939, an apparently paradoxical alliance between the communist and national

Socialist ideologies, and the Soviet aggression against Finland did not promote a favorable climate of opinion in Switzerland toward the USSR, even among the Swiss left in which there was a traditional indulgence, even an unspoken admiration, for the communist revolution. As Switzerland's return to full neutrality was recognized by the League during the European tensions of 1938 so that it no longer participated in the League's sanctions, it abstained in 1939 from the vote that excluded the USSR following the war against Finland.[8] But the Federal Council, before Parliament, approved the decision and publicly stigmatized the aggression that the Swiss people condemned unanimously.

Meanwhile, in spite of everything, attempts at rapprochement at the level of commercial relations were sketched out between the representatives in Berlin, and then, on Russian invitation, in Moscow.[9] An agreement was reached in March 1941. The German aggression of that June made these efforts inoperative for practical reasons, and in addition the Federal Council hastened to block Soviet funds deposited in Switzerland, although only temporarily. However, the passage of the Soviet Union to the Allied camp and the strength of Soviet resistance after the rapid progress of the Germans led to reconsideration of the idea of resuming diplomatic relations. Up to then, Pilet had opposed the move; the Soviet alliance with the Axis was added to all the previous controversies. But with the breakup of that alliance and with Russia passing to the democratic camp, at least militarily, and proclaiming in May 1943 that it would stop its international propaganda from the Comintern, the ideological obstacles weakened, and some in Parliament and certain economic circles began to recommend full diplomatic recognition.

Pilet noted his reservations on the matter. He estimated, as he had often stated, that during wartime, neutrality imposed maintenance of the status quo in diplomatic relations: thus, some countries that had momentarily disappeared from the map kept their representation in Bern. And in the same way as the recognition of a state taken out of the war, a change of relations with the USSR could appear to the Axis as an exception to neutrality, a tilt toward their Soviet adversary. But with the progress of the Soviet armies, economic and political pressure mounted for resuming relations.

On March 29, 1944, Pilet, in replying to a motion of the Socialist Reinhard, appeared to bend the Federal Council's position.[10] The 1941 trade agreement remained in force, even though total trade had declined from 64 million francs in 1941 to zero, due to transportation difficulties. Pilet added that: "Switzerland, traditionally neutral, with a neutrality that is neither conditional nor directed, but general and shining . . . has only one desire: to maintain correct and, if possible, trusting relations with all nations: correct, that is to say, in conformity with the law of nations, with proven international customs, inspired by respect for independence and domestic autonomy, led by the desire to settle issues that arise equitably, realistically and with good sense and proportion, and by no means with force of any kind, to take on conflicts to try to resolve them and not cut them off."

With these reservations, which could have constituted a reference to the recent past of Soviet policy, Pilet stated he was ready to renew diplomatic relations with the Soviet Union, because there could not be true and lasting peace for the continent without Russia's cooperation. But he resumed the argument—which as it happened was debatable—of the status quo ante (1939) which he believed was tied to the credibility of neutrality. "Diplomatic relations as we understand them . . . are the preservation of the de facto relations we must first develop so that they become thereafter their safeguards." The Swiss people's feelings of hostility to Communism further required only steady and prudent progress.

If the Federal Council could not accept the imperative character of the Reinhard motion, it did consider it as a postulate, a vow to be pursued "with diligence and vigilance." It was further in the development of those "relations in fact" that he had encouraged and would incite the Swiss representatives in Ankara, Sofia, Teheran, and Rome between 1942 and 1944 to make contact with Soviet diplomats. Pilet wrote to the minister in Rome in 1944 that, "If Swiss diplomats were to encounter Soviet diplomats in third party locations, we would not wish them to avoid contact. On the contrary, we would prefer that they seek as much as possible to have contacts without being obliged to compromise themselves, and that, far from believing that they should behave coldly, they should make efforts to maintain correct and courteous relations with them. Further, there would be nothing against establishing contact with the Soviet intelligence services in the trade areas, and certain administrative questions could be handled by notes verbales, if that should turn out to be possible and judicious."[11]

Pilet pushed these measures further, notably in London with the support of diplomats at the Foreign Office. In March 1944, when Thurnheer, the chief of legation in Great Britain, was ill, he sent one of his close collaborators, Clemente Rezzonico, who was familiar with conditions in Britain, to London on reconnaissance. Rezzonico had occasion, by the intermediary of a French diplomat, to meet Soviet Ambassador Lebedeff, who had been authorized by Moscow to do so. The Swiss diplomat evoked the neutrality policy, its services, its contributions to peace, and its difficulties, alluding to Reinhard's intervention in Parliament and expressing the view that it would lead to progress in relations. Lebedeff reportedly asked sarcastically if Switzerland was expecting the Soviet army to reach its borders.[12]

The illnesses, first of Minister Thurnheer, then of his successor Paul Rüegger, unfortunately delayed the moves in London. Rüegger, a brilliant diplomat who specialized in international law, had been expelled from the legation in Rome on the demand of Mussolini, who reproached his lack of enthusiasm.[13] But Pilet, citing Rüegger's health, requested Minister Bruggman in Washington on June 1 to resume his personal relations with the Soviet ambassador to the American government, "and in confidence, to exchange views on future relations between Russia and Switzerland."[14] At that time, an exploration would in practice be "reduced to a spectacular gesture whose consequences could be most disagreeable, if not worse."

Very likely Pilet meant the hostile reactions that could not fail to be expressed in Switzerland. "But since the situation abroad is more open, it will be easier. I am personally convinced that diplomatic relations with the Soviets will be necessary and useful when hostilities come to an end." Of course diplomatic relations must not be confused with adopting Communism. "While waiting: contacts of a preparatory nature, but discreet, are completely in conformity with my intentions."

After the unfortunate interregnum at the Swiss Legation in London, Rüegger returned to his post, equipped with instructions dated July 5 that looked to a resumption of diplomatic relations with the USSR. Meanwhile in Switzerland, the supporters of resumption (the Socialist left and businessmen) were losing patience. National Councilor Reinhard resumed his crusade, and his March speech was transmitted to Molotov by Léon Nicole, head of the extreme left in Geneva.[15] The inevitable Hausamann participated in the discussion and suggested the mediation of Eduard Beneš, the former president of Czechoslovakia who was living in London but who enjoyed a privileged relationship with the Kremlin.

Finally on September 7, Soviet Ambassador Gusev[16] received Rüegger in London. He listened carefully to the Swiss emissary but could not give him a reply since he had to refer the matter to his government. He requested a written memorandum from Rüegger, declining for the moment to see him again without authorization from Moscow.

Five days later, Pilet presented a report on the general situation to the Foreign Affairs Committee of the National Council, which brought out the need for vigilance at the border, the prudent exercise of the right of asylum, and the need of substantial help for people affected by the war. "The Confederation of course will do its part in money and in kind." Then he brought up diplomatic relations:[17]

"Our relations with England are good as far as may be judged, which does not mean that the English will forget their interests to defend ours. . . . The Americans know us less well. They are more direct and perhaps more brutal in their methods, as we have seen in our economic relations; but they will do nothing to annoy us or harm us unless they absolutely have to. They will help us if we need it. The arrest of Marshal Pétain has led us to give up our representation in Vichy. We have exchanged delegations with the French authorities in view of the liberation. We must keep our reserve and our dignity and avoid being carried away by passion when dealing with a Germany of whose defeat we are convinced."

Concerning relations with the Soviet Union, on which he had said little up to then due to the conversations then under way, Pilet noted a report of July 21 from the consul general in New York to the effect that "Moscow would be happy to resume trade relations with Switzerland." Before his departure for London, Minister Rüegger was given very precise instructions on the contacts he was to have with representatives of the USSR, one of the most important points of the mission he would be fulfilling in London. His instructions were based primarily on the principles of Switzerland's desire to first resume normal relations with the USSR within a short time after the resumption of communications and second, the abstention of each country from any interference in the internal affairs of the other.

The second point would appear to go without saying in relations between sovereign countries, but not necessarily for the USSR; Edgar Bonjour, however, would have preferred to take it out "in order not to hold up the procedures."[18]

Pilet also mentioned the telegrams of August 16 and 29 and September 8 from the Swiss Legation in London, reporting on the first contacts. "We will continue to pursue this discussion diligently, but with all vigilance required."

At the end of September, Rüegger, with the collaboration of British diplomats, wrote the memorandum the Soviet ambassador had requested and forwarded it to Pilet, who submitted it to the Federal Council. The latter approved it with some minor modifications, and Rüegger put it in the Soviet ambassador's hands on October 13.

The text, written in English,[19] referred to Pilet's explanation to the National Council on March 29, expressing the desire of the government and Parliament, in conformity with Switzerland's democratic traditions. It contained the following points:

1. Switzerland sincerely desires to maintain normal relations, based on the rules of law and international custom, with all the powers. It regrets the circumstances that have interrupted their course and hopes for the resumption of normal relations with the USSR.
2. It believes that relations between the two countries can be established on a clear basis that will enable the development of mutual understanding. The former problems and those that remain can be resolved in friendship and equity.

3. Technical relations (postal service, railroads, telephone) have not been interrupted, to the extent that the war allowed. The establishment of normal diplomatic relations will enable the development of these relations in the interest of our economies.
4. Existing relations will undoubtedly be improved if the Swiss administration and its consular agents can exercise their functions, officially and unofficially, in the areas occupied by the Soviet Union, in favor of Swiss interests or the interests of the powers that have entrusted their representation to Switzerland, with the consent of these powers.
5. The Swiss government hopes that relations between the two countries will develop favorably and that the resumption of diplomatic relations by mutual consent can be accomplished as soon as possible after the reopening of communications and transport between Switzerland and the Allies. Diplomatic relations being established on the basis of mutual recognition of existing legislation in the two countries will allow Switzerland to participate at the side of the USSR in the problems of reconstruction and the organization of the world of tomorrow by bringing to it the cooperation of a neutral country in its vocation of universal relations.

In deploring this document, Bonjour noted that it "hardly shows that Switzerland judged the Soviet Union's war effort favorably. Nor is there the slightest allusion to the fact that the Soviet conqueror had contributed to freeing Switzerland from German pressure."[20] However, it is worth remarking that the memorandum did not give itself over to hypocritical complacency, which would certainly not have deceived the Soviet government. In circumstances that carried more immediate threats, the speech of the Federal Council of June 25, 1940, which that Basel historian had so severely criticized, had undoubtedly restricted itself to ambiguity, but, in its biblical moralism, Pilet had had the decency and pride to let no word emerge that glorified the triumph of the conqueror in order to gain his good will. And the memorandum certainly did not bring out Stalin's proposal to the Allies of invading Switzerland. The Soviet conqueror had undoubtedly "contributed to freeing Switzerland from German pressure,"[21] though without specifically desiring to do so. But the historian could not ignore the role played by the Molotov-Ribbentrop Pact in the outbreak of the conflict, the decisive role played by American intervention in the liberation of Western Europe, and the Soviet contribution to the victory. As to the Soviet contribution to this liberation, it is enough to note the forty years of totalitarian alignment imposed on Eastern Europe afterward to appreciate its significance. He was again happy that the Anglo-Saxon troops had kept Western Europe from that Soviet "liberation." And so the Federal Council, even if it could thereby have compromised its approach, was to be praised for not having strewn it with the flowers of compliance and having shown its good will without conceding its principles.

However, without doubt, and whatever text was sent, the government in Moscow, encouraged by its Swiss correspondents, set store by imposing a lesson on this small, impertinently democratic country and at the same time impressing the other neutrals and other countries that were still basking in the mirage of recovered liberty. The Federal Council had the courage to harbor no illusions as to Soviet behavior or intentions.

Meanwhile, the Soviet press was picking on the neutral countries, especially Switzerland. The USSR refused to take part in an international aviation conference that was to be organized in Chicago on November 1. It gave as its reason the fact "that Switzerland, Portugal, and Spain had been invited to this conference, countries with which the Soviet Union did not have relations and which for several years had pursued a profascist policy hostile to the Soviet Union." According to a Soviet diplomat, Switzerland was in particular included in that classification. Certain Swiss newspapers, caught up in the Soviet euphoria, were outbidding each other in pointing out the guilty party: "We are now paying for the first time on an international level for the policies of Motta," wrote the *Tagwacht* on November 4.

From that time, a negative decision from Moscow on the question of diplomatic relations was expected. Brutal and laconic, it came on November 3 through the Soviet ambassador in London and was broadcast the following day from Moscow and London:

"The Soviet government has studied the proposals of the Swiss government concerning the resumption of diplomatic relations between Switzerland and the Soviet Union contained in the aide-memoire sent by the Swiss minister in London to the Soviet ambassador. This aide-memoire, referring to the ancient democratic traditions of Switzerland and the fact that the Swiss Federal Council is prepared to discuss existing problems frankly, is mute on the policy which the Swiss government has pursued all these years with respect to the Soviet government, when it is well-known that the Swiss government, violating its old democratic traditions, has for several years pursued a profascist policy toward the Soviet Union, which, with other democratic countries, is in the process of combating Hitler's Germany in the interests of peace-loving peoples.

. "In view of the preceding, the Soviet government refuses to accept the proposals of the Swiss government for the resumption of diplomatic or other relations with Switzerland because up to now the Swiss government has not in any way disavowed its previous policy hostile to the Soviet Union."[22]

The Federal Council did not allow itself to be upset by the Soviet response, which was a little surprising. It did not hold an extraordinary session as it did in serious cases; that would have betrayed its emotion and caused concerns. It could have noted that the USSR was not in a position to designate as pro-fascist a country that had made its independence in neutrality respected, while the USSR itself had associated itself with Hitler to dismember Eastern Europe. It was not appropriate to go on bended knee and make amends, but it would have been equally inconvenient and imprudent to pour oil on the fire. Instead, the Federal Council contented itself with a laconic communiqué which, after briefly noting the situation, concluded:

"The reproach of pursuing a hostile policy toward the USSR does not correspond to reality or to any impartial observer who is directly and completely informed on the attitude of Switzerland, its government, and its people. The facts are so clear in this connection that the Soviet government cannot fail to persuade itself of them. In addition, the Federal Council continues to hold the views that led to the negotiations, now interrupted, which correspond to its general wish to maintain good and pacific relations with all countries."[23]

Press commentary in the Allied countries was different and contradictory. Certainly the British and Americans had been firmly against Stalin's proposal to invade Switzerland to punish the "swine" who lived there, as Churchill relates in his memoirs and a note from Bruggmann to Petitpierre of 1946 confirms.[24] But the western Allies did not intend to aggravate the tensions that were cropping up between themselves and the Soviets. Was not the brutal refusal to the Swiss a way of marking the Soviet desire to play a decisive role in Central Europe?

In a situation analogous to Switzerland's, Swedish Foreign Minister Günther confided his explanation of the event to Swiss Minister Dinichert in Stockholm. Certainly the real reasons for certain acts of Soviet diplomacy were often difficult to ascertain. The USSR liked to surprise and disconcert. The reproaches to Switzerland were not going to convince anyone. But if Moscow took up the reference to Switzerland's democratic traditions, it was in the framework of the Soviet idea that Communism is an expression of democracy.[25]

Dinichert reassured Günther, who feared that the Soviet response would cause a division in Swiss public opinion as it had not failed to do in Sweden. But the Swiss minister explained to him that "[t]he overwhelming majority of people would not accept anyone casting doubt on their convictions and the logic of their institutions." The Swede regretted that Switzerland had not established relations with the USSR before the war. Dinichert tried hard to explain the reasons to him. Further, he learned from one of Günther's collaborators that the Swedes had had some bad experiences in seeking to use the intermediation of London or Washington in their relations with the USSR. Moscow was mistrustful of these attempts, but some irrational reactions could not be excluded.

Dinichert was not wrong about the Swedes' reactions. André Lasserre, who in *Les années sombres* took the temperature of the press and public opinion and found that—with the exception of the philo-communist extreme left—the great majority, including the Socialists, rejected the accusation of profascism formulated in the Soviet reply. "Diplomatic relations should not be confused with domestic politics . . . Sovereignty is not an object for sale." "After having resisted Axis pressure for five years we were not going suddenly to throw in the towel and give in to threats in the opposite direction."[26]

The majority of public opinion and the near unanimity of the press thought as Willy Bretscher, in the *Neue Zürcher Zeitung* of November 6, that "the attitude of the Soviet government toward the small neutral country cruelly shed a disturbing light on relations between the colossus of the east and the rest of the world."[27]

"Reacting to the Soviet affront, all the Swiss newspapers agreed in rejecting the reproach of profascism, which was regarded as absurd," Bonjour himself noted.[28] "Under no account will Switzerland allow itself to be treated like any Balkan country," wrote the *Volksrecht*. The Soviet rebuff provoked Swiss unity in response, with the exception of the extreme left. But there was disagreement on the conclusions to draw from the Soviet action. Certain overcautious moves showed the same alignment reflexes that had appeared in 1940 with respect to the triumphant Third Reich. Hausamann, who held onto his prey, tried to persuade Kobelt on November 6 that "Moscow has made the first unfriendly move; other larger ones will surely follow. But for each of these blows, aggravated by the uproar it causes in the country, we will be in a more difficult position. We will always have a hard time getting close to the Russians while we save face and preserve our dignity before our own people and the world. . . . We need to have something happen soon that will keep Moscow from inflicting another blow."[29]

This "something" was the departure of the head of the Political Department, in the view of Hausamann, the Socialists, and many bourgeois, who had always been allergic to Pilet. However, there was no unanimity in this matter. Many people, more numerous than some had thought or than Bonjour would have us believe, recognized the capacities of Pilet the statesman, without liking him personally. If he had caused mistrust or general hostility and if the country's interests had required, it had long been possible to make him hear it by kid-glove maneuvers in the corridors of Parliament; but he was reelected in 1943 with a two-thirds majority, which certain estimable federal councilors after him were hard put to attain. Further, many thought rightly that it would not be appropriate to have him resign, as that would look like a concession to the USSR or a confession of weakness and irresolution before these foreign difficulties. "Many bourgeois newspapers," Lasserre noted, "were extremely severe in judging this desertion, which could only play into the hands of the Socialists and communists, who had finally gotten rid of their enemy and were convinced of their own influence."[30] Perhaps some of them were counting on the entry of some of their number into foreign affairs, a thorough revision of foreign policy, and a renewal of the diplomatic service.

It was one of their number who struck the final blow, in the *Tagwacht* of Bern on November 7: "Foreign policy, according to the Constitution, is within the jurisdiction of the Federal Council; but if this policy endangers the people and their interests, the people can exercise a right of necessity and this right takes precedence over the legal quibbling of the vain man from Vaud. Mr. Pilet, it's time!"[31] Without worrying about "legal quibbles," it would be right to ask where the people's interests did lie and, supposing that the newspaper did define them, what "right of necessity," formulated by whom, could take precedence over institutional procedures. But this blow was irremediable, and the fact that Pilet was from Vaud constituted an aggravating circumstance for the elegant finesse of the Bern newspaper.

The following day a delegation from the Socialist Party met with Pilet, Kobelt, and von Steiger to plead less publicly with a request for Pilet's resignation. In one way, in its usual more delicate manner, this radical group from both houses of Parliament would probably have come to the same conclusion and conveyed it to their fellow radical, Pilet.

But Pilet's decision had already been made. The letter of resignation he addressed to the president of the Federal Assembly is, in fact, dated November 7. In the absence of Pilet himself and of Swiss President Stampfli, Etter informed the Federal Council at its meeting of November 10. He expressed his regrets, but the decision was already well known, and there was no going back. With his colleagues, Etter expressed to Pilet the heartfelt appreciation of the Swiss government and people.[32]

The Federal Council's communiqué stated that Pilet had made his decision on November 7 but had requested to postpone the announcement so as not to anticipate the discussion of relations with the Soviet Union. The resignation letter, dated that day, read as follows:

Mr. President:
   The negotiation to resume diplomatic relations between Russia and Switzerland, which I had long desired to conduct to a successful conclusion, has not succeeded at this time.
   Circumstances will soon show the real and underlying causes of the Soviet refusal.
   As we await developments, we must not let this refusal compromise domestic cohesion and unity, which are indispensable in the most difficult years ahead.

I have always thought and often stated that for us, the wartime foreign minister should not and could not be the same person who serves in the postwar period. The times require fresh and intact forces. But my decision is made, and I anticipate only a few more weeks in office.

It is for this reason that I have the honor to convey to you my resignation on the date it will please the Assembly to set.

With all its members, I hope that our dear, small country can maintain its independence and liberty as in the past.

In his commentary on the resignation, Edgar Bonjour posited a direct relationship between what he joyfully refers to as the "Russian slap in the face" and Pilet's departure. "A latent disease has finally come to light after several years. Already in 1940 the head of the Political Department had ceased to inspire the people's confidence; he could never regain his credit after that. It is because Pilet no longer enjoyed the support of a certain number of political friends that the Russian slap in the face forced him to go. The fact that this slap caused his downfall proves once again that even in Switzerland, foreign policy and domestic policy cannot be separated. The Parliament and the people will not long stand for being kept out of foreign policy. In decisive and critical circumstances they can impose their will, as was seen when international treaties had to be submitted to a referendum. If Pilet, in his foreign policy, had also taken the people's will into consideration, he probably would not have been led to yield to ideas that a deeply democratic people repudiated, ideas which definitively led to the Soviet refusal."[33]

These serious words from the pen of the official historian accuse Pilet of evil intent. Bonjour spurns objectivity with his claim that Pilet had been led "to yield to ideas that are contrary to democracy," in justifying the Soviet rebuff. He saw a good lesson in democracy coming from a country so totalitarian that in 1944 it had already brutally enslaved the countries it was claiming to liberate.

It is true that Pilet could not always develop and maintain constant and trusting relations with the people. Was it possible or reasonable, in a period of high tension, to keep the people constantly informed of the threats, the hypotheses, and the possible options? The permanent unease, the hysterical susceptibility of the Nazi leaders never could force the Swiss leaders, the Federal Council—for the council was concerned and not just Pilet—to deny in their ideas and acts the values of independence and democracy. Nor could they express all the emotions, sometimes versatile and occasionally contradictory, which emanated from popular feelings during this time of crisis in their diplomatic relations. Discretion is required for diplomatic continuity, and press campaigns and variations in the polls cannot convince us of the contrary. They are less the expression of the popular will than pressure from political, media, or economic lobbies.

To attribute the conduct of Swiss foreign policy exclusively to Pilet totally lacks objectivity; it was sometimes positive in spite of partisan whimpering. If that policy did not derive, thank God, from daily opinion polls, which are versatile and very often manipulated as can be seen, it was under the responsibility of a Parliament that had been democratically elected in 1939 and in 1943, under the active and critical control of committees, and under the authority of a government, including Pilet, that was comfortably reelected in 1943. For a historian, it would be a serious mistake to ignore the allergy of the Swiss body politic to personal power. There was a jealous republicanism, the principle of collegiality of executive authority, which expressed the constructive spirit of a team that was united in the best of cases, but which also, on occasion, displayed dogged resistance, open or muffled, by the organization, to him who would claim to be lifted on his shield in the manner of a Celtic chieftain and conduct the country's destiny as he wished. Pilet, with his perfect knowledge of his brief, analytic intelligence, and decisiveness, could be persuasive and at times exercise predominant influence. He was not the only one to lead the country, even though after the fact, between two misdeals or a caustic allusion, one or the other could cheerfully shuffle off his responsibility and give vent to his feelings to satisfy his tablemates.

Willy Bretscher, that brilliant journalist and member of Parliament, wrote, in the *Neue Zürcher Zeitung* of November 11, 1944, concerning Pilet's resignation in both objective and humane terms:[34]

"The cold lucidity of the head of the Political Department did not give way at the moment of his resignation to impulse or momentary depression. Federal Councilor Pilet was used to controversy and for many years it was with the serenity of a Saint Sebastian that he supported the innumerable poisoned arrows they shot at him. But the recent attacks concerning the Soviet "no" have surely confirmed the precarious vulnerability of his office, the times we live in, and the strong need of liberation, both personal and political. The foreign minister of the war years is not leaving his post because he has failed—it would be grotesque to speak of failure and incompetence, as does the *Weltwoche*. He is leaving because he is aware that he will serve the country by giving up his duties to a new man who is not committed in this field. This new man will not be reproached automatically with each diplomatic difficulty, each domestic political incident (such as a speech of four years ago that has long been forgotten abroad), where people will not find the cause of failure or accidents on the way. Internal cohesion is necessary to assure the credibility of our foreign policy. Pilet has certainly understood that in this complex of imponderables and irrational

reflexes he had himself become a stumbling block, an obstacle to that cohesion, and it is for that reason that he is leaving.

"The Soviet refusal is not the reason for his resignation. The bitterest critics of our foreign policy up to now have not brought forward any argument
that criticizes Pilet's person or method in this matter."

"But unfortunately, the federal councilor did not possess the art and gift of
communication. He was not able to maintain enough contact with the people
and the press to make his policy appreciated; he was lacking in democratic
'sex appeal.'"

However, history will in time do him justice, Bretscher believed, as do now
"all those who refuse to accuse of incompetence and incapacity, as do certain
critics, the magistrate who led our foreign policy through five years of war,
under the most difficult of conditions."

Bretscher's brilliant analysis refuted in advance the trial of his interpretation and intent that the official historiography was to put Pilet through and the
distorted image of him that was long hawked in public rumor.

Pilet's resignation was both premature and justified. It was really only
slightly premature but, coming as it did at the time of the Soviet rejection, it
gave the impression at home and abroad that the USSR could impose its will
and decisions on Swiss democracy. One must deplore the haste of both parties, the spite of some, and the cowardice of others, to urge on the decision.
With Pilet's intention blocked, it would have been possible (with the party
leaders informed in confidence) to put off the announcement. The rumors
could not have been avoided—they had been circulating for a long time—nor
could the leaks. However, it would have been possible to save the political
gesticulations, the corridor intrigues, or the indecent invectives, which made
the departure appear forced, like a punishment that was far from merited, for
a policy pursued with prudence, ability, and firmness under the most difficult
conditions. The haste of the decision gave to his departure the tone of abandonment and threw discredit on a course for which Parliament had stood
surety during the five most dramatic years of the twentieth century—with the
exception of some visceral sensibilities, some incidents, and some states of
mind—because it had safeguarded what was essential: peace in independence
and liberty. A delay of a month in the resignation would have been enough to
handle coolly the tempering emotions, partisan fervor, and necessary relief.

Resignation was necessary because of the physical and moral tension to
which the critical leadership had subjected him and because of the conditions
and new issues the prospect of peace and the reorganization of Europe and the
world posed. "The position of foreign minister in wartime should not and
could not be the same person for the postwar period. A new situation requires

fresh and intact forces," Pilet himself wrote in his letter of resignation. Finally the resignation was necessary because democracies are ungrateful by their nature, and a feeling of liberation willingly arises with respect to those who bring much to the people without their realizing it and at the same time have courageously required much of them. Churchill was to live through that same ingratitude at the hour of victory. The small democratic country could not celebrate a victory. It had to content itself with having lived through the torment unleashed by the caprice of the powers and having safeguarded the peace in independence, liberty, and honor. It was a singular privilege, compared to the lot of others and to so many innocent victims.

NOTES

1. *Documents Diplomatiques*, vol. 13, 416–21.

2. *Documents Diplomatiques*, vol. 13, 606–42.

3. Erwin Bucher, *Zwischen Bundesrat und General*, 586–87.

4. Edgar Bonjour, *Neutralité*, vol. V, 401–4.

5. Edgar Bonjour, *Neutralität*, vol. II, 260–81; Paul Schmid-Amman, *Die Wahrheit über Generalstreik 1918* (Zurich 1968), 34–41, 165–75; and Willi Gautschi, *Der Landesstreik 1918* (Zurich, 1968), 156–71.

6. *Documents Diplomatiques*, vol. 11, 204–8.

7. Hans Rudolf von Salis, *Giuseppe Motta* (Zurich, 1941), 410–18.

8. Edgar Bonjour, *Neutralität*, vol. III, 203–81; and Hans Rudolf von Salis, *Giuseppe Motta*, 450–54.

9. Edgar Bonjour, *Neutralité*, vol. V, 365–416.

10. Edgar Bonjour, *Neutralité*, vol. V, 380–83.

11. Edgar Bonjour, *Neutralité*, vol. V, 384.

12. Edgar Bonjour, *Neutralité*, vol. V, 385.

13. Edgar Bonjour, *Neutralité*, vol. V, 273–86.

14. *Documents Diplomatiques*, vol. 13, 409.

15. Edgar Bonjour, *Neutralité*, vol. V, 386–87.

16. Edgar Bonjour, *Neutralität*, vol. IX, 351.

17. *Documents Diplomatiques*, vol. 13, 606–12.

18. Edgar Bonjour, *Neutralité*, vol. V, 387.

19. *Documents Diplomatiques*, vol. 13, 667–68.

20. Edgar Bonjour, *Neutralité*, vol. V, 388.

21. Edgar Bonjour, *Neutralité*, vol. V, 389–91.

22. *Documents Diplomatiques*, vol. 13, 705.

23. Edgar Bonjour, *Neutralité*, vol. V, 392.

24. Edgar Bonjour, *Neutralité*, vol. V, 399, note.

25. *Documents Diplomatiques*, vol. 13, 718–19.

26. André Lasserre, *La Suisse des Années Sombres*, 320–22, cites the *Volksrecht* and the *Thurgauerzeitung*.

27. Willy Bretscher, "Das Russische Nein," in *Neve Zürcher Zeitung, 1933–1944: Siebzig Leitartikel von W. Bretscher* (Zurich, 1945), November 6, 1944, 196–99.

28. Edgar Bonjour, *Neutralité*, vol. V, 417.

29. Edgar Bonjour, *Neutralité*, vol. V, 391, note.

30. André Lasserre, *La Suisse des Années Sombres*, 321.

31. Edgar Bonjour, *Neutralité*, vol. V, 417; and Walther Bringolf, *Mein Leben: Weg und Umweg eines Schweizer Sozialdemokraten* (Bern, 1965). Recalls the interview with the Socialist delegation, 369–74.

32. *Documents Diplomatiques*, vol. 13, 725–26.

33. Edgar Bonjour, *Neutralité*, vol. V, 417–26.

34. Willy Bretscher, "Bundesrats Pilets Rückritt," in *Neve Zürcher Zeitung, 1933–1944: Siebzig Leitartikel von W. Bretscher* (Zurich, 1945), November 11, 1944, 200–202.

Chapter Twenty-Two

Bitter Ingratitude of Power

Professor Edgar Bonjour's severe judgment of Pilet-Golaz and his policies left me with a feeling of unease, because this judgment uniquely concerns the statesman who had the most difficult and the most thankless task of all the Swiss. It is really too easy to make a scapegoat of him.

Jean Rodolphe de Salis
Sonntagsjournal, June 20, 1970

Marcel Pilet, head of the Political Department without expressly desiring it, and in addition president of Switzerland in the crucial year of 1940, held the leadership of the neutrality policy in the dangerous field of diplomacy. He maintained as far as possible the universality of diplomatic relations in a world at war, in a surrounded country living under threat, in the middle of a Europe subjugated by the totalitarian Reich. As foreign minister of a neutral country, he was aware of his exposure to a convergence of contradictory criticism from the belligerents, who reproached him for what they claimed were concessions to their adversaries and complained that he refused to give in to their individual requirements. Paradoxically, the Axis side often showed itself more understanding of neutrality than did the Allies, who wanted to force Switzerland into the anti-German blockade.

To the critical challenge of the belligerents in both camps, a natural situation for a neutral, were added the incessant domestic political shafts of the parliamentarians, who for the sake of political advantage spied out the least fault of the most exposed department head. This occurred less in public debates, it should be said, than in the quiet corridors of the Federal Palace, the chatty terraces of the nearby cafés, or the first-class federal train compartments, all encouraging secrecy.[1]

Certainly the difficulties of Pilet's position were augmented by the rough edges of his character. He was aware of his duty but also of his own worth and he was little inclined to that cordial conviviality which flatters and reassures. His adversaries accepted still less the acid humor of his rebuttals than his traditionally conservative opinions. His polished language, often in search of literary originality, disturbed a good number of German speakers, who mistrusted his too rapid eloquence and a humor they were hard put to follow in the subtlety of his expressions. Irony wounds more than argument, and resentment is long lasting. Uneasiness and unanswerable mistrust echoed through public opinion.

Léon Savary, a writer and journalist covering the Federal Palace, who, with his alert and sharp pen, portrayed the leading figures of the Swiss Confederation without indulgence in his *Lettres à Suzanne*, took up Pilet's defense with vitality:[2]

> The Swiss do not desire great men, and in politics, they are afraid to have them. What they like in a public figure is honesty and average aptitude to manage public affairs like a shop. They mistrust superiority and, let us frankly admit, they are horrified at genius.
>
> No geniuses, no saints. Even talent is suspect. . . . It is enough to say that a politician who showed signs of surpassing the low water mark would be promptly subject to public discredit. Edmond Schulthess, one of our most remarkable statesmen, was cordially detested, and the blackest of calumnies were poured on him. He had been bold enough greatly to exceed this average, above which people became disturbed. Pilet-Golaz, who saved us from invasion during the last war and who is a man of superior intelligence, but with a detachment and irony that are odious to our compatriots, was savagely and perfidiously attacked, even in his home canton of Vaud. . . . I am not speaking of German-speaking Switzerland: at any given moment it is enough to pronounce Pilet's name to make our fellow Swiss furious. When he resigned after working day and night for four years for our safety, I was precisely the only one [Savary is exaggerating here] in the Swiss press to support and honor him without reticence. I am happy to have been literally berated because of my fidelity to Pilet. If there are some unforgettable moments in my life, there are also those where one is scolded and blamed, but where one can say: I know I am right. . . . Pilet had his principles, something most rare among our statesmen. He had a line of conduct he followed decisively, but he also had the flexibility required of a foreign minister.

Edgar Bonjour was not ready to share this enthusiastic fervor. This painstaking, prolix, and conscientious historian contributed, in the voluminous *Histoire de la neutralité suisse* in nine volumes written at the request of the Federal Council, toward magnifying discredit on Pilet rather than giving him praiseful recognition. The mass of documents consulted and cited, the nearly official caution of Bonjour's work, and the obvious bias of this unique and solitary author betray a formidable process of intent which is astonishing, coming from the pen of a historian whose honesty, however, would be difficult to deny.

Curious and disturbed to understand the reason for this bias, I put the question to Bonjour himself. As justification, he cited Pilet's jest mentioned in Chapter 2. Pilet, then vice president of the Federal Council, on meeting the young historian, posed the question, "What good are the archives anyway?" "How could I trust a politician who had such contempt for history?" Pilet's place in history had fallen into infamy.

Nevertheless, I would not want to ascribe the historian's bias to an ill-understood joke. I would rather seek the reason for it in the explanation in Bonjour's foreword to his French edition.[3] He states honestly that "the historian never ceases to bring value judgments to bear, even if he is unaware of it," that the abundant material should give him "the courage to leave things out, to abandon the idea of pushing the meaning of nuances too far." "His duty before all else is to bring his moral and political judgments to bear without softening them, even at the risk of casting the purity of his intentions in doubt." Hence, Bonjour refers to a moral and directional concept of history where the value judgment, according to ethical or ideological criteria, should take precedence over objective analysis of the facts. He states a little farther on, with no fear of contradicting himself, that "the historian should be the partisan of no single idea and should free himself from all prejudice."

But is he not the one concerned with a moral interpretation of history, tied to a patriotism that is praiseworthy in itself but expressed in terms of a pure, hard, absolute, and intransigent neutrality, with little care for nuances, as he himself would require of the historian? Pilet understood that neutrality, to which he was attached as the guarantee of the country's independence, would not succeed by intransigence alone. In the factual situation that Switzerland could not escape, one sometimes had to negotiate the inevitable to affirm the essential or negotiate the provisional to consolidate the durable. The integrity of the historian cannot bend to political pragmatism, no matter how well founded the politics were.

From then on, Bonjour did not forgive Pilet for one single error or tactless statement. He promoted a picture of a foreign minister believing nearly to the end of the war in the victory of the Third Reich and being subservient to its requirements. In the chapter devoted to the end of Pilet's career, the historian starts off with an indictment. Doubtless, he recognizes Pilet's attractive gifts: a sharp wit, his legal training, the gift of grasping the most difficult problems quickly, his psychological intuition, his facility in discussion, a sparkling eloquence, and even patriotism. But all this was to buttress the view "that [Pilet] was far from having the international reputation of Motta. . . . He was attached to tasks he could not conclude successfully. . . . He did not give the

impression of a man fully convinced of his mission, expressing his high-
flying thoughts. . . . It was not clear that the flame of the purest patriotism
guided him who was seeking his purposes by obscure paths, nor that the cold
mask could conceal the warmth of his sentiments. . . . His deeds did not correspond to the image the people created of a senior Swiss official (It is true
that he wore a Basque beret.)"

Bonjour reproaches Pilet for his lack of consideration for General Guisan.
It is true that these two men from Vaud, who were paradoxically given the
heaviest responsibilities in this time of crisis, complemented but hardly appreciated each other. However, the differences that arose between the political authority (not necessarily Pilet) and the army's commander in chief were
in a way tied to their missions, whether it was the issue of repatriating German aviators and aircraft that had been interned or shot down for violating
Swiss airspace, debatable military promotions, or troop levies where the general's proposals were not always followed by the government. This was especially the case after the Allied landing of June 1944.

Serious disagreements, on principle as much as prestige, led Pilet and
Guisan to oppose each other concerning the intelligence services.[4] Pilet, who
thought highly of Masson, paid homage to his enthusiasm and his work but
reproached his emotionalism and his confidence, which was too easily extended to some problematic collaboration. Chiefly, Pilet did not admit interference by the intelligence service or its collaborators in the country's domestic or foreign policy.

Thus, at the time of the "officers' conspiracy" of 1940, Pilet had requested
that Ernst and Waibel, who were its leaders, be dismissed from the service,
which would have deprived Masson of his most effective collaborators. He
expressed some doubts about the Franco-Swiss general staff contacts of
1939–40 and the nature of the commitments that might have been given. But,
with the Federal Council and Defense Minister Karl Kobelt in particular, Pilet
reacted especially vigorously to the Schellenberg-Masson connection and to
the enigmatic meetings in Biglen and Arosa in 1943 between the SS general,
Himmler's right arm, and the commander in chief of the Swiss army, whatever might have come out of them. These incidents show that Pilet was concerned above all to maintain respect for the authority of the Federal Council,
which General Guisan, pushed by the eager officers on his personal staff, was
sometimes hard put to accept.

Pilet was far from showing a bias against the army. Had he not himself
commanded a battalion? However, although he appreciated the value and
qualities of the military command, he thought it unwise to give it a signed
blank check, and he was determined to exercise his criticism and political responsibility as much as necessary. "Pilet did his duty entirely," stated Léon

Savary. "If he sometimes resisted the general in the area where national defense touched on politics, he acted as he should have. Even in time of war, we have one executive authority in Switzerland and one only: the Federal Council. I revere General Guisan; we must be grateful for what he has done for us. But the Federal Council was sometimes obliged to set clear limits on the attributes of both of them; and if Pilet, as head of the Political Department and responsible for our foreign relations, sometimes strongly asserted the rights of the government, he was assuming his constitutional role.[5]

The historian Erwin Bucher, in the methodical study he published in 1981 under the name of *Zwischen Bundesrat und General* [Between the Federal Council and the General], has applied himself with tenacity and courage (he needed them) to oppose the historical current and overturn the public image of a Pilet-Golaz ready to grasp every opportunity and hoping for a German victory.[6] He refutes Bonjour's imputations with precision, showing that if Pilet feared a German victory, as did many others, he neither celebrated it nor desired it in his unfortunate speech of June 25, 1940, and since that time he doubted a definitive German success. "We must guard against taking the future for the present," as he said.

Despite some ambiguity on the exercise of authority in that speech, which had been approved by the Federal Council and was heard by three out of four Swiss from the German voice of his colleague Philipp Etter, Pilet did not declare an authoritarian reform of the institutions any more than the government did. "Practiced with wisdom, without confusion of powers, without dispersion of authority and responsibilities and without a multiplicity of instances, (our institutions) are healthy in principle," he said in Lausanne in September 1940.[7]

It was at the instigation of certain of his colleagues and Switzerland's attorney general that Pilet ill-advisedly received the delegates of the *Mouvement National*, among them the poet Jakob Schaffner, who was well-known in that capacity. Pilet's objective was to sound out the intentions of these activists. This led to the position that caused the movement to be banned two months later, but Pilet received the blame.

Finally Bucher, in a detailed and exact argument, dismantles the plot, established very likely out of whole cloth by Hausamann, to destabilize Pilet by accusing him of lending his support to a separate peace between Germany and the Anglo-American allies and trying to compromise Guisan.

But the best refutation of Bonjour's bias and imputations should come from Bonjour himself. In his portrayal of Pilet, Bonjour emphasizes "what was false in Pilet's foreign policy," and afterward hurls him with historian's justice from "the Tarpeian rock, which exists in small Switzerland too" and which punishes solitary pride. After refusing him "a choice place in history,"

Bonjour executes an unexpected reversal and concludes his portrait with homage that contrasts with the acrimony that had dominated up to that point:[8]

"Combining prudence and boldness in true Swiss fashion in the midst of a hostile world, [Pilet], however, struggled resolutely for the independence of his country, with the same purpose in mind as Guisan. The mission of the statesman was more extensive and complex than that of the military man, and it required more subtle behavior. Here is a case of classic antagonism between the art of governing and the art of war. Pilet had a less heroic and more thankless role to play than the general. He was forced to appear extremely sensible and prudent in his relations with the representatives of a country intoxicated with its victories. A political man who had read Machiavelli, he meant to defend his country by all appropriate means, even by deception: 'If I cannot be a lion, at least I want to be a fox.' If in his efforts he sometimes offended the foreigner and even the Swiss people by his roundabout methods, one thing, however, is certain; Pilet was animated by the most ardent patriotism and he struggled with all his strength for the independence of Switzerland. If Switzerland had not practiced a policy of extreme flexibility allied with quiet firmness, which allowed it to gain the confidence of the two adversaries decided on destroying themselves, the country would have scarcely succeeded in staying out of the conflict. Pilet was firmly aligned with the group of federal councilors who, assuming the heaviest responsibilities in those war years, helped steer the Swiss ship of state over the reefs without damage in the midst of mortal danger. He clearly had the hardest task of all, and this has not been adequately memorialized."

Coming from Edgar Bonjour, who seems to have remembered it reluctantly, this surprising confession of praise for Pilet derives all its value. We must grant to the historian that he knew, in his final overall assessment, how to rid himself of the bias that had otherwise systematically animated his writing and contributed greatly to the discredit of Pilet and from him to the government and the country.

NOTES

1. Edgar Bonjour, *Neutralité*, vol. V, 417–43, 16; *The Fall of Pilet*, 17; and Alfred Bonnet, *Le Grand Mérite du Conseiller Fédéral Marcel Pilet-Golaz*, 57-page brochure, no date, privately printed. This short work by a journalist covering the Federal Palace is preceded by a preface by Georges Perrin, a parliamentary journalist.

2. Léon Savary, *Lettres à Suzanne* (Lausanne, 1949), pp. 56–59.

3. Edgar Bonjour, *Neutralité*, vol. V, 8.

4. Erwin Bucher, *Zwischen Bundesrat und General*, 532–35.

5. Léon Savary, *Lettres à Suzanne*, 129–30.
6. Erwin Bucher, *Zwischen Bundesrat und General*, especially 509–98.
7. Erwin Bucher, *Zwischen Bundesrat und General*, 525.
8. Edgar Bonjour, *Neutralité*, vol. V, 441.

Chapter Twenty-Three

The Challenge Met

END OF THE WAR

The resignation of Marcel Pilet-Golaz put an end neither to the war nor to the troubles Switzerland still faced until the return to a stable situation that people would try to call peace.

The war was not over. In the west, the German armed forces, with the exception of some knots of resistance, were driven out of France and easing back to the German borders. But they were still capable, like a cornered boar, of a few thrusts, such as the Battle of the Bulge through the Ardennes at Christmas 1944. This breach in the Allied lines was soon closed by the Americans, but they did not reach the Rhine until March 6, 1945. Meanwhile, along Switzerland's northern border, the French army of General de Lattre de Tassigny, which had plodded along the length of the Jura, advanced toward Lake Constance before penetrating into Austria. To the east, the Soviet armies would soon surround Berlin and threaten Vienna.

Since March 1945, contacts had been established in Bern between SS General Wolff and British and American generals with a view to an at least partial capitulation in Italy, but these contacts only irritated the Soviets, who feared a separate peace.[1] A Swiss intelligence officer, Major Max Waibel, had acted as mediator without the knowledge of his superiors, as we have seen, in the negotiations that ended with the surrender of the German troops in Italy on May 2. General Eisenhower in Rheims on May 8 and Marshal Zhukov in Berlin on May 9 received the surrender of the German armies. However, on May 12, 1945, Prime Minister Churchill warned President Harry S. Truman, who had recently succeeded Franklin Roosevelt, that an "iron curtain" had fallen over Europe, behind which the USSR was imposing communist domination on the countries it had liberated, to the detriment of democracy and in violation of the Yalta Agreements. The tensions of the Cold War were taking the shape they were to assume for nearly half a century after the bloody encounters of World War II.[2]

But the Swiss people foresaw none of this. Giving up all business, abandoning classes, counters, shops, and offices, they poured into the streets at the news of the German surrender, waving Allied banners and giving no thought to the troubles to come. They had not experienced war, its victims, or its ruins; occupation by a foreign military power and the agents of the Gestapo; "voluntary" work abroad; deportation to the death camps; or the heroic but sometimes equivocal doings of the resistance, with its informing and repression. They had not known famine, but they felt at one with those who had suffered this scourge, fought against it with conviction or by force, and supported it with resignation. Even though they were aware of the privilege of protected peace, the Swiss people felt a certain moral isolation in the presence of so much suffering in which they had not participated but which they had nevertheless tried to alleviate by private actions and public assistance.

The Swiss people had to make a transition between the crude requirements of wartime and those of the earlier peace which had been forgotten, along with illusions lost, and they had to adapt to a different pace of life. They had to resolve wartime disputes, and normal relations had to be reestablished with the winning side, which was preparing to endow the world with an organization claiming to outlaw war definitively. This effort, however, would not be an easy task because cracks that were to expand to crevasses had opened up between the great powers well before the end of the fighting. The latter, after having won the victory, took in hand the fate of peoples and began quarreling over influence without worrying much about the smaller countries, willingly making those who had been allowed to remain neutral dance to their tune.

THE PRICE TO PAY FOR NEUTRALITY

Switzerland had been a neutral by customary law since the sixteenth century and thereafter by recognized international law guaranteed by the great powers since 1815. It now found itself under the most difficult conditions of encirclement and permanent threat of invasion, but it applied itself strictly to maintaining its neutrality and preparing for its defense, while showing its sympathy with peoples in conflict.

However, this neutrality did not have the benefit of unanimous recognition among the belligerents near and far, victors or vanquished, or heartfelt gratitude for the services Switzerland was able to render because it was neutral.

When Stalin, perhaps irritated by some Swiss comrades, proposed that the Allies invade Switzerland, Winston Churchill paid homage to us in a letter to Anthony Eden, his foreign minister:[3]

> Of all the neutrals, Switzerland has the greatest right to distinction. She has been the sole international force linking ourselves with these terribly divided nations. What does it matter if she was unable to give us the commercial advantages we desire, or gave too many to the Germans, to keep herself alive? She has always been a democratic state, defending her freedom among her mountains, and in spite of race, largely on our side in thought.
>
> I was astonished at Uncle Joe's [Stalin's] savageness against her, and much though I respect that great and good man, I was entirely uninfluenced by his attitude. He treated them as swine and he does not use that sort of language without meaning it. I am sure we should stand by Switzerland, and explain to Uncle Joe why it is we do so.

But even if few Allied countries shared Stalin's opinion of Switzerland, they did not all agree with Churchill. Whether they were engaged in the conflict deliberately or by alliance, or whether they were dragged into it by force, the countries that had known violence and seen the victims and ruins of war were not going to carry in triumph those who in their neutral refuge, with the help of providence, looked down on the bloody conflict from the balcony of the Alps and enjoyed the benefits of peace, liberty, and also undeniable economic advantage in contrast to the general distress.

The belligerents and those who had joined them, willingly or unwillingly, inevitably sought flaws in the virtues of neutrality and claimed to detect indulgence to and connivance with the losers. They calculated the list of benefits and inventoried the capital fled. They compared their cities and factories in ruins to the flourishing cities of the neutral country, its cultivated fields, and its intact factories ready to profit from peace even more than they had during the war.

Several states and numerous refugees from war-torn countries gave witness to their gratitude for Swiss aid, for the work of the International Committee and the Society of the Red Cross, for the dispatch of food and medicine, and the welcome accorded refugees and internees and for official, private, and clandestine assistance. But many whose governments had, however, deliberately contributed to the Holocaust complained that the welcome was conditional and that numerous refugees threatened with persecution had been rejected at the border. "Was the Swiss boat really full?"

But this bitterness, even if it unjustly struck at the principle of neutrality and the actions taken in its name, was understandable on the human level. The return of Switzerland to the concert of powers, which had some trouble adopting this attitude, turned out to be as difficult diplomatically as the exercise of neutrality had been during the war.

REJOINING THE POSTWAR WORLD

This would be the task of Max Petitpierre, who was elected to succeed Pilet-Golaz on December 14, 1944 and assumed direction of the Political Department in February 1945. This jurist from Neuchâtel, a lawyer by education, vocation, and profession who had a temperament that combined logical construction with an awareness of reality, was conciliatory by nature and experience. Had he not had the skill to reunite the two evangelical reformed churches in Neuchâtel, separated for more than a century of formal but tenacious prejudice, often more stubborn than the diversity of profound beliefs? On a vastly greater, thankless, and dangerous field Petitpierre was careful, courteous, discreet, and modest, not very talkative but tenacious in his purposes. He brought Switzerland progressively back into the community of nations, without alliances or blame.[4]

Assuming the neutrality of wartime, he also stated the reason for it generally, its vocation in the service of peace and assistance among peoples, and the universality of its relations. This solidarity, tied to neutrality, should be able to find expression, whether or not Switzerland joined the United Nations then being formed, or later, the institutions that would be given to Europe and the world, as Switzerland continued to maintain its reserve and its political independence.

Here Petitpierre shared the views of William Rappard. This eminent Swiss historian of economics, diplomacy, and public law, who established the reputation of the Institute of Advanced International Studies in Geneva, had warmly defended the League of Nations, for which he had worked. His expertise in economics and his American connections had made him a very effective asset for Swiss diplomacy both before the war and in the financial negotiations with the Allies in 1945 and 1946. Although he had been an ardent defender of the principles and institutions of the League of Nations, he expressed reservations regarding the United Nations Organization as it emerged from the talks at Dumbarton Oaks in 1944. Rappard feared that the Security Council, by the powers with which it was endowed, would be just "the dictatorship of the three or four great imperial powers over the rest of the world." Switzerland could not sacrifice its neutrality for that state of affairs. His recommendation was therefore "neither passive and sullen abstention, nor prompt and unreserved adherence."[5]

On April 12, 1945, Petitpierre briefed the Federal Council's delegation for foreign affairs on the policy he foresaw for the new world organization in San Francisco which was about to define its structure and its goals for safeguarding peace. Switzerland was not to be invited, and the neutral countries were not even to have the opportunity to send an observer.[6]

Was Switzerland to stay passive? If not, what position would it take with respect to the new organization? It seemed unlikely that the conference would fail. If the negotiations were to succeed, it must be anticipated either that the neutrals would not be invited to participate in the new organization or that they would be faced with giving up their neutrality, wholly or in part.

"The provisions of the project for the preparatory conference at Dumbarton Oaks," Petitpierre noted, "concerning the participation of the neutral states in the economic and military sanctions . . . left scarcely any doubt on the subject: Switzerland, in the new world security organization, would be hard put to benefit from a privileged position comparable to the one granted it within the League of Nations."

"If we have decided to maintain neutrality, it would be well to establish a 'Swiss doctrine' from this moment on. This should declare that our country, even if it remains outside the international organization, would not be indifferent to its actions. It should try to dissociate the purely political organization from the various technical organizations subordinate to it, such as the International Court of Justice at The Hague, and the social, economic, and humanitarian commitments."

Petitpierre then addressed the need to defend the idea of neutrality within Switzerland. The Federal Council would have to promote its policy clearly against its critics. We must also defend Swiss interests in maintaining at least part of the new institutions in Geneva, in the League of Nations buildings. The United Nations Security Council could be established at Gex, in France near Geneva.

Without bringing up here the diligent and effective activities of the sixteen years that Federal Councilor Petitpierre was to spend at the head of Foreign Affairs, we should state to his credit, during the liquidation of the wartime controversies, the resumption of diplomatic relations with the USSR, the problematical return of the Soviet internees to their country, and the settlement of the financial disagreement between Switzerland and the Allies.

THE FINANCIAL AGREEMENTS

Neutrality could not be an absolute idea, and a neutral state could not live in isolation in the redoubt of its virtues, isolated from a world at war. International conventions admit and guarantee the universality of diplomatic, economic, and financial relations, allowing a neutral state to survive by participation in international exchanges which continued in spite of the war. But it is true that, in the conditions of encirclement to which events had reduced it and in spite of maintaining, at the height of the conflict, the universality of these exchanges, Switzerland closely depended for its economic survival on the Third Reich, which in normal times had been its most important trading partner, rather than the Allied countries from which it was separated by war and the sea. Did it have to allow advantages to Germany that exceeded all bounds, departing from its duties as a neutral?

On January 19, 1945, President Roosevelt had sent a message to Swiss President von Steiger,[7] announcing that the moment had come to renegotiate certain aspects of the trade agreements and that he had called on his personal advisor, Laughlin Currie, to lead the American delegation assigned to discuss it.

Roosevelt declared, "We have respected the traditional neutrality of your country and have sympathized with the past difficulties of your position. We forbore pressing our demands when you were isolated by our enemy and were in no position to do other than carry on a large trade with him. Now, however, the fortunes of war have changed. We are now in a better position to meet your most urgent needs if they are threatened. I know in these circumstances that you will be eager to deprive the Nazis of any further assistance. It would indeed be a trial to any freedom-loving Swiss to feel that he had in any way impeded the efforts of other freedom-loving countries to rid the world of a ruthless tyrant."

Roosevelt showed himself all the firmer because each day was costing the lives of many of his fellow citizens.

This was not the first time that the Allies, especially the Americans, had requested the Swiss Confederation to join the blockade against Germany and to cease all trade and transit relations with the Axis countries. Switzerland, in keeping with its neutrality, had refused, which led in 1944 to a marked slowdown in imports from the Allies. However, the German clearing debt had swollen greatly, and with Germany being less and less in a position to meet its delivery commitments, trade had fallen a good deal.

The Allied commission, chaired by Laughlin Currie and made up of American, British, and French delegations met in Bern from February 12 to March 8, 1945 and intended to scrutinize Swiss economic policy during the war and the manner in which it had respected neutrality.[8] The commission requested the cessation of deliveries to Germany, which had already been reduced to the portion agreed on; the end of north-south transit; and the sequestration and inventorying of German assets in Switzerland. It also opposed Switzerland's receiving in gold the sums due it from the Reich. In exchange, the Allies would lift the blockade that had been so detrimental to both Swiss imports and exports in the preceding months. They promised to facilitate maritime and rail transport.

The Swiss delegation stuck to the law. It would have been contrary to neutrality to cease all trade with the Reich, and the interruption of transit would have violated the Gotthard Convention which guaranteed north-south civilian traffic between Italy and Germany. Switzerland did not accept a breach in its trade relations with Germany or a suspension of transit. It reached a modus vivendi with the Reich on February 28, which did not break off trade relations but limited them to strict reciprocity. In fact, the collapse of the German economy was soon to interrupt trade and transit relations. The Allies adjusted to this de facto situation without demanding a rejection of neutrality. France obtained from Switzerland a loan of 250 million francs for reconstruction.

At the end of the talks, a communiqué announced that the resulting agreement did not call into question the neutrality Switzerland that observed: "The Allied governments recorded their full understanding of Switzerland's special neutrality, which they have always respected. But without departing from this principle, Switzerland could take a series of steps requested by the Allies. Concessions were made on both sides without putting Swiss relations with the two belligerents into question."

Chairman Currie of the Allied delegation noted that several misunderstandings had been cleared up and that he came to appreciate the qualities that allowed the Swiss people to safeguard their independence during the war: "We are grateful for the existence of a strong democracy in the heart of Europe. It is comforting for us to know that people live there who share our ideas and act the way the American people do, people who condemn aggression and a proud and arrogant dictatorship, people who understood the need for tolerance and the rights of reason."[9]

Remaining to be settled was the fate of the capital that had been transferred to Switzerland, whether it should be returned or confiscated, according to its origin. The Allies, even before Germany's surrender, had succeeded in having these funds blocked. They were thinking less of demanding, as they had in 1919, that the Germans pay reparations for their wartime expenditure than of preventing German domination of foreign economies and a rebirth of National Socialism from funds placed abroad. In the reparations conference held in Paris in January 1946, the western Allies looked to the neutral countries, requesting the sequestration of these assets, their liquidation, and payment of the proceeds.

In February and March 1946 in Washington, Americans, British, and French bitterly debated the issue with the Swiss. The Confederation obtained the unfreezing of Swiss funds long blocked in the United States, notably the gold deposited by the Swiss National Bank, as well as the cancellation of the blacklists that had enabled the boycott of firms which had worked with the Germans. On the other hand, in spite of its contesting the principle at law, Switzerland was obliged to deposit 250 million francs by way of participating in reparations to the Allied countries.

At the time of the debate in the National Council of June 24, 1946, the Geneva deputy François Perréard, the French language reporter, summed up the results of the Washington Agreement.[10] They certainly had their disadvantages, in particular the takeover of the German assets entrusted to Switzerland as a reserve against the funds belonging to Germans resident in Switzerland, which that country refused to expropriate, but the Confederation was to participate in their distribution. If Switzerland had opposed the agreements, it would have incurred the reproach that in protecting German capital invested in its country, it would have preserved funds that could finance a new conflict. It would have seen its gold reserves deposited by the National Bank in the United States blocked. It would have made the resumption of exchanges with the Allies problematical.

The advantages were more numerous:

• The reestablishment of confidence in Switzerland,
• A final settlement, on the national and international plane, of the issue of German assets in Switzerland,
• At least partial safeguarding of Swiss interests in Germany and being held harmless for damages undergone there,
• Renouncement of all action against the Swiss National Bank and the Swiss Confederation for the gold ceded by the Reichsbank,
• Unblocking of Swiss assets in the United States, and
• Cancellation of the blacklists of those firms that had worked for Germany.

Under the Washington Agreement, Switzerland committed itself through its delegation to consider the claims that Holocaust victims or their survivors might make on the funds deposited in Swiss banks that would be returned to them. The banks, which were not party to the agreement, did not bring a burning zeal to bear on the restitution required by the Swiss federal government. This explains the heated controversy that erupted in 1995 in New York between the Swiss banks and attorneys for Jewish organizations concerning the "escheat funds" unduly in the possession of Swiss credit institutions and whose total amount was alleged, wrongly, to be more than 12 billion Swiss francs. With the agreement of the Swiss government, an international commission chaired by Paul Volcker, former chairman of the American Federal Reserve, was given the mission and power to investigate these escheat funds held by Swiss banks.

In September 1998, including the exhaustive investigation of the Volcker Commission, which was then underway, Professor Lambelet estimated at approximately 70 million Swiss francs the escheat funds held in Swiss banks, only 10 to 15% of which concerned Holocaust victims. At the time of the rise of National Socialism, the German Jews were very intelligent not to place their fortunes at the mercy of a raid by Hitler. The refugees in the Western Hemisphere were both more confident and less exposed to government inquisitions.

As they awaited the conclusions of the Volcker investigation, under threat of an American boycott, the Swiss commercial banks reached an agreement with the main American Jewish organizations. In order to settle the entire matter, the banks committed themselves to deposit 1.25 billion dollars.

The Washington Agreement of 1946 lifted a burden that had weighed heavily on Swiss diplomatic relations. It marked the end of a state of war in the financial field, at the same time that Petitpierre was undertaking Switzerland's return to the diplomatic community.

At the end of the debate in the National Council, which accepted the agreement by 142 to 29, Federal Councilor Nobs, head of the Finance Department, gave a pertinent conclusion. "In the tragic dilemma where it had been placed, there is no shame or dishonor for Switzerland to have acted as it should, in order to escape the war."

This homage to the Confederation's policy during the conflict had its effect. Did it suffice to justify neutrality?

NEUTRALITY IN THE BALANCE

An interpretation of the neutrality policy followed by Switzerland between 1939 and 1945 should not be limited to the highly honorable appraisal of the Allies and their experts, nor to the fact that the country was able adroitly to "escape the war." It deserves a more extensive justification of the reasons for being neutral and the way neutrality was in fact carried out.

Opinions on this subject differ today. "A scarcely glorious period in our history" a journalist stated pompously on the fiftieth anniversary of the end of the Second World War. And one of the most brilliant of our German-language writers recently told a French newspaper, arming himself resolutely with retroactive courage, that he was ashamed not to have fought at the side of our neighbors and to have remained a cowardly neutral. Others find in neutrality the flavor of an outdated folklore in a world and a Europe where supranational institutions should impose peace in respect for law, collective security, and prosperity in economic and monetary integration.

Did Switzerland derive an economic benefit from its neutrality? Certainly, the territory of the belligerents invaded and bombarded, the human losses at the front and under bombardment of civilian populations, the destruction of buildings and factories, the transport and communications network that it was spared conferred an obvious advantage on a neutral country over the countries engaged willingly or not in the furnace of war. This justifies an active effort to assist those trapped by the scourge on the part of the countries that were spared. For Switzerland, the actions of the International Committee of the Red Cross in particular fulfilled this role. However, a neutral country cannot be required to assume all the responsibilities and all the burdens of a conflict it had neither desired nor caused nor could have prevented.

Switzerland's neutrality did not derive an economic profit from the war. The period 1939–1945 was marked, as we have seen (in Chapter 16 above), by a net decrease in foreign trade in tonnage and value and therefore in production. Real revenue per inhabitant fell in Switzerland by approximately 10%, while it increased substantially for certain belligerents.[11]

We have put Swiss participation in the German war effort in its context: in exchange for iron and coal that allowed us to reinforce our defense, and we have noted that closing the windows of the National Bank to the Reichsbank's gold would not have prevented Hitler from pursuing the war. [12]

It is true that neutrality gives no claim to glory. It leaves the honor to the survivors of the battlefields. But, resolved to fight in its own defense, Switzerland refused the reproach of evasion, the blame, and the dishonor. The decision for neutrality was an act of independence, the refusal to be ruled by national quarrels, or ideological, ethnic, or religious differences. Customary law for four centuries, recognized and guaranteed by the powers, neutrality is for Switzerland an international engagement which it could not abandon without losing both credibility and political independence.

Although Switzerland was aware of the danger represented by totalitarianism and although it was close to the French and British democracies, it would not have saved these liberties by participating by their side in the beginning of the conflict. Rather, it would have shared their defeat and sanctioned their diplomatic differences, their lack of firmness, and their lack of military preparedness. Switzerland would certainly have been occupied and dismembered according to the German-Italian plans and controlled by a foreign administration; it would have been forced to work more intensely for the benefit of the Axis. "Voluntary" workers would have been mobilized for the German factories, and a legion of Swiss SS would have enrolled for the eastern front. On the other hand, certainly a resistance movement would not have failed to rise up, bringing repressions and reprisals with it.

Armed neutrality spared Switzerland from this fate. The challenge was nevertheless formidable. Everything but the hostility of the great majority of the Swiss people, their certain desire to resist, and the useful role of the neutral country on the international plane, would have led the Axis countries to invade: the strategic and logistic mastery of the alpine bastion, the material and financial reserves, and the provocation, in the heart of an aligned Europe, of a small free and democratic country, which in spite of the rules of prudence did not hide its hostility to dictators and its refusal to be swallowed up into a "greater Germany."

From June 1940 to 1944, the threat of invasion was constant, with different degrees of intensity. The plans drawn up jointly by the German and Italian general staffs demonstrate both that intention and the effect of dissuasion caused by the resolve to resist and the grouping of the bulk of Swiss forces in the alpine redoubt. However, as essential as the military defense was, it required tenacious action by a very adroit diplomatic service, for allaying suspicion, but also basically to enable the country to survive economically without detracting from neutrality and the universality of its trade, to the extent that the wartime conditions and transport allowed it.

The challenge of neutrality was met by a twofold effort of military dissuasion and maintenance of diplomatic and economic relations with all countries. An unarmed Switzerland would certainly have been invaded and subjected. The universality of diplomatic relations and the representation and defense of the interests of countries at war assured permanent contact with the belligerents and contributed, alas in too relative a way, to the search for peace and respect of international law. This universality facilitated the activities of the International Committee of the Red Cross, and assistance, however partial, was given to victims of war and racial and political persecution. It was certainly the natural vocation of the neutral country to extend asylum to millions of deserving beings. The encirclement of Switzerland, the precarious nature of its food supplies, and the impossibility of transferring refugees to a country that would take them in made a strict and arbitrary limitation on these entries inevitable. Yet what other frontiers could have been so generously opened to the innumerable candidates deserving to find refuge from the horror of the "final solution?"

Under these sad constraints, the challenge of neutrality was met, and Switzerland did not align itself with the totalitarian order. The credit, with providence extending its protection, with the British and then the Americans fighting for liberty and restoring it and assuring it to Western Europe, goes to the solidarity and cohesion of the Swiss people in its vocation for liberty and its will to resist. General Guisan was the emblematic personification of this vocation in the army and in the people. But the credit goes equally to the Federal Council, which gave him his mission and the means to maintain it, extending to him the necessary resources. The government assured the conduct of foreign policy through a collegiality that was not seriously weakened and its economic survival assured in the most critical of conditions. With a Minger leading military preparation, and a Pilet-Golaz at the head of foreign relations, the Obrechts and Stampflis heading the economy, Etter seeing to Swiss cultural conscience, they all assured the will to exist, to defense and liberty, the material means and the indispensable social cohesion. Neither heroes or saints, but men with their weaknesses, mistakes, unfortunate utterances, varying temperaments, and personal dislikes, exposed to criticism and intrigue, experiencing ingratitude, unpopularity or led by their popularity, sometimes divided in their humor, but united firmly for the same goal, the liberty of their country, devoting themselves to it with the same sense of duty.

Neutrality is neither glory nor virtue. It does not give rise by itself to either heroes or legendary myths. It is an act of reason, a will to liberty, duty, and solidarity. It is achieved by popular awareness and the will of the political leaders, knowing that the country that is not engaged in the capricious play of power struggles will better serve peace and international solidarity.

NOTES

1. Edgar Bonjour, *Neutralité*, vol. VI, 119–27.

2. Winston Churchill, *The Second World War*, vol. VI, *Triumph and Tragedy* (Boston: Houghton Mifflin, 1953), 572–74.

3. Winston Churchill, *The Second World War*, vol. VI, *Triumph and Tragedy*, 712.

4. Max Petitpierre, *Seize ans de Neutralité Active: Aspects de la Politique Étrangère de la Suisse (1945–1961)*, contributions, speeches, and notes on public meetings published by Louis Edouard Roulet (Neuchâtel, 1980); Alfred Zehnder, *Die Aussenpolitische Lage der Schweiz am Ende des Zweiten Weltkrieges*, 13–32; Pierre Michel, *Les Grandes Lignes de la Politique Étrangère Conduite par Max Petitpierre*, 33–39; and Gérard F. Bauer, *La Coopération et l'Intégration Économiques Européennes et la Politique Suisse (1947–1961)*, 83–101.

5. Daniel Bourgeois, "William Rappard et la Politique Extérieure de la Suisse à l'Époque des Fascismes (1933–1945)," in *Etudes et Sources* 15, 1989, 7–76.

6. *Documents Diplomatiques*, vol. 15, 1048–50.

7. *Documents Diplomatiques*, vol. 15, Letter of F. D. Roosevelt, 844–45; and von Steiger's reply, 969–71, congratulating him on the results of the conference, thanking him for sending a medallion with Roosevelt's portrait, and sending another to the American president in commemoration of the battle of Saint Jacques sur la Birse.

8. Edgar Bonjour, *Neutralité*, vol. VI, 441; *Documents Diplomatiques*, vol. 15, 883–96, 906–12, 920–28, 937–41, 986–89, 1015–32, 1036; and Marco Durrer, "Les Négociations Économiques entre Alliés et Suisses à la Veille de la Défaite du IIIᵉ Reich," concerning the Anglo-American point of view, in *Relations Internationales*, no. 30, (1982).

9. Edgar Bonjour, *Neutralité*, vol. VI, 353–80.

10. *Bulletin Sténographique de l'Assemblée Fédérale*, National Council, session of June 1946, 347–407.

11. Jean Christian Lambelet, *Le Mobbing d'un Petit Pays: Onze Theses sur la Suisse Pendant la 2ᵉᵐᵉ Guerre Mondiale* (Lausanne: L'Age d'Homme, 1999), 97–98.

12. Jean Christian Lambelet, *Le Mobbing d'un Petit Pays*, 183–85.

Appendix

Switzerland in 1938

Switzerland in Figures

	Area (km2)	Population (millions)	Foreign Trade (millions of SF)
Switzerland	41,000	4	2,900
France	550,000	41	9,500
Germany	470,000	66	18,850
Italy	310,000	43	4,889
United States	7,839,000	122	21,893

A confederation of cities, towns, and small mountain cantons originally united since 1291 to deliver themselves from the control of the Holy Roman Empire (which included Germany and Austria), Switzerland has seen its political independence and neutrality recognized in European conflicts as well as by the Congresses of Westphalia in 1648 and Vienna in 1815. In 1848, in a Europe where the great national states of Germany and Italy were taking shape, and where nationalistic fervor was flourishing, Switzerland felt the need to reinforce its cohesion and, while leaving the cantons with a large portion of sovereignty, adopt an effective central power; a common foreign policy, army, and currency; and a coordinated economic and social policy. The Swiss Confederation of cantons became a federative state like the United States.

Since 1848, the Parliament of the Swiss Confederation, reflecting the American system, has been composed of two chambers. One, the National Council, is elected by the people of the cantons in proportion to their population and consisted of 187 deputies in 1938. The cantons, regardless of their population each elect two deputies to the second chamber or Council of

255

States. The powers of the two councils, which debate and vote separately, are identical. United in the Federal Assembly, they elect the seven members of the Federal Council who make up the government; the judges in the federal courts; and, in times of conflict requiring the mobilization of the army, a general who takes command of it.

The Federal Council is a collegiate authority in the fullest sense of the term: "It is a college of equals that has no chief" (Jean-François Aubert). There is no head of state, monarch or president of the republic. The president of the Confederation is elected for one year by the Federal Assembly in rotation among the seven members of the council. He may not be reelected immediately and does not have any special authority over his colleagues. During his year in office, he remains at the head of one of the departments, which correspond to ministries in other governments. Thus, there is no head of State, as other governments understand the term. Rather, there is the government which embodies it collectively as it receives visits from foreign heads of state as a body.

The Swiss recognize four official languages. In 1938, 72% spoke German or German dialects, 20% spoke French, 6% Italian, and 1% Romansh. They thus reflected the three cultures of the neighboring countries and felt their influence. During the war of 1914–18, the sympathies of the German-speaking majority were mostly for Germany. The Latin minority supported France and its allies. Without putting neutrality at risk, there were some heated controversies. Such was not the case in 1939. Except for some isolated fanatics, private persons tied to the interests of the fascist countries, the great majority of public opinion and the press was hostile to the totalitarian regimes of the neighboring dictatorships and bore witness to their attachment to independence in neutrality and the military defense of the country. This was also the conviction of the Parliament, in the radical, conservative, and agrarian parties that held two-thirds of the seats in the Assembly and all the seats in the Federal Council. This was also the opinion of most of the Socialist Party– a quarter of the electorate—which had renounced its revolutionary ideology and its hostility to national defense. It supported the government with critical vigilance and entered the Federal Council in 1943.

National defense was assured by a militia. Men between the ages of twenty and forty-eight—and up to sixty since 1939—were subject to military service unless physically incapacitated. Beginning in 1936, they were sent to a school for recruits for two to three months beginning in 1936 and were periodically assembled for three week refresher courses with the unit to which they belonged. Besides a small number of professional officers and noncommissioned officers, the army cadres, who were also in the militia, were specially trained and participated in troop training. Officers and soldiers kept their weapons and personal equipment at home. They could therefore be mobilized very quickly, often near their homes, especially at the border. In this way, the government was able to field 440,000 men in two days in September 1939. Just before mobilization, the Federal Assembly had elected Corps Commander Henri Guisan to become general and commander in chief of the Swiss armed forces.

In the economic area, Switzerland, with scarcely any natural resources and whose agriculture, active as it was, was not sufficient to feed it, depended on foreign commerce to survive. At nearly three billion francs, foreign trade exceeded a third of the gross national product. Germany was the principal supplier at 24%, and it took 20% of our exports. Switzerland's dependence was heightened still more by the absence of direct access to the sea, and the need to utilize its neighbors' railroad networks, which made it vulnerable to a blockade. It thus was forced into difficult negotiations with the belligerents on both sides to ensure both its economic survival and respect for its rights as a neutral and freedom to trade, especially after 1942 when the Axis powers controlled all the Swiss borders and access to the sea.

Bibliography

Altermatt, Urs. *Conseil Fédéral*. Biographic dictionary of the first hundred federal councilors. French edition. Yens, 1993.

Bonjour, Edgar. *Geschichte der Schweizerischen Neutralität*. 9 vols., the last 3 being devoted to documents. Basel, 1946–76.

Bonjour, Edgar. *Histoire de la Neutralité Suisse*. French translation by Charles Oser. Tomes IV to VI. Neuchâtel, 1979.

Bonjour, Edgar. *La Neutralité Suisse Synthèse de son Histoire*. French translation by Charles Oser. Vol. I. Neuchâtel, 1970.

Bourgeois, Daniel. *Le III Reich et la Suisse, 1939–1941*. Neuchâtel, 1974.

Braunschweig, Pierre Th. *Geheimer Draht nach Berlin: Die Nachrichtenlinie Masson-Schellenberg und der Schweizerische Nachrichtendienst im Zweiten Weltkrieg*. Zurich, 1989.

Bucher, Erwin. *Zwischen Bundesrat und General: Schweizer Politik und Armee im Zweiten Weltkrieg*. Saint-Gall, 1991.

Ernst, Alfred. *Die Konzeption der Schweizerische Landes-Verteidigung 1815–1966*. Frauenfeld, 1971.

———. *Die Ordnung des Militärischen Oberbefehls im Schweizerishen Bundestaat*. Basel, 1948.

Freymond, Jacques, and Oscar Gauye, eds. *Documents Diplomatiques Suisses, 1848–1945*. 15 vols. National Committe for Publication of Swiss Diplomatic Documents, 1979–.

Frölicher, Hans. *Meine Aufgabe in Berlin*. Private Edition, 1962.

Gautschi, Willi. *Le Général Guisan: Le Commandement de L'Armée Suisse Pendant la Seconde Guerre Mondiale*. French translation by Corinne Girard. Lausanne, 1991.

Guerres Mondiales et Conflits Contemporains. Publication of l'Institut d'Histoire de la Défense, ed. Guy Pedroncini. Paris: PUF.

Kurz, Hans Rudolf. *Histoire de L'Armée Suisse de 1815 à nos Jours*. Lausanne, 1985.

Lasserre, André. *La Suisse des Années Sombres*. Currents of opinion during the Second World War.

Les Dossiers de la Seconde Guerre Mondiale. Published under the auspices of the International Commission for the Teaching of History. Collection of Marabout University. Verviers, 1946.

Les Etats Neutres et la Seconde Guerre Mondiale. Proceedings of the international conference organized by the History Institutes of the Universities of Neuchâtel and Bern 1983. Neuchâtel: Louis Edouard Roulet, 1985.

Marguerat, Philippe. *La Suisse Face au III Reich.* Lausanne, 1991.

Pilet-Golaz, Marcel. *Aperçu Destiné à Monsieur le Conseiller Fédéral Petitpierre, Chef du Département Politique, sur les Dangers Auxquels la Swisse fut Exposée au Cours de la Guerre Mondiale 1939–1945.* Typewritten. Federal Archives.

Rau, Jean-Philippe. *Marcel Pilet-Golaz.* Thesis submitted to the Faculty of Letters of the University of Geneva, under the direction of Professor Jean-Claude Favez, 1971.

Relations Internationales. Quarterly review published by la Société d'Etudes Historiques des Relations Internationales Contemporaines, l'Institut Universitaire de Hautes Etudes Internationales (Genéve), l'Institut d'histoire des Relations Internationales Contemporaines, and l'Institut Pierre Renouvin, under the direction de Pierre Guillen. Paris and Geneva.

Renouvin, Pierre, ed. *Histoire des Relations Internationales.* Tomes VII et VIII.

——. *Les Crises du XX Siecle.*

Revue d'Histoire de la Deuxième Guerre Mondiale. Quarterly publication by the Committee on the History of the second World War, under the direction of Henri Michel. Paris, PUF, 1960–.

Revue Suisse d'Histoire (Schweizerische Zeitschrift für Geschichte, Rivista Storica Svizzera). Published by the Société Générale Suisse d'Histoire (Allgemeine Geschichtforehende Gesellschaft, Società Generale Svizzera di Storia). Basel.

Ruffieuz, Roland. *La Suisse de l'Entre-deux Guerres.* Lausanne, 1974.

Salis, J. R. von. *Weltgeschichte der Neuesten Zeit.* Vol. III, bk. 2, *Die Grosse Krise und der Zweite Weltkrieg.* Zurich, 1980.

Schwedische und Schweiserische Neutralität im Zweiten Weltkrieg. Published by Rudolf Bindshedler, Hans Rudolf Kurz, Wilhelm Carlgren, and Sten Carlsson. Publication undertaken on the initiative of the Swedish Ambassador and the head of the Swiss Military Department. Basel, 1985.

Senn, Hans. *L'Etat-Major Général Suisse.* Vol. VI and VII. In Vol. VI, *Erhaltung und Verstärkung der Verteidigungsbereitschaft Zwischen den Beiden Kriegen.* Basel and Frankfurt am Main, 1991.

Studien und Quellen. Etudes et Sources. Studi e Fonti. Brochures published since 1975 by les Archives Fédérales Suisses, 1975–.

Urner, Klaus. *Die Schweiz muss noch Geschluckt Werden: Hitler's Aktionspläne gegen die Schweiz.* Zurich, 1990.

Index

About the Author

George-André Chevallaz was born February 8, 1915 in Lausanne, Switzerland. In 1937 he earned his Licentiate of the Faculty of Philosophy degree at the University of Lausanne. He continued his studies at the Ecole Pratique des Haute-Etudes in Paris, but World War II interrupted, and Chevallaz became a lieutenant in the infantry.

In 1942 he assumed a position as professor of History and French at the School of Commerce in Lausanne. In 1949 he obtained his PhD in economic history and was elected to his first political position as a member of the municipal legislature of Lausanne.

He remained in his position at the School of Commerce until 1955 and then was appointed Director of the Cantonal Library in combination with a position as associate lecturer for History of Diplomacy at the University of Lausanne. It was during the late 50s that politics became his main occupation.

In 1957, Chevallaz was elected mayor of Lausanne. The next year, he was elected to the National Council. He held both positions until 1973.

During his tenure in the National Council, Chevallaz presided over, among other things, the commission debating the laws regarding promotion of university studies in 1968, the commission for foreign affairs in 1970–71, and the commission debating the repeal of the Jesuit articles of the Swiss Constitution in 1972. Between 1970 and 1973 he was also the president of his party in the United Federal Assembly.

During these years, Chevallaz published numerous historical writings. He also wrote a weekly column for the *Feuille d'Avis de Lausanne* (now *24 Heures*). In 1967 he published a political essay, "Switzerland or the Sleep of the Just," in which he promoted, among other things, his views on political positions and responsibilities.

In 1973 Chevallaz was elected to the Federal Council. During his tenure, he headed two departments, the Department of Economic Affairs from 1974–1979 and the Federal Military Department from 1980–1983. In 1980, he became the President of the Confederation for that year.

At the end of 1983, Chevallaz retired. He returned to his home in Epalinges, where he continues to write and publish many historical studies and political essays. He is collaborating on a historical lexicon of Switzerland and is president of the Kornhaus Stiftung in Burgdorf, the future Swiss Museum for Folk Music. He is also a member of the board of directors for Tradition, a financial company.